Automotive
Electrical Systems

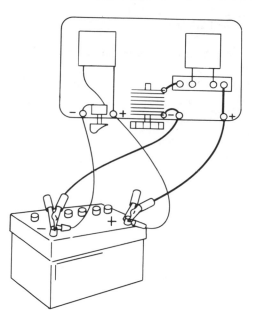

HERBERT E. ELLINGER

Associate Professor
Transportation Technology
Western Michigan University

Automotive Electrical Systems

Prentice-Hall, Inc.
Englewood Cliffs, N.J.

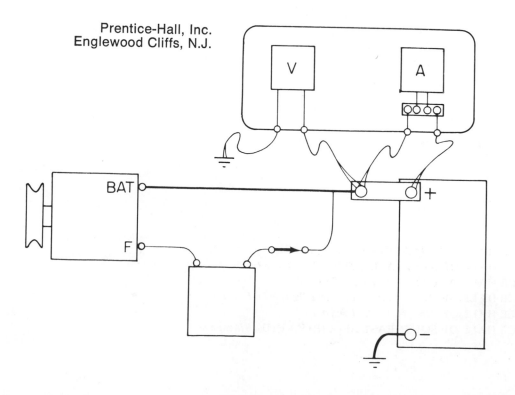

Library of Congress Cataloging in Publication Data

ELLINGER, HERBERT E.
    Automotive electrical systems.

    Includes index.
    1.   Automobiles—Electric equipment—Maintenance
and repair.   I. Title.
TL272.E639   629.2'54   75-23225
ISBN   0-13-054262-8

© 1976 by Prentice-Hall, Inc.
Englewood Cliffs, New Jersey

10   9   8   7   6   5   4   3

Printed in the United States of America

PRENTICE-HALL INTERNATIONAL, INC., *London*
PRENTICE-HALL OF AUSTRALIA, PTY. LTD., *Sydney*
PRENTICE-HALL OF CANADA, LTD., *Toronto*
PRENTICE-HALL OF INDIA PRIVATE LIMITED, *New Delhi*
PRENTICE-HALL OF JAPAN, INC., *Tokyo*
PRENTICE-HALL OF SOUTHEAST ASIA (PTE.) LTD., *Singapore*

To My Colleagues

who provided encouragement and
useful information as this book was being written.

Contents

Contents

Preface

Electricity is one of the most complex matters the automotive technician must deal with. To complicate the situation, cars are being equipped with more and more complex electrical and electronic equipment. Experimental engines are operated with electrical components that replace familiar mechanical, vacuum, and hydraulic items in the ignition and fuel systems. It is therefore essential for the technician to understand electricity and to be able to service electrical systems. This book has been designed to help the technician understand how the electrical system operates, how it is tested, and how it should be serviced properly.

Test and diagnosis procedures specified by car manufacturers often differ from those specified by the test equipment manufacturers. Car manufacturers' test procedures are keyed to the type of test equipment they require their dealers to have. Equipment manufacturers, on the other hand, have devised test equipment that can be used more rapidly to test the car's operating systems and thus allow the technician time to do more jobs in one day, thereby increasing his income.

The most common of these test procedures are explained in this book. Manufacturers often recommend test procedures that are somewhat different than those presented here. It is always advisable, therefore, to review the manufacturer's Service Manual for any special procedures that may have to be followed before making unfamiliar tests or working on unfamiliar types of cars.

I have attempted to combine similarities of the different types of electrical systems and the similarities of the electrical operating units in an orderly fashion without discussing details of the systems used by each manufacturer for his cars. These specific details can be found in the applicable Service Manual and in annually produced reference manuals.

This book is organized by first presenting the principles of electricity and the repair procedures that are common to electrical system service. This is followed by a discussion of the major automotive electrical systems. Each electrical system is presented in three ways. First, a description is given showing why and how each system works. This is followed by a discussion of methods used to test the system operation. The subject is completed by a description of typical system servicing procedures.

For a thorough understanding of the ignition system it would be helpful if you are acquainted with engine operation, with emission control, and with fuel, lubricating, and cooling systems. Study Chapter 9 if you do not have that background, so that you will understand the interrelationship of the engine electrical system with the other electrical systems. The basic function and testing procedures of the auto chassis electrical systems are introduced in Chapter 12 to help you service the complete automotive electrical system. Each chapter is followed by review questions listed in the order the information is presented in the book, which makes it easy for you to find the correct answer to any question.

I wish to express my sincere thanks to all those who have helped make this book possible. Special thanks must go to the automobile manufacturers and equipment companies that provided many excellent illustrations: they are listed in the Acknowledgments. Thanks should also go to Steve Weaver who spent many hours preparing photographs and to Gerald Helsley, who was very helpful in correcting early drafts of the manuscript. The unrestricted use of the Automotive Laboratories, automotive equipment, and training aids at Western Michigan University to take many of the photographs is especially appreciated. Help was received from the automotive teaching staff and automotive students who brought new and unusual items to my attention for inclusion in this book. My thanks also to Gertrude Lamoreaux and Linda Campbell for typing the manuscript. And to my wife Christine, my affection; without her encouragement this book would not have been written.

HERBERT E. ELLINGER

Acknowledgments

A great number of individuals and organizations have cooperated in providing reference material and illustrations used in this text. The author wishes to express sincere thanks to the following organizations for their special contributions:

Allen Test Products
American Motors Company
Champion Spark Plug Company
Chrysler Motors Corporation
Ford Motor Company
General Motors Corporation
    AC Spark Plug Division
    Buick Motor Division
    Cadillac Motor Car Division
    Chevrolet Motor Division
    Delco Remy Division
    Oldsmobile Division
Kal-Equip Company
Marquette Corporation
Modine Manufacturing Company
The Prestolite Company
Sun Electric Corporation

Principles of Electricity

After electrical phenomena were first recognized, scientists pieced together enough information to allow them to successfully use electricity, even though they did not understand its nature. Early useful sources of electricity were the dry cell and the battery. These were followed by generators which were more useful than batteries because they produced a continuous source of electricity for light, heat, and power. Benjamin Franklin thought that electricity acted like a type of fluid flowing from one terminal to the other. He suggested the names *positive* and *negative* for the terminals. He further suggested that electrical current flowed from the positive terminal to the negative terminal. The Franklin current theory became firmly implanted in technical literature because it was accepted by scientists, engineers, authors, and teachers for a number of years. When the science of electronics developed it proved that electricity was actually the *movement of electrons* through conducting material. The electrons actually move in the electrical circuit from the negative terminal toward the positive terminal, directly opposite to the accepted Franklin current theory. Because Franklin's current theory has been thoroughly implanted in textbooks and reference material and so many tradesmen still think in these terms, many automotive training and reference sources still describe electrical current flow in terms of this well-known current theory (positive to negative) rather than using the technically correct electron flow theory (negative to positive). It really makes no difference which theory is used when one works with automobile electrical circuits as long as one does not get into the automotive electronic circuits or semiconductor circuits that are now being used to operate and control specialized units in the automobile. Throughout this text the electron theory approach is used, describing the electrical flow from the negative terminal to the positive terminal.

1-1 NATURE OF ELECTRICITY

All matter is composed of *atoms*, which are made up of particles called *protons, electrons,* and *neutrons*. The structure of the atom is often compared to that of the solar system. The center of the atom, called the *nucleus,* is made of neutrons and protons. Neutrons have a neutral electrical charge and protons have a *positive* electrical charge. The nucleus is surrounded with rapidly spinning electrons that are *negatively* charged particles. These lightweight electrons weigh only 1/1800 as much as a proton or a neutron.

It is difficult to comprehend the fact that atoms, even in solid matter, are mostly space, like the solar system. To rationalize this, it might be helpful to consider an analogy using an airplane

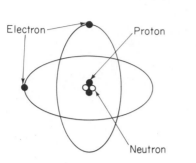

Fig. 1-1 Particles of an atom.

propeller consisting of two blades. When the propeller is spinning it appears to be a flat disc, even though there is mostly space between the blades. This spinning disc would act more like a solid than like empty space if one tossed a rubber ball at it because the ball would be hit by a blade and would bounce off. If this spinning disc could be tumbled fast enough, it would look and behave like a solid ball. The atom appears much the same. Electrons rapidly spinning around a nucleus at velocities as high as 4000 miles per second produce an object that is called solid.

When the number of electrons in an atom equals the number of protons, the atom has a neutral charge. The negative charge of each electron will balance the positive charge of each proton. Electrons spinning about the nucleus rotate at different distances away from the nucleus. As they rotate, they form shells at different energy levels. The electrons rotate in a fashion similar to a satellite rotating around the earth. Satellite orbits

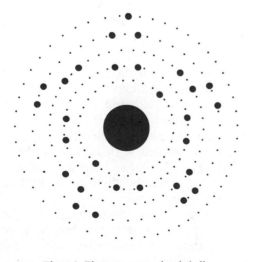

Fig. 1-2 Electron energy level shells.

may be close to the earth or they may extend into space, depending upon the energy or velocity of the satellite. Electrons in the lower orbits are bound tightly to the nucleus, while electrons in the outer orbits of many materials are loosely bound. Electrons may be removed from or added to the loosely bound outer orbit of these materials.

An atom is an extremely small particle. Usable matter is made up of large groups of atoms or combinations of atoms. For instance, water is made from hydrogen and oxygen atoms, petroleum is made from hydrogen and carbon atoms, and steel is made from iron, carbon, manganese, phosphorus and sulfur atoms.

The electrons from the outer shell of the atoms in conducting matter may detach from their orbit and enter the orbit of another atom or they may become free electrons. The electrons move through materials in a random fashion or *drift* so that the net change is zero. That is, every electron that leaves the orbit of an atom is replaced by an electron from another atom. Metallic materials have many free drifting electrons. These materials are called *conductors*. Conducting materials have three or less electrons in their outer orbits. Materials with five or more electrons in the outer orbit have a tighter bond to the nucleus with few drifting electrons. These materials are called *insulators.*

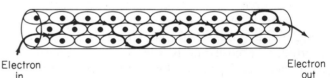

Electron
in

Electron
out

Fig. 1-3 Electron drift.

Atoms that pick up an extra electron in their outer shell have more electrons than protons and therefore the atom is said to have a negative charge. If an atom were to give up one of its electrons to a neighboring atom, it would have one more proton than electron. It would then have a positive charge. Atoms with either extra or missing electrons are called *ions*. If they have an excess of electrons, they are *negative ions*. When they are missing some electrons, they are *positive ions*.

Copper is a good conductor because it has many free electrons drifting within it. Most conductors in automobile electrical systems are therefore copper. If the conductor has one end connected to a source of extra electrons and the other end connected to an object that lacks electrons, the general drift of electrons in the conductor will be away from the portion having excess electrons and toward the part that lacks electrons. This drift of electrons occurs because *like charges repel* and *unlike charges attract* each other. The forced drift from the collision of the electrons will produce an *energy wave* that moves through the conductor at a speed approaching the speed of light. This wave proceeds like a series of rear-end collisions on a crowded highway, where the collision rate proceeds much faster than the movement of any one of the vehicles involved in the collision.

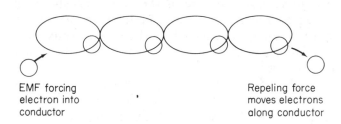

EMF forcing electron into conductor

Repeling force moves electrons along conductor

Fig. 1-4 Electron drift in one direction.

The net drift of electrons through a conductor in one direction is *electricity*. The rate of drift is called *current* expressed in *amperes* (A). The electrical force that causes directional electron drift is called *electromotive force* (EMF). In automobiles, the initial electromotive force is produced by a battery or charging system. The electromotive force or amount of electrical pressure is expressed as *voltage* (V). The higher the voltage, the greater the electrical force that is capable of moving electrons within the conductor.

1-2 SERIES ELECTRICAL CIRCUITS

If voltage is applied to an open conductor, free electrons will fill the conductor, but they will not flow. A complete circuit is required to have an electron flow. With a complete circuit, electrons will flow and cause an electrical current whenever voltage is applied to the circuit. In a given conductor, as the voltage decreases, amperage will decrease. Current cannot flow unless there is an electromotive force or a voltage difference at the ends of a conductor to cause the electrons to move within a closed circuit.

As current flows in a conductor, the forced drift of the free electrons is hindered by collisions with atoms in the conductor. This produces heat, which in turn increases free-electron activity. Free electrons provide the force required to dislodge an electron from the outer shell around an atom, but in the process, some of the energy of the free electron is absorbed. Energy absorbed by collision

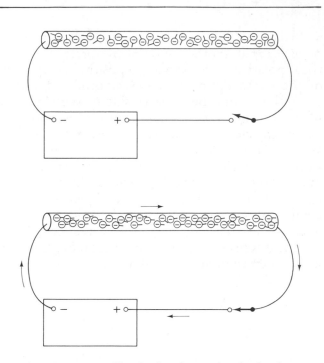

Fig. 1-5 Current will only flow in a series circuit when the switch is closed.

with atoms and by dislodging electrons is responsible for *resistance* to the electron drift or flow. Resistance to electron movement is measured in units called *ohms*.

There is a fixed relationship between the electrical pressure, *volts;* the electrical current, *amperes;* and the electrical resistance, *ohms.* This relationship is expressed in an algebraic expression, ohms = volts/amperes, and it is called *Ohm's Law.* If two of these values are known, the third may be calculated. If a circuit resistance in ohms is constant, the ampere flow in a conductor is directly proportional to the circuit voltage.

A complete electrical circuit can be illustrated by a circle with an electrical source at one point in the circle to provide circuit electromotive force

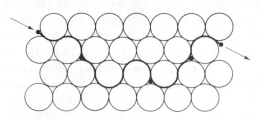

Fig. 1-6 An added electron within the conductor repels an electron.

and a device that uses electricity, called an electrical *load,* at another point of the circle. The electrical polarity of the circuit is positive on one side of the circle and negative on the other side. Electrons flow from the negative side of the electrical source through the load and return to the positive side of the electrical source. The electrons will flow as long as the circle is complete. The rate of current flow in the circle is determined by the electromotive force (electrical pressure) difference on each side of the source, measured in volts, and the amount of resistance provided by the load and conductors. The current flow will be reduced if the electrical resistance of the load becomes greater or if the electromotive force is lowered.

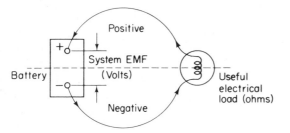

Fig 1-7 Electrons flow in a complete electrical circuit.

In automobile electricity the maximum electromotive force is the battery voltage when the engine is not running. When the charging system is operating the maximum electromotive force is the regulated voltage (except in special circuits within some electronic accessories).

For purposes of illustration, the automobile battery will be considered to supply the maximum circuit electromotive force (voltage). The battery produces electrical current through interaction of the chemicals that it contains. As electrical current is drawn from the battery, chemical reactions produce additional free electrons. Battery-terminal voltage remains constant as long as the chemical reactions within the battery can supply the required current. If the electrical load increases it will allow more current to flow than the battery can readily produce, and battery terminal voltage will decrease. This lower voltage will force less current to flow through the circuit so that the current will stabilize. The circuit electromotive force in volts times current flow in amperes equals elec-

trical power in *watts* (watts = amperes × volts). For instance, if a starter were cranking at 10 volts drawing 160 amperes the starter would be using 1600 watts of power. One horsepower equals 746 watts, so the starter produces 2.28 hp (1600/746 = 2.28).

For example, a battery in a circuit has a given amount of electrical power. As resistance in this circuit is reduced, current flow will increase and that, in turn, lowers the system voltage. In contrast, system voltage will rise as the circuit resistance is increased and current flow will decrease. Maximum system voltage occurs when the system resistance is infinite, which occurs when the circuit is opened with a switch.

The total resistance of a conductor increases as the length of the conductor increases, as its cross section decreases, and as its temperature increases. Wires normally used in automobile applications are selected to be as small in cross section as possible without causing excessive resistance, in order to minimize cost.

The resistance of a conductor or wire can be determined by measuring the voltage difference at the ends of the conductor and the amperes that it is carrying; then by using Ohm's Law (ohms = volts/ amperes) resistance can be calculated. In automotive service, specification for maximum resistance is usually given in terms of *voltage drop.* While a known current is passed through the circuit in question, the voltage across that part of the circuit is measured. Using this method, the voltage drop can be used as a measure of circuit resistance any time the current passing through a conductor is known. It is also true that no current will flow unless a voltage drop is present.

In the circuit illustration, system voltage is measured by placing one voltmeter lead on *each side* of the source or load. Voltage drop is measured along a conductor with both voltmeter leads on the *same side* of the source and of the load while current is flowing. In nearly all of the automobile electrical circuits the positive side of the circuit is an insulated wire conductor. The negative side of the circuit is the vehicle body and engine metal.

The starter-circuit voltage drop can be used to measure resistance by applying Ohm's Law. The starter circuit resistance in the example is 0.0613 ohms, while the starter has a cranking voltage of 9.8 V and a starter draw of 160 A.

$$\text{ohms} = \frac{\text{volts}}{\text{amperes}} = \frac{9.8}{160} = 0.0613$$

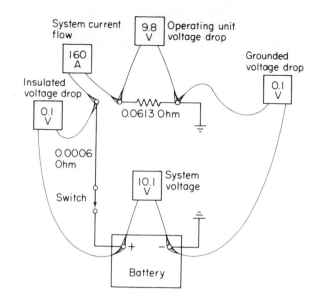

Fig. 1-8 Voltage drop in an operating circuit.

scale voltmeter (1-4 V full scale) at *each end terminal* of the conductor being checked while the starter is *cranking.* Any voltage reading on the voltmeter indicates resistance. The greater the voltage reading, the greater the resistance, assuming constant ampere flow to the starter.

Each conductor, switch, and connector causes some resistance to current flow. When these current-carrying units are connected, one after the other, as they are in the starter circuit, they form a *series* electrical circuit. Resistances in series add directly in ohm units. Voltage drops across the conductor, switches, and operating units in a circuit will add up to equal the measured battery voltage while current is flowing. Remember that voltage drop is a measure of resistance. No voltage drop exists when current is not flowing. Full battery voltage will be measured across an open switch. It should be noted that the voltmeter is used without disconnecting any circuit connections.

Series resistance is similar to a line of traffic going into a raceway. The restrictions are the drive-in gate, the ticket salesman, and the ticket collector. Each car that goes through the gate also

Note that battery-terminal voltage in this example is only 10 V while a 160 A current is flowing. The battery is only acting fast enough to maintain 10 V at this current draw. When the circuit is opened the chemical activity of the battery will immediately catch up to bring the battery electromotive force back to 12 V. Resistance of the insulated and ground sides of the circuit allow 9.8 V to operate the starter.

Resistance in a circuit will increase with temperature change, loose terminals, and added resistors. If the resistances are added, one after the other, so that the only electrical path is through each resistance in turn, the resistors are said to be connected in *series.* Series resistances, measured in ohms, add directly. The sum of the curcuit resistances in series equals the total circuit resistance.

$$R = R_1 + R_2 + R_3$$

A number of resistances are present in a starter circuit. Each cable, each junction, and each switch in the cranking circuit has some resistance. The starter motor itself provides the major circuit resistance while the starter is cranking. The *SAE Handbook* specifies that the maximum allowable voltage drop is 0.2 V per 100 A for cables between the battery and starter. Resistance in most starter circuits is well below this value. Voltage drop in the starter circuit is the result of the cable size, and the number of wire strands in the cable.

The starter-circuit voltage drop can be measured by placing one of the terminals of an expanded-

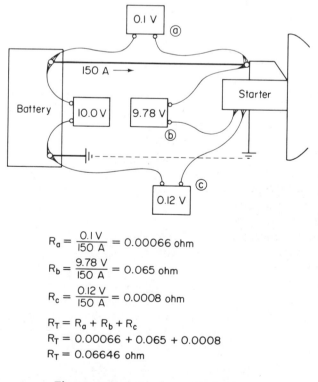

$$R_a = \frac{0.1\ V}{150\ A} = 0.00066\ ohm$$

$$R_b = \frac{9.78\ V}{150\ A} = 0.065\ ohm$$

$$R_c = \frac{0.12\ V}{150\ A} = 0.0008\ ohm$$

$R_T = R_a + R_b + R_c$
$R_T = 0.00066 + 0.065 + 0.0008$
$R_T = 0.06646\ ohm$

Fig. 1-9 Voltage drop in a series circuit.

goes through each of these restrictions in series, one after the other.

The grounded portion of the starter circuit is just as important as the insulated side. All of the current that flows through the insulated and switch side of a series circuit also flows through the grounded side. The grounded side of the circuit is often overlooked when automotive electrical circuits are tested. It is tested in the same manner as the insulated side of the circuit.

1-3 PARALLEL ELECTRICAL CIRCUITS

The remote starter switching circuit is in operation along with the cranking circuit while the engine is being cranked. Current that flows through the switching circuit is not the same current that flows through the starter circuit. Current from the battery splits, some going through the switching circuit and some going through the starter circuit. Systems that split the current are called *parallel* circuits. Parallel circuits are sometimes called *shunt* circuits. It is obvious that as more circuits are connected in parallel, more current will be able to flow. The only way more current is able to flow with a fixed battery voltage is to lower the circuit resistance. The parallel circuit does this.

Here again, think of the raceway entrance. If a walk-in gate is opened in addition to the drive-in gate, more people can get into the raceway than through the drive-in gate alone, even though the walk-in people are restricted by ticket sales and ticket collectors.

Each restriction or resistance to current flow is measured in ohms. Resistances added in parallel provide more paths for current to flow. The formula for adding the total resistance in a parallel circuit is:

$$R = \frac{1}{1/R_1 + 1/R_2 + 1/R_3}$$

For example, if the starter circuit resistance is 0.0625 ohms and the starter switch circuit resistance is 2 ohms the total resistance of the parallel circuits would be:

$$R = \frac{1}{1/0.0625 + 1/2} = \frac{1}{16/1 + 1/2} = \frac{1}{32 + 1/2} = \frac{2}{33}$$

$$= 0.0606 \text{ ohms}$$

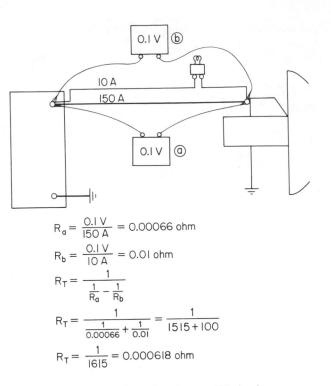

$$R_a = \frac{0.1 \text{ V}}{150 \text{ A}} = 0.00066 \text{ ohm}$$

$$R_b = \frac{0.1 \text{ V}}{10 \text{ A}} = 0.01 \text{ ohm}$$

$$R_T = \frac{1}{\frac{1}{R_a} - \frac{1}{R_b}}$$

$$R_T = \frac{1}{\frac{1}{0.00066} + \frac{1}{0.01}} = \frac{1}{1515 + 100}$$

$$R_T = \frac{1}{1615} = 0.000618 \text{ ohm}$$

Fig. 1-10 Voltage drop in a parallel circuit.

As more resistances are added, the total circuit resistance will decrease. Resistances used in parallel form an electrical *load*. An example, starting with voltage drop, is shown in Figure 1-10.

Another common electrical circuit that has application in automobiles and in test equipment is the *Wheatstone Bridge.* It can be used to illustrate the principle that no current will flow when the voltage is the *same* on both ends of a conductor.

The Wheatstone Bridge in Figure 1-11 is connected across a battery. This completes the circuit and current will flow. The voltage drop across R_1 is the same as the voltage drop across R_2, when

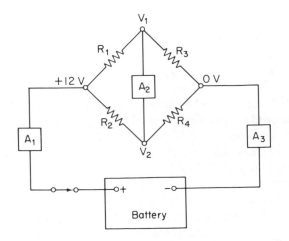

Fig. 1-11 Wheatstone Bridge Circuit.

the resistances are equal. The voltage at V_1 is the same as the voltage at V_2. No current flow will be shown on ammeter A_2 because the voltage is the same at both of its terminals. The current flow on ammeter A_1 is the same as the current shown on ammeter A_3 because the total current flowing in one series part of the circuit is the same as the total current flowing in any other series part of the circuit.

1-4 MAGNETISM

There is a very specific relationship between electricity and magnetism. This relationship is used in all electric motors, relays, solenoids, generators, alternators and electrical test instruments. A brief review of magnetism will be helpful in understanding the interrelationship of electricity and magnetism. Magnetism was first observed in curious stones called *lodestones* that when suspended would turn to the same alignment with one end, or *pole*, pointing north and the other end pointing south. Lodestones were first used as compasses aboard ships for navigation. Studies of their unusual nature led to the discovery that *like poles repelled* and *unlike poles attracted* each other. Lodestones, or *magnets* as they were later called, also attracted iron. If a sheet of plastic is placed over a bar magnet

Fig. 1-13 Magnetic field around a horseshoe magnet used in an instrument.

and iron filings are sprinkled on the *plastic*, the filings will collect in lines. These are called *magnetic lines of force*. All of the lines together are called a *magnetic field*. The lines form even when the bar magnet is rotated. This proves that the lines of force are actually a section view of a magnetic field which consists of a number of magnetic shells that never cross each other. They come together at each pole. The magnetic force is considered to be directed from the north to south pole of the magnet along the outside of the magnet. If the bar magnet is bent in the form of a horseshoe the poles would form on the ends of the horseshoe and lines of force would concentrate between the poles.

Magnetic fields have other interesting features. If a soft iron object is placed in the magnetic field the field will be displaced as the lines of force concentrate in the iron rather than moving through air. An iron bar is often placed across the open end of a horseshoe magnet to act as a *keeper* by forming a path that is easier for the magnetic lines to move through than through air. This characteristic of iron to concentrate magnetic lines of force is due to the low *reluctance* of iron compared to that of air. Magnetic lines of force move through other materials, such as copper, aluminum, and plastic, in nearly the same way they move through air.

If a magnet is cut it will form two magnets, end to end, each having a north and south pole. Each cut will produce a smaller but a complete magnet. If this example were carried to the extreme, one atom would be left and it would still be a magnet.

Fig. 1-12 Effects of polarity. (a) Unlike poles attract, (b) like poles repel.

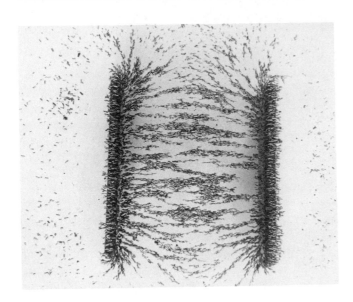

Fig. 1-14 Magnetic field around small sections of a bar magnet.

1-5 ELECTROMAGNETISM

An atom acts like a very small magnet, having north and south magnetic poles. Current flowing through a conductor will tend to polarize the electrons around the atoms so their magnetic poles are generally headed in the same direction. Polarity align-

ment of the electrons produces a magnetic field that surrounds all current-carrying conductors. The magnetic field is considered to be directed from the north pole toward the south pole. If one places his left thumb pointing in the direction of electron movement, the fingers will be pointing in the direction that the magnetic field surrounds the conductor. This is called the *left hand rule.*

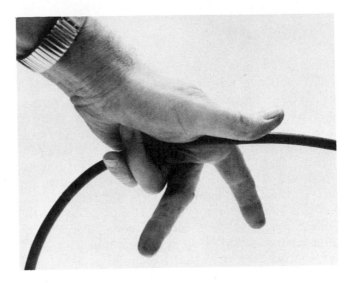

Fig. 1-16 Left hand rule with the thumb pointing in the direction of electron flow and fingers pointing in the direction of magnetic flow.

The strength of the magnetic field surrounding a current-carrying conductor is proportional to the current strength flowing in the conductor. If more current flows, the magnetic field becomes stronger and produces more magnetic lines of force. When two magnetic fields that surround adjacent conductors run in the same direction between the conductors, their fields are displaced outward. This occurs when current flows in opposite directions in each of the adjacent conductors. The force of the displaced fields tends to force the conductors to separate or repel the conductors.

When the magnetic lines of force that surround current-carrying conductors normally move in opposite directions in the space between the conductors, the lines of force will join up. This forms a large displaced magentic field that produces a force which will tend to pull the conductors together or attract the conductors. This force occurs when the current flow in the two adjacent conductors is flowing in the same direction. Magnetic forces try to move the conductor to the *center* of the magnetic field. Used in this way the device is called an *electromagnet.*

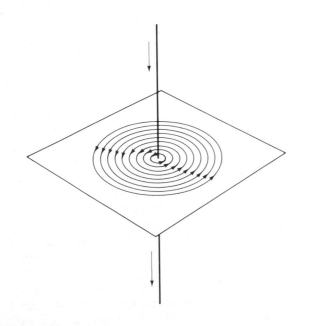

Fig. 1-15 Magnetic field around a current-carrying conductor.

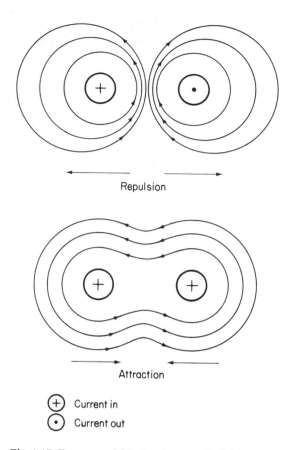

Repulsion

Attraction

⊕ Current in
⊙ Current out

Fig. 1-17 Forces resulting from magnetic fields around adjacent current-carrying conductors.

Motor solenoid and electrical relay operation makes use of attracting and repelling magnetic forces that surround current-carrying conductors.

Electrical instrument operation is another important use of electromagnetism. High quality instruments are based on a galvanometer D'Arsonval movement which uses a moving coil suspended in the magnetic field of a horseshoe magnet. As cur-

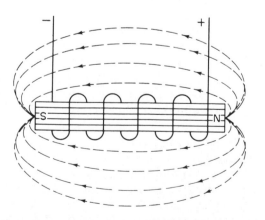

Fig. 1-18 Drawing of a typical magnetic field produced by an electromagnet.

rent flows through the suspended coil an electo-magnetic field is produced. The interrelationship of the two magnetic fields produces a reaction that causes the moving coil to rotate and assume a new position. This movement is shown by a pointer that is attached to the moving coil and sweeps past a calibrated dial as the coil rotation takes place.

The moving galvanometer coil is a winding of many turns of very fine wire wound on a non-magnetic frame. The frame has a short shaft on each end supported by and pivoting in jeweled bearings. This allows free rotation of the coil around an iron core that is held in place with a plastic support. A hair spring on each short pivot shaft holds the meter coil and its indicator pointer in the "at rest" position. Electromagnetism of the moving coil rotates it against the hair spring force. The hair springs also serve as electrical leads between the instrument terminals and the movable coil. Calibration is accomplished by adjusting the hair spring anchors. The back anchor is used for basic meter calibration when the meter is manufactured. The front anchor can be changed with a small screw on the instrument cover to provide the meter zero setting.

Most electrical test instruments used in automotive service have meters built in this way. The test instrument is provided with electrical circuits, switches, resistors, and shunts that sense the electrical signal of the item being measured and convert the signal to a voltage at the meter terminals. Current flowing through the moving coil of the meter is directly proportional to the voltage at the meter terminals because the moving coil has a fixed resistance.

The meter is used as a voltmeter. With the correct size resistances connected in series through appropriate switch positions the meter will read different voltage ranges. The same meter is also used as an ammeter to measure current by connecting the meter terminals to the ends of a fixed-resistance shunt through which current is flowing. The meter measures voltage drop across the shunt, which is proportional to the current flow. The current flow is indicated on the calibrated dial. Different sized shunts are used to measure different ampere ranges.

The basic galvanometer instrument can be connected into other circuits when the test signal is modified by electronic components within the

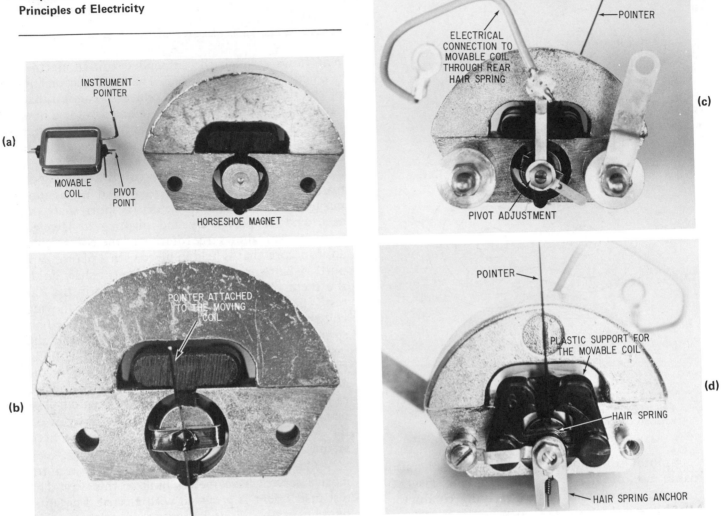

Fig. 1-19 Instrument movement. (a) Major parts, (b) coil in the magnetic field, (c) back side of instrument, (d) front side of instrument.

test instrument which convert the test signal to a voltage. Instruments of this type measure engine speed, dwell, ohms, microfarads, ignition output, hydrocarbons, carbon monoixde, etc.

1-6 INDUCTION

If the lines of force in a magnetic field are made to cut across a conductor in opposition to their normal action, they will cause the electrons in the conductor to attempt to drift in one direction. The more magnetic lines of force that are made to cut the conductor, the stronger will be the force attempting to move the conductor's free electrons.

This electromagnetic force is measured in volts, the same units that are used for the electrical pressure of batteries. Producing an electromotive force through relative motion between a conductor and magnetic field is called *electromagnetic induction.* The strength of the electromotive force depends on the number of magnetic lines of force cutting across the conductor each second.

The alternator is one of the common automotive devices using the principle of electromagnetic induction. The rotating part of the alternator, the *rotor,* is an electromagnet with a magnetic field surrounding it. As the rotor is forced to rotate by a drive belt, the magnetic lines of force cross the wire coils of a stationary conductor, the stator, lo-

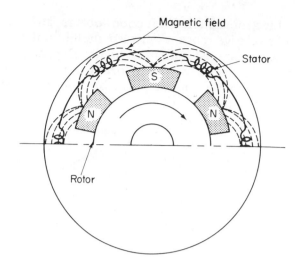

Fig 1-20 Electromagnetic induction.

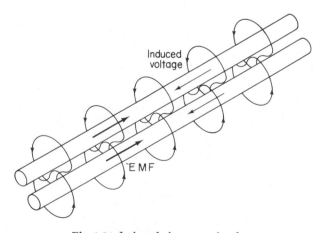

cated in the alternator frame. This produces a voltage in the stator coils which forces a current to flow through the automotive electrical system. In this case electromagnetic induction results from moving magnetic lines of force cutting a stationary conductor.

Current flowing in an alternator reverses itself, increasing and decreasing as it alternates. As the current flow increases in the stator, it forms a second expanding and contracting magnetic field around the stator winding. This newly-formed moving magnetic field cuts across the adjacent conductors within the stator coil winding. This moving field produces a counter voltage in the adjacent conductors of the stator coils which opposes the initial voltage that was induced by the rotor magnetic field. This principle of inducing a counter voltage in a coil wire that is carrying an increasing or a decreasing current is called *inductance.*

Fig. 1-21 Induced electromotive force in a section of a coil.

Maximum alternator current output is limited by the induced counter voltage. As counter voltage approaches the alternator output voltage, the alternator amperage output stabilizes at a maximum safe value.

Inductance is only present when there is an increasing or decreasing current flowing in adjacent conductors. When the current change rate is one ampere per second inducing one volt, the system has an inductance unit of one *henry.* Henry units are not used in automotive servicing. They are used in electrical equipment design and may be used as an aid to understanding the equipment operation.

A similar type of electromagnetic induction occurs in the ignition coil. When the ignition contact points are closed, current will flow through the heavy primary windings of the coil to make the coil into an electromagnet with a surrounding magnetic field. When the ignition points open, the primary ignition current stops and the magnetic field collapses. As the field collapses, the magnetic lines of force rapidly move through the coil secondary windings. These rapidly moving magnetic lines of force induce a high voltage in the coil secondary windings. This high voltage produces the arc or spark at the spark plug. Here again the lines of force move through a conductor to produce a voltage. The faster they cross the conductor the more voltage is produced.

Electromagnetic induction also occurs in motors. As the armature turns it cuts through the magnetism of the motor field. This produces an electromotive force that is in a direction opposite to the electromotive force imposed on the starter by the battery. It is, therefore, called a *counter electromotive force* (CEMF). Counter electromotive force strength is proportional to armature speed. As motor speed increases, its counter electromotive force increases. When the mechanical load plus the counter electromotive force equals battery electrical energy, the motor will not rotate faster and its speed will stabilize. In this case the conductor moves in a stationary magnetic field to produce voltage. A weaker magnetic field produces less counter electromotive force at the same armature speed and so the armature speed will increase until it produces a counter electromotive force that balances system voltage.

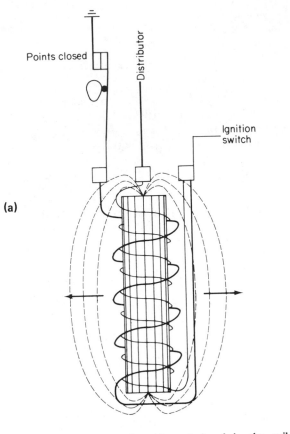

(a)

Points closed

Distributor

Ignition switch

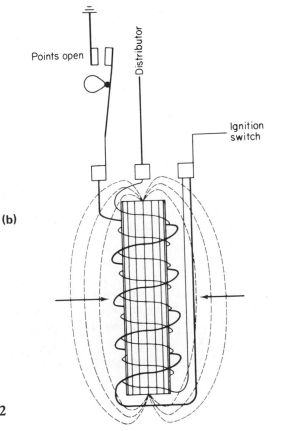

(b)

Points open

Distributor

Ignition switch

Fig. 1-22 Induction coil. Voltage induced in the coil secondary by the changing primary magnetic field cutting across the coil windings. (a) Magnetic field builds up while the points are closed, (b) magnetic field collapses when the points open.

Electromagnetic induction occurs any time there is relative motion between the lines of force of a magnetic field and a conductor. Expanding or contracting magnetic lines of force can move across a conductor or the conductor can be moved through a stationary magnetic field.

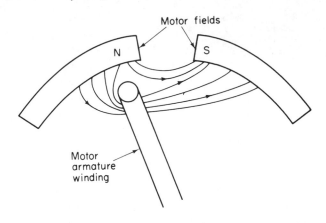

Motor fields

N   S

Motor armature winding

Fig. 1-23 A conductor moving through a magnetic field.

1-7 CAPACITANCE

Capacitance is another electrical property that affects the electrical system, especially the ignition system. When two conductor materials are close together but insulated from each other, the negative electrical charges in one conductor will attract the positive electrical charges in the adjacent conductor. These electrical charges will remain as long as the conductors are insulated from each other.

Condensers are the easiest capacitance devices to understand. They are made from two long strips of electrically conductive foil called *plates*, separated by insulating paper. The number of electrons that can accumulate on one side of a plate is limited by the plate size and the distance between it and the adjacent plate. The larger and closer together the plates are, the more electrons they can store. The ability to store electrons is called

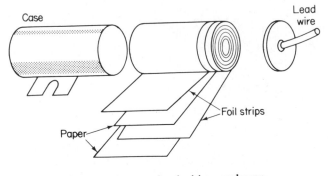

Case

Lead wire

Foil strips

Paper

Fig. 1-24 Parts of an ignition condenser.

capacitance. The electrical measurement of capacitance is a *farad.* It is a very large unit, and so
the smaller unit, *microfarad* (mfd = 1/1,000,000
farad) is used to describe the electrical capacity of
automotive condensers.

In addition to condensers, a number of other
parts of the automobile electrical systems have
capacitance. Any two current-carrying conductors
that are close together but insulated from each
other have capacitance. A good example of this is
a wire coil, such as is used in an electromagnet or
ignition coil. In addition to carrying the required
current these coils have capacitance which affects
the way in which they function. This function will
be described in more detail in the chapter on
ignition systems.

1-8 DIODE—SEMICONDUCTORS

It is necessary to understand the operation of
diodes if one is to understand rectification of alternator current in the automobile charging system.
Diode operation is based upon semiconductor
principles.

It has been previously stated that metallic
atoms with less than four electrons in the outer
shell are good conductors and atoms with more
than four electrons are good insulators. Atoms
with exactly four electrons in the outer shell are
neither good conductors nor good insulators. Silicon
and germanium represent materials of this type. In
pure crystalline form, adjacent atoms share the
electrons of their outer shells and, in effect, they
each have eight electrons in their outer shell. This
makes them good insulators.

But if silicon, for example, is slightly con-
taminated or "doped" at a rate of 1:10,000,000
with impurity material that has five electrons in
the outer shell, such as phosphorus, arsenic, or
antimony in crystalline form, there would not be
enough space in the shared outer shell for nine
electrons and so a free electron would be left. This
type of doped material would be called a *negative*
or *N-type* material because it already has excess
electrons and would *repel* a negative charge or an
electron.

If, on the other hand, the silicon were con-
taminated or doped with impurities, such as small
particles of boron or indium crystals, which have
only three electrons on their outer shell, a gap or
hole without an electron would remain in the shared
outer shell. A *hole* is the absence of an electron
needed to complete an atom's outer shell. Doped

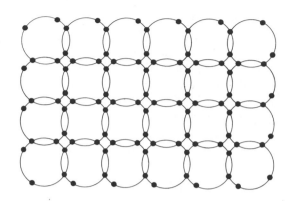

Fig. 1-25 Atom with four electrons in a structure.

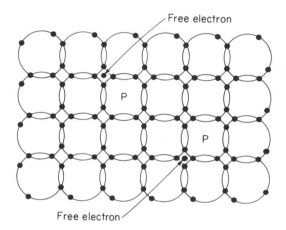

Fig. 1-26 Two atoms of phosphorus having five electrons
within a structure made of atoms with four electrons.
This leaves two free electrons.

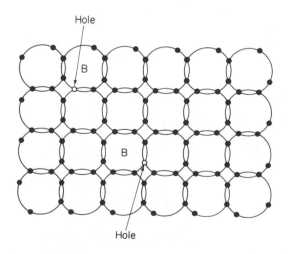

Fig. 1-27 Two atoms of boron having three electrons
within a structure made of atoms with four electrons.
This leaves two holes.

material with holes is called *positive* or *P-type* material because it would attract a negative charge or an electron.

Movement of electrons and holes can be compared to heavy slow-moving traffic. Assume that the cars are in a line of traffic and the first car (*A*) moves up one space. Each following car (*B, C, D,* etc.) successively moves into the space ahead of it. The cars progress forward while the space moves backward. Electrons can be compared to the car and holes can be compared to the space. Electrons and holes move in opposite directions.

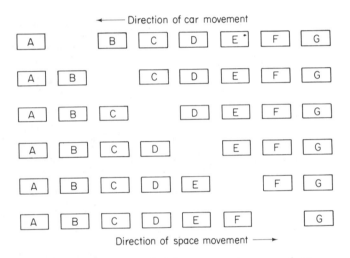

Fig. 1-28 Electron and hole movement compared to vehicle movement in traffic.

Diode Construction. The P-type and N-type materials are called *semiconductors.* In certain combinations of materials and of circuits, semiconductors will conduct current. In other applications, they will act as insulators. In automotive applications, semiconductors are used in *diodes* and in *transistors.*

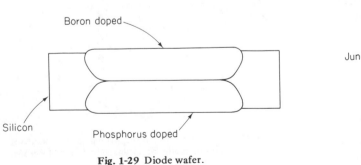

Fig. 1-29 Diode wafer.

Fig. 1-30 Encapsulated diode wafer.

The diode semiconductor is made under very closely controlled conditions from a thin wafer of crystal silicon. Boron is painted on one side and phosphorus on the other side of the crystal to make a *junction* of P-type and N-type semiconductor materials. The doped wafer is put into a high-temperature furnace and heated until the doping materials are fused into the silicon. Following this, the semiconductor wafer is plated for good electrical contact; it is then broken into chips 3/16 in. × 3/16 in. (4.6 mm × 4.6 mm) square and 0.007 in. (0.175 mm) thick, that can be encapsuled for easy assembly into electrical circuits.

Diode Operation. Within the diode, the holes in the P-type material attract electrons from the N-type material toward the *junction,* which is a thin region between the P-type and N-type materials in the crystal. As the electrons move toward the junction, they leave positive ions behind them that prevent the electrons from crossing the junction into the P-type material. Some electrons do drift across the junction. However, this drift is

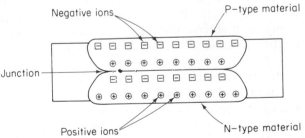

Fig. 1-31 Electron and hole movement in a diode with no voltage applied.

14

an insignificant amount of electron flow and does not measurably affect diode operation.

If the diode is connected into a circuit with the negative side of the circuit connected to the N-type material and the positive side of the circuit connected to the P-type material, a current will flow across the diode. This is called a *forward bias.* Electrons from the circuit put additional electrons on the N-type material. These electrons will satisfy the positive ions that had been holding electrons from crossing the junction. With this restraining force satisfied by new electrons, the electrons at the junction move across the junction and on through the circuit, resulting in a current flow.

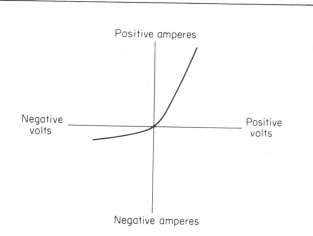

Fig. 1-33 Curve showing how a diode conducts current as voltage changes.

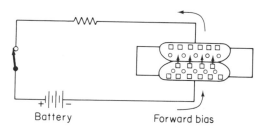

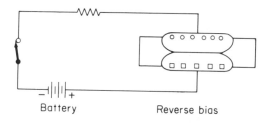

Fig. 1-32 Electron and hole movement with a forward bias and a reverse bias.

If the polarity of the diode is reversed, forming a *reverse bias,* the electrons in the negative side of the circuit are attracted by the holes in the P-type material. The electrons of the N-type material are attracted to the positive side of the circuit. This results in moving both the electrons of the N-type material and the holes of the P-type material away from the junction. The tendency to move in opposing directions allows an insignificant current flow across the junction. In effect, there is no reverse current flow through a diode.

The diode is used as a one-way electrical check. It will allow current to flow in one direction (forward bias) by acting as a conductor and will stop the current back flow (reverse bias) by acting as an insulator.

Excessive voltage, either forward or reverse biased, will force an abnormal current to flow across the diode junction, rapidly heating the diode. If the voltage is high enough to force excess current across the junction, the diode will be ruined by overheating. Some special diodes are heavily doped so that they will withstand large reverse-biased currents without damage. When made in this way, they are called *Zener diodes* and are used in systems that require voltage control. At less than the designed reverse-bias voltage, they act as a normal diode conducting only a forward bias current. Above this designed voltage, they will conduct a reverse-bias current.

Diodes used in alternators are designated either as positive or as negative diodes. When they

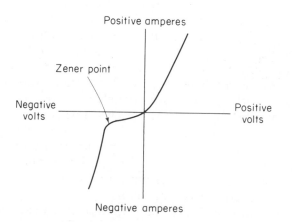

Fig. 1-34 Curve showing how a Zener diode conducts current as voltage changes.

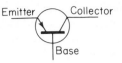

are encapsulated their exterior case looks similar; in the negative diode, the P-type material is connected to the case and the N-type material is connected to the diode lead. In the positive diode, the N-type material is connected to the case and the P-type material is connected to the diode lead. Positive diodes have their part number printed in red and negative diodes have their part number printed in black.

1-9 TRANSISTOR—SEMICONDUCTORS

The transistor is another of the many uses for semiconductor material. Diodes used in automotive applications are usually made of doped silicon crystals. Many transistors are made from germanium crystals using indium to dope P-type material and antimony to dope N-type material. Silicon transistors are used in high temperature applications. A diode is made of two materials, P-type junctioned to N-type. Transistors add another junction to the diode, forming either PNP or NPN transistors having two junctions. Most automobile applications use PNP-type transistors in discrete circuit and hybrid circuit construction. The NPN-type is used in monolithic voltage regulators that are designed to be placed inside the alternator case.

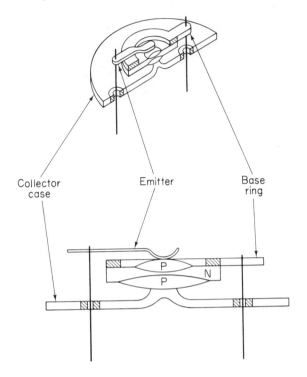

Fig. 1-35 Transistor construction.

Transistor Construction. A simplified description of the transistor manufacturing procedure follows, with a PNP-type transistor used as an example. The procedure starts with a germanium crystal that has been doped with antimony. It is cut into thin slices to make a wafer of N-type material. Pure germanium crystals are applied to each side of the N-type wafer. Indium is then placed on each side of the pure germanium surface crystals and heat is applied to fuse the indium into the surface of the germanium crystals that are on each side of the N-type wafer. This forms a single crystal wafer consisting of three regions, N-type material in the center and P-type material on each side, forming a PNP transistor. The P-type materials are close together with a very thin layer of N-type material between them.

When assembling the transistor in a case, the outer edge of the N-type material of the original thin wafer is attached to a metal ring with one of the P materials fitting through the hole of the ring.

An extension from the ring is used to attach the electrical conductor. The center N-type material of the transistor is called the transistor *base.* The transistor with its base connection is placed in a copper container so that the largest P-type material area rests against the heavy bottom of the container's inner surface. The container serves as an electrical connection called the transistor *collector* as well as a heat sink to keep the transistor cool. A strip of metal connected to the smaller P-type area located in the ring hole serves as an electrical connection called a transistor *emitter.* This transistor assembly is brazed together and sealed in a case. The wire from the emitter is run through an insulator in the transistor case so that an electrical connection can be made. Some transistors will also use a wire-type connector for the collector. The actual transistor is only the small crystal wafer. Connections and case make up the bulk of the transistor assembly.

Some transistors are integrated in a complete monolithic or one-piece circuit. These circuits start with a silicon wafer. The wafer is coated with

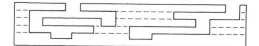

Integrated circuit build up
(side view)

Fig. 1-36 Typical integrated circuit buildup.

a ceramic insulation and an emulsion that masks some of the insulation material. Where it is not masked, the ceramic insulation is removed by etching to expose silicon. Doping material is fused into the silicon, the wafer again is ceramic coated, masked and etched in other places, and then another doping agent is used. In some places conductors are developed, in other places resistors and capacitors. This process gradually builds up a complete circuit with transistors, conductors, resistors, and capacitor within the wafer. The wafer is scribed and broken into chips. Each chip is a complete electronic circuit with all required operating parts. These complete circuit chips are encapsuled and have electrical leads for circuit connections.

Transistor Operations.   A PNP-type transistor will be used to describe transistor operation. The N-type material in the central region is the base. It is made as thin as possible. The P-type material in the outer regions form the emitter and collector. The emitter is connected through the operating unit to the positive or insulated side of the battery. The collector is connected to the grounded or negative side of the battery. The transistor base circuit is used to control transistor operation.

Electricity is movement of electrons. It has been previously shown that as the electrons move in one direction, holes will move in the opposite direction. It is easier to understand PNP-type transistor operation if a simplified explanation is given in terms of hole movement rather than electron movement.

Assume that the emitter is connected through the operating unit to the positive battery terminal. The collector is connected through ground to the negative battery post, with the base circuit switch open. Whenever possible, electrons fill holes to make neutral atoms. Excess holes supplied by the battery collect along the junction between the emitter and base. Holes in the collector are attracted toward the negative or grounded side of the battery. As the holes move toward the grounded side of the battery, free electrons are left behind in the emitter side of the transistor, and these hold the holes in position.

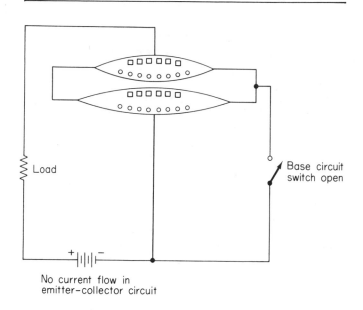

Load

Base circuit
switch open

No current flow in
emitter–collector circuit

Fig. 1-37 Transistor circuit with open base circuit.

When the base circuit switch is closed (having the same polarity as the collector) holes will move from the emitter to the base and back to the battery ground. As the holes from the emitter cross the base junction, their energy carries most of them across the second junction into the collector. This produces a current in the operating circuit. The base current is about 2.0% of the total emitter current. When the base circuit is reopened, hole

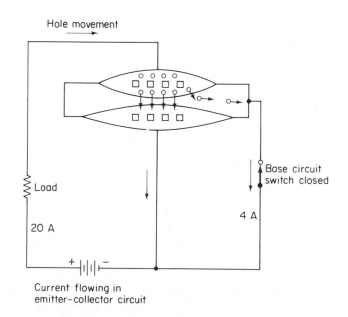

Hole movement

Load

20 A

Base circuit
switch closed

4 A

Current flowing in
emitter–collector circuit

Fig. 1-38 Transistor circuit with a conducting base circuit.

17

movement stops, the transistor charges become neutralized, and hole movement to the collector stops, stopping the current flow from the emitter to the collector. In this way the transistor is a solid-state electrical switch with no moving parts.

Its switching operation is controlled by controlling base current of the transistor.

Summary. A thorough understanding of electrical principles and basic electrical circuit components will aid the reader in understanding the operation of automotive electrical systems. This understanding will be invaluable in helping the reader to diagnose a malfunctioning electrical system.

REVIEW QUESTIONS

1. Why is the flow of electricity called a current?

2. What is all matter composed of?

3. What particles make up atoms?

4. What kind of atoms is water made of?

5. How many electrons do atoms of a conductor have in their outer orbit?

6. How many electrons do atoms of an insulating material have in their outer orbit?

7. What is electricity?

8. What is required for electron flow when voltage is applied?

9. What is required to have a current flow?

10. What produces heat in a conductor as current flows?

11. When the engine is not running, what controls maximum electromotive force in the electrical system?

12. In what units is electrical power measured?

13. What causes system voltage to increase?

14. When is the system voltage at a maximum?

15. What increases the resistance of a conductor?

16. Why is battery voltage below 12 volts when the starter is cranking?

17. What must be necessary in a circuit to measure voltage drop?

18. What are systems called that split the current that is flowing?

19. How can current flow be increased when a battery supplies the electrical energy?

20. How does one magnetic pole affect another?

21. What makes up the magnetic field?

22. What way is the magnetic field directed?

23. How is a meter needle set at zero?

24. What part of an alternator is an electromagnet?

25. What limits alternator output?

26. What will a weakened magnetic field do to an electric motor, assuming all other factors remain constant?

27. What electrical function does a condenser perform?

28. What is the characteristic of an atom with four electrons in its outer shell?

29. What happens when a material having four electrons in the outer shell is doped with one having five atoms in the outer shell?

30. What prevents electrons in the N-type material from crossing the junction into the P-type material when no voltage is applied?

31. Describe a diode operation.

32. How can an encapsulated diode be identified as negative?

33. What three parts make up a transistor?

34. What is a complete circuit in a "chip" called?

35. How does the movement of holes compare to the Franklin current theory?

36. What is the name given to a solid state electrical check valve?

2

Routine Service Operations

The useful service life of an automobile can be extended by promptly repairing any obvious malfunction and by providing preventive maintenance. Except for a change in appearance or performance, these two conditions are the only reason a customer will have his automobile serviced by a technician.

Anyone working on a vehicle should make a conscious effort to work in a safe manner that prevents personal injury or damage to the vehicle being worked on. To start with, he should wear appropriate clothing. Loose clothing may catch on a moving part to cause injury. Long sleeves will help protect the arms from becoming burned on hot engine parts. It is advisable to remove rings and wrist watches so that they do not catch on parts and injure one's hands. Metal in these items may contact an electrical junction and cause a severe burn when the ring or watch heats up as it conducts electricity. Proper safety glasses are recommended during any automotive service to minimize the chance of eye damage.

Fender covers and seat covers should be used to protect the vehicle from scratches and soil from tools and dirty vehicle parts. It is much easier to cover the vehicle than it is to clean it after it has become dirty or to repair scratches.

Routine service work that an automobile technician will perform includes lubrication, oil changes, filter changes, seasonal service, and tune-ups. The automobile technician will be expected to

repair faulty items rapidly and correctly. Faulty small electrical components are usually replaced, but major electrical units, such as starters and alternators, are disassembled and the faulty subassembly replaced. Connecting wires are usually repaired. The biggest problem the technician faces is the identification of the specific part that is causing the malfunction. This is especially true in electrical systems. Checking the system to identify a faulty part is called diagnosis. Flow charts in the applicable service manual are especially useful in diagnosis when they are carefully followed.

2-1 LIGHTS

The most usual failure in a lighting system is light bulb failure. Some manufacturers call the light bulb a lamp. Light bulb life depends on the bulb construction, the system voltage, the time the light bulb has been in use, and the amount of jarring it receives as the vehicle operates over rough surfaces. Many light bulbs will last as long as the automobile is in use while others may need to be replaced several times during the lifetime of the vehicle.

Lights are safety items. The exterior lights help the driver light the roadway and warn other drivers that a vehicle is there. They also indicate that the driver intends to decelerate or to change direction. The interior lights give the passengers

19

Fig. 2-1 Typical automotive lamp bulbs.

light for entry into and exit from the automobile. Instrument lights help the driver to keep track of the vehicle operating conditions to prevent dangerous or destructive malfunctions. Any time a light does not function it becomes a factor contributing to vehicle safety.

Bulb Identification. Light bulbs are given a commercial designation that is used by both the bulb manufacturer and automobile manufacturer. Bulbs are designed with different bayonet base sizes (some are baseless), locking pin arrangements, single or double contacts, voltage and amperage requirements, as well as other technical design features. The technician will be most concerned with the base size, the locking pins and contact arrangement, and the correct voltage range. This information is available in the owner's handbook that is usually kept in the glove box, the applicable automotive service manual, and in bulb manufacturer's catalogs. If these are not available, the bulb should be replaced with the same number as the bulb removed. This should always be the last resort, because someone may have installed an incorrect bulb, and this may be the reason it burned out.

Bulb Replacement. Turn-signal lights, marker lights, and some tail lights are designed to be sealed from dust and moisture. They consist of a lamp body mounted in an external body panel. The lamp body is covered with a lens; there is a gasket

seal between them. The bulb is usually replaced by removing phillips head lens-mounting screws, and then lifting the lens off. The bulb can be removed by pushing it inward and turning it counterclockwise to release the pins; then the bulb can be lifted from its socket. If the lens seal does not function correctly or if moisture follows the wire into the bulb socket the bulb may corrode and seize in the socket. In this case special bulb-removing tools are

Fig. 2-2 Replacing a lamp bulb after removing the lens.

available to aid in its removal. When these special tools are not available the bulb can be covered with a shop towel and the glass broken. The bulb base can then be forced sufficiently with pliers to remove it. In some cases the base is corroded so badly that the entire socket will have to be replaced. Be sure to seal the new socket properly so it will not seize again.

The new bulb base is pressed into the socket and turned clockwise to secure it in place. Check the bulb operation. If it is normal, install the gasket and lens.

Some tail light reflectors have removable sockets so that the bulb can easily be changed from inside the trunk. Spring clips on the socket hold it in the lamp body. From inside the trunk the socket is merely pulled from the lamp body. The bulb is replaced in the socket as previously described; then the socket is replaced in the lamp body. Be careful to line up the tab that correctly positions the socket.

Fig. 2-4 Replacing a lamp bulb from inside the trunk.

Fig 2-3 Typical lamp socket assembly.

Instrument panel lights are designed with removable sockets. When the instrument panel is wired, the socket is similar to replaceable tail light sockets. Most modern instrument panels have printed circuits, and so the socket is made of molded plastic with fingers to contact the printed conducting surfaces. The sockets are difficult, if not impossible, to see under the dash panel so that one learns to feel for the socket. The technician should not wear rings and watches while doing this, to avoid burns. The voltage under the dash is so low that it will not shock a person's hand if he makes contact without a metal conductor, but the metal can short a circuit. The current flow will make the metal hot.

The instrument bulb socket is turned counterclockwise to remove the socket from the printed panel circuit. If the bulb is baseless it is inserted in the socket and the socket is then reinstalled in the panel and checked to see that it is operating correctly.

Other interior light bulbs can be replaced by removing the lens to reach the bulb. Interior lights are not sealed. The lens may be fastened with screws around a frame or the lens may be made of flexible plastic that can be slightly distorted to release tangs, then lifted from the lamp body. The bulb is removed and replaced as previously described.

Sealed-beam headlight bulbs are held in an adjusting ring by a retaining ring. This is often covered by a trim panel called a door or bezel. The headlight door or bezel must be removed, usually by removing phillips head screws, to reach the retaining ring. The retaining ring can be removed without changing the position of the adjusting ring. Care must be exercised to be sure to turn only the retaining ring screws and not the adjusting ring screws to avoid upsetting the headlight aiming. When the retaining ring is removed the sealed-beam headlight bulb can be lifted out and the wiring socket removed from the bulb base.

The socket is plugged on to a new sealed-beam bulb of the correct size and type, then the light is turned on to see that the new bulb functions properly before the unit is assembled. Both high and low beams should be checked if the bulb is a type-2 bulb. If it is working correctly, the bulb should be properly seated in the adjusting ring and the retainer ring installed, followed by the door or bezel.

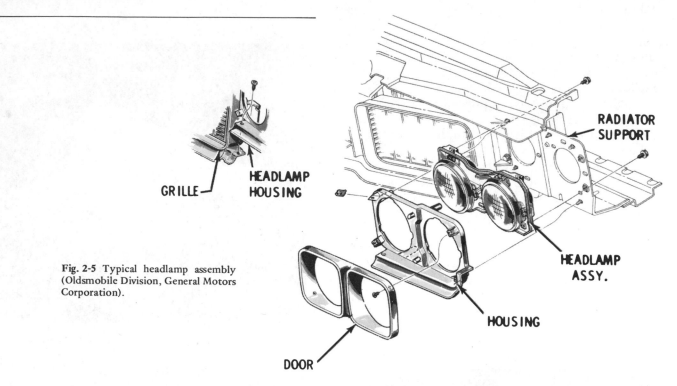

Fig. 2-5 Typical headlamp assembly (Oldsmobile Division, General Motors Corporation).

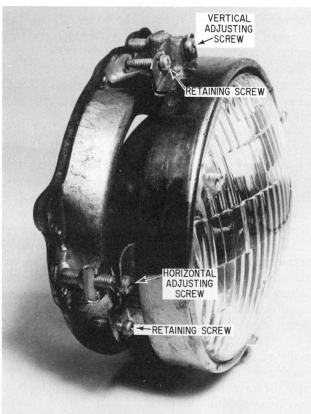

Fig. 2-6 Typical headlamp adjustment details.

Fig. 2-7 Identification numbers on headlamps.

If the headlight requires adjusting, aiming should be done before the door or bezel is installed because adjusting cannot be made on some cars when it is installed.

Headlight aiming can be done in a darkened area with the automobile on a level surface facing a wall. The lens of each headlight should be twenty-five feet from the wall. Vertical and horizontal lines are placed on the wall so that they cross directly in the front-center of each sealed-beam unit. The adjusting screw, either at the top center or bottom center of the adjusting ring, can be turned to raise or lower the beam. The adjustment screw on the side of the adjustment ring is used to move the beam sidewise. Type-2 bulbs are adjusted on low-beam position and type-1 bulbs on high-beam, so that the bright spot appears as on Figure 2-9.

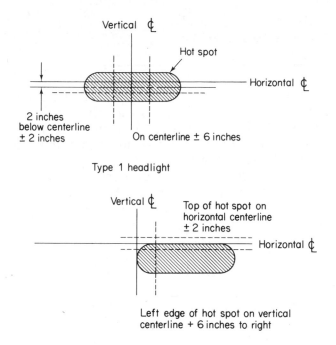

Type 1 headlight

Type 2 headlight

Fig. 2-9 Viewing screen patterns of the headlamp hot spot aiming area.

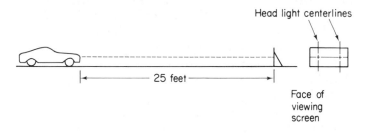

Fig. 2-8 Headlamp aiming principles.

Most shops do not have the available space and are too light to aim headlights as described; these shops depend on mechanical headlight-aiming devices. One of these aimers presents the equivalent viewing screen through optics, similar to a camera.

Fig. 2-10 Mechanical headlamp aimers (Cadillac Motor Car Division, General Motors Corporation).

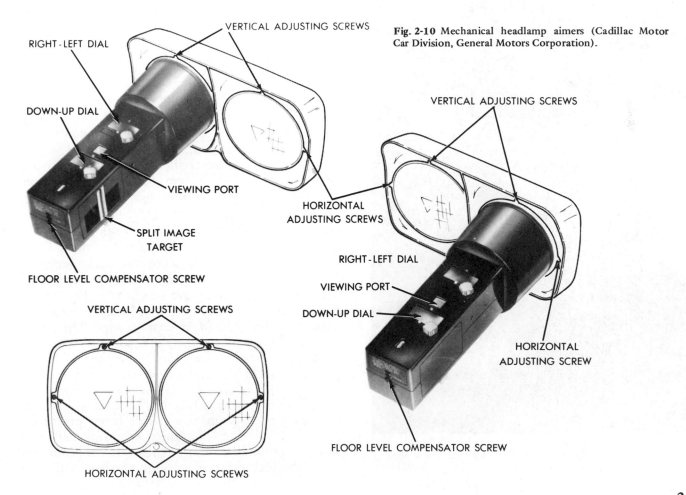

Most aimers mechanically aim the bulb. One aimer is attached to each bulb so that the aimer seats against three lugs molded into the sealed-beam lens. The two aimers are interconnected with strings or with alignment mirrors.

Before the aimer can be operated, the floor slope must first be measured so that this angle can be set on the aimers. This allows the bulb to be given the correct vertical elevation even when the floor is not level. The interconnection between the aimers allows the sidewise beam angle to be positioned correctly. When mechanical aimers are used properly there is no need to have the vehicle on a level floor or to have the lights turned on. Adjusting methods of any specific make of aimer are printed on the instrument or in an instruction book that accompanies it.

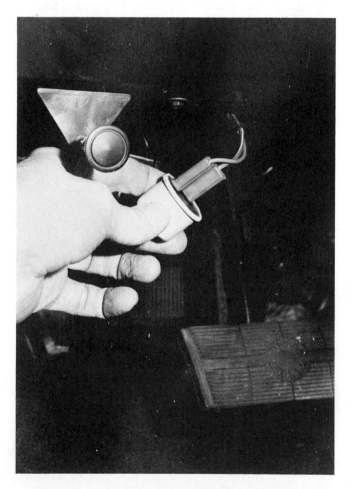

Fig. 2-11 Turn signal flasher unit lowered below the instrument panel for replacement.

2-2 FLASHER UNIT REPLACEMENT

When a flasher unit fails to operate in one direction it may be due to a burned out bulb that can be checked and replaced as previously described. One easy way to check the condition of a turn-signal bulb is to turn on the emergency hazard flasher, then observe which bulb fails to operate. If the turn signal fails to operate in both directions it is very likely that the flasher unit has failed. The flasher unit is usually mounted under the dash. It is a small enclosed can with wires connected on one end, or it is plugged into a junction on the fuse block. Sometimes it is clipped into a bracket and other times it hangs freely. Again the technician may have to reach under the dash and feel for the flasher. Once found, the flasher unit can be pulled low enough so that the socket can be removed and a new flasher installed. Most automobiles use two flasher units, one for the turn signals and one for the hazard warning lights. Be sure to check both systems before starting to work on the flashers, then check them again when the flasher is removed to be sure the correct flasher is being replaced. Check the system operation with the new flasher unit installed before putting the flasher in its retaining clip.

2-3 FUSES

Fuses are placed in circuits to protect the circuit from excess current flow that could lead to overheating and cause a fire. Circuits having continuous heavy current demand, such as windshield wipers, radio, hazard warning flasher, heater, and air conditioner, have an individual fuse in each circuit. Circuits having intermittent use, such as courtesy lights, trunk lights, and glove-box lights, are grouped together, and use one fuse. If the entire circuit fails to operate the failure is most likely caused by a blown fuse. Fuses are easily replaced. Most fuses are located under the lower edge of the dash panel or in the glove box where they can be viewed. In some cases the fuse block is hinged so that it can be lowered for easy viewing. The circuit that the fuse protects and the fuse type are usually identified on the fuse block. The burned fuse is pulled from the clip and a new one inserted.

One should always seek the reason for a blown fuse. The only way a fuse can blow is to have excess current flow in the circuit being protected. This could be due to a faulty operating unit, to a short or grounded wire, or to accidental grounding while the technician is working on the circuit. The

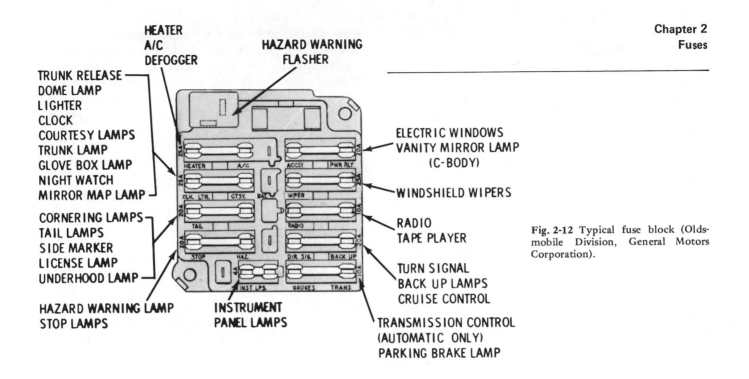

Fig. 2-12 Typical fuse block (Oldsmobile Division, General Motors Corporation).

cause of excess current should be determined before a new fuse is installed or the new fuse could blow, too.

If a fuse were replaced with a larger capacity fuse it could allow sufficient current to flow so that a partly malfunctioning unit would be completely ruined. This, of course, would increase the repair cost to the customer.

Circuit breakers are used in the headlight circuit instead of fuses. A high current draw in the headlight circuit will overheat the circuit breaker. The circuit breaker will open the circuit before damage occurs to the wiring. The circuit breaker cools quickly and closes the circuit to momentarily relight the headlights and this "on-off" action provides sufficient illumination to bring the vehicle to a safe stop.

A third type of safety device used in automobiles is a fusable link. Fusable links are short pieces of wire four sizes smaller than the wire they are protecting. The fusable link has a heavy heat-resistant insulation and so it looks like a large wire. This link will burn out before any damage is done to the circuit. Some fusable links are equipped with terminals so that they can be attached to connectors while others must be soldered into the circuit. An electrical dead short is about the only malfunction that will cause a fusable link to burn out. The short should be corrected before the link is replaced.

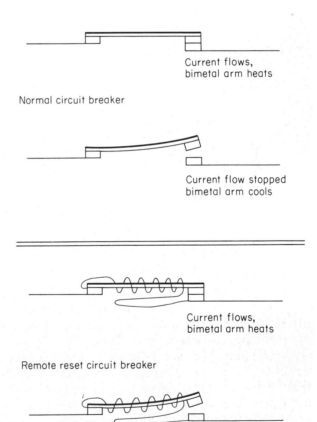

Fig 2-13 Principles of typical circuit breakers.

2-4 TESTING ELECTRICAL CIRCUITS

When functioning normally, electrical current flows through the wires and conductors to make a complete circuit. The battery or the alternator is the source of electrical current. Current flows from one of the source terminals through the conductor to the unit being operated, such as a light bulb, electric motor, solenoid, instrument, etc., then through another conductor to the opposite source terminal. Automobiles use a grounded system for almost all of their electrical circuits. The automobile frame, body sheetmetal, and engine are connected to the battery and alternator negative terminal to form one of the conductors to the operating units. This is called the grounded circuit. The other conductor is an insulated wire connecting the operating unit with the battery and alternator positive terminal.

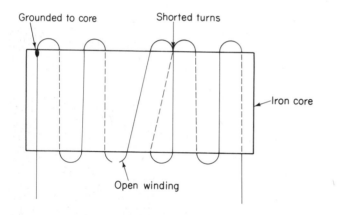

Fig. 2-14 Principles of shorts, opens and grounds (The Prestolite Company).

This part of the circuit is called the insulated circuit. When the circuit is complete the circuit has *continuity*. If the circuit is broken in any place and therefore the current cannot flow, the circuit is said to be *open*. This occurs when a switch is *off* or when the wire or conductor is broken; it also occurs when excess current flowing in a circuit opens the fuse, circuit breaker, or fusable link. When a circuit has continuity but the insulation is broken, current can flow from the circuit; this causes an electrical

leak. Electrical leakage between two wires is called a *short*. If the electricity leaks directly to the vehicle frame or body sheetmetal it causes a *ground*. Opens, shorts, and grounds are the electrical circuit problems usually encountered by the technician in automobile electrical system service.

Opens occur when a junction in the circuit does not make contact, when vibration breaks a wire or connection, or when the circuit has mechanical damage. Shorts and grounds can occur when vibration causes the insulation to wear through or when a wire is pinched or cut during installation.

The conductor size and the type of operating unit limit the amount of electrical current that can flow through the circuit with a specific electrical pressure (volts) at the source. Small conductors limit the flow more than large conductors, just as small pipes limit air flow more than large pipes in the shop air lines. The limiting factor in electrical systems is called resistance.

Electrical circuit problems are very difficult to solve by trial and error. They can be found by a straightforward test procedure using electrical test instruments. With the correct use of simple equipment it may take a little while to identify the cause of a problem. The correct use of elaborate equipment will pinpoint the problem quickly. This discussion will stress the use of simple electrical equipment. The two most useful tools are a 12-volt test light and a DC voltmeter. Both can be used to determine if voltage is available at any point in the circuit. The test light draws some current and the brightness is an indication of the voltage. The voltmeter does not draw any appreciable current and will give a direct reading of the voltage.

When an electrical unit fails to operate, the test light or voltmeter should be connected between the insulated wire at the unit terminal and a good ground (black voltmeter terminal to ground). When the electrical unit is turned on the test bulb should light or the voltmeter show a voltage reading. If there is no indication of electricity the unit will have to be disconnected and the wire itself rechecked in the same manner. If electricity is indicated at the terminal wire with the unit removed, the unit is faulty. If no electricity is available at the terminal wire, the circuit is open and the circuit will have to be tested in small sections to pinpoint the open. More detailed directions for circuit testing are given in Chapter 12.

(a)

Fig. 2-15 Testing the electrical circuit at an electrical unit. (a) Test light, (b) voltmeter.

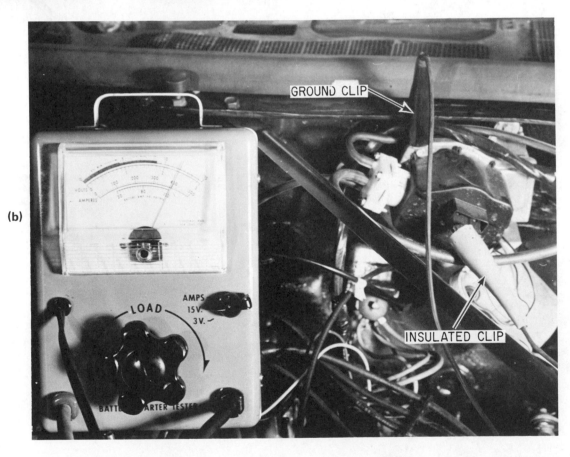

(b)

2-5 REPAIRING ELECTRICAL CIRCUITS

Once the specific electrical problem has been located it can easily be repaired using standard electrical repair procedures. If a wire is shorted or grounded as a result of breaks in the insulation with no other damage, it can be repaired by tightly wrapping the damaged wire with plastic electrical tape. If further electrical wiring damage exists or if opens occur, the faulty portion of the electrical system will have to be replaced.

If the problem is in a wire, the ends of the wire can be spliced or a new short piece of the same size and type of wire spliced between them. The splice must be mechanically strong and electrically sound. Splicing can be done by stripping the insulation from the wire, then wrapping the two wires being spliced around each other to make the joint mechanically strong. The joint is heated with a soldering iron until it is hot enough to cause rosin core solder to flow through the splice.

Fig 2-16 Making an electrical wire repair. (a) Stripping insulation, (b) crimping a connector, (c) crimping a terminal, (d) taping the connector.

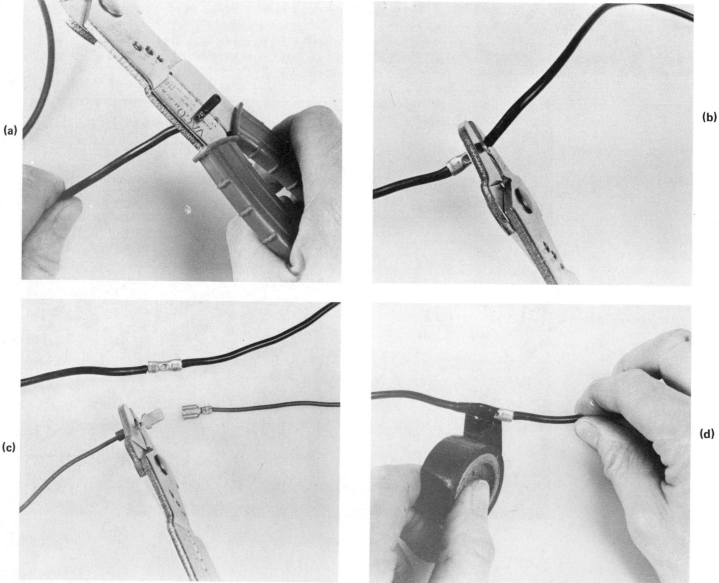

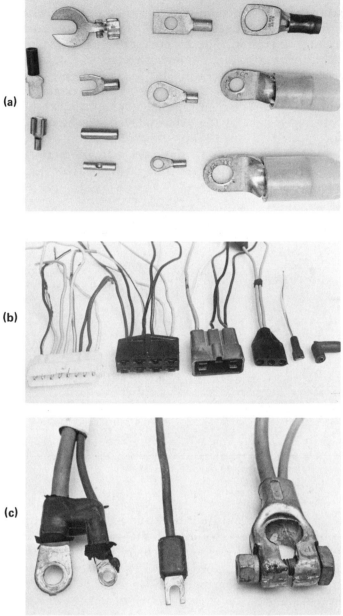

(a)

(b)

(c)

An alternate and faster means of making an electrical splice is to use a crimp-type terminal covered with tape or a plastic sleeve. Enough insulation is stripped from the wires so that the bare wire fits the connector being used. The insulating sleeve is placed on one of the wires, then the connector is put on the wire. A special crimping plier is used to squeeze the connector around the wire to make a mechanically strong and electrically sound joint. The second wire is placed in the other end of the connector and crimped. The splice is finished by centering the insulating sleeve over the splice or by wrapping the splice with plastic electrical tape.

Wire end terminals are available in a number of different sizes and shapes. They may be attached to the wire by rosin core solder or by crimping, depending upon the terminal type. A group of terminals may be held together in a junction block to interconnect the wiring between separate parts; for example, in the headlight wiring junction at the body fire wall bulkhead where all of the front body wiring is connected with one junction block. This makes a quick assembly procedure during manufacture with minimum chance of misconnecting the wires. The junction also provides a good location to separate the system to check the electrical circuit for opens, shorts, and grounds.

A useful test light can be made while one practices electrical repair procedures. The test light in the accompanying illustration is made from a readily available electrical socket, a number 67 bulb, wires, and clips. It is designed to incorporate a variety of repair procedures used in electrical systems.

Fig. 2-17 Typical electrical terminals. (a) Crimp type, (b) connector junction block, (c) molded insulation on terminals.

Fig. 2-18 Method of fastening terminals in connector junction blocks. They can be released with a small screwdriver blade.

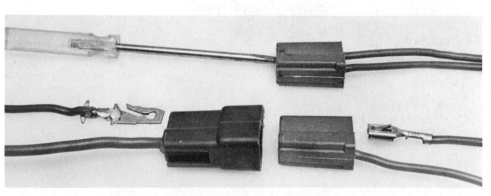

All automotive primary wiring is made of stranded wires covered with plastic insulation. The insulation is adequate to keep the electricity from leaking to ground. The number and size of strands in the wire are large enough to carry the current without adding excess resistance. If the wire size in new automobiles were larger than necessary to carry the required current it would increase the cost and weight of the vehicle. Oversize wires used for repair will not reduce the effectiveness of the circuit. Wires smaller than the original will increase the circuit resistance and reduce the circuit efficiency.

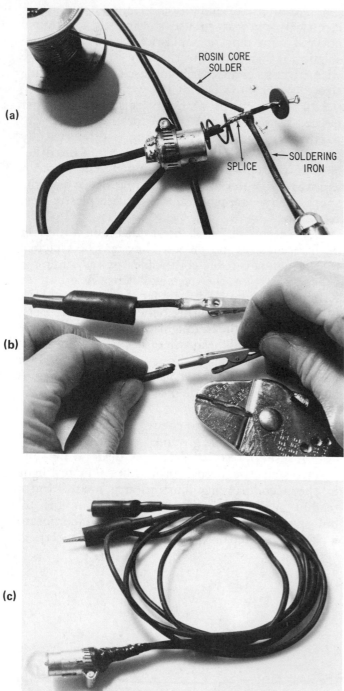

(a)

(b)

(c)

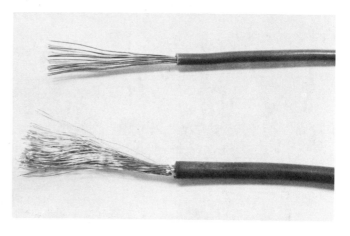

Fig. 2-20 Wire types used in automobiles. Standard primary wire above and flexible wire below.

The more and finer the strands in an electrical cable the more flexible and the more costly the wire is. Some locations, such as the distributor primary-lead wire, need to be flexible because they must withstand continuous movement. These wires are made from a large number of small strands. Wires under the dash and wires in the vehicle body do not usually flex in use so they can be made of less expensive primary wire using fewer large strands. Replacement wires should be of the proper type. Comparative examples are shown in the accompanying illustration.

After the wires are repaired they should be properly supported in brackets and clips. This reduces the chance of the wires failing again from vibration or from contacting hot engine parts.

Fig. 2-19 Making a test light. (a) Splicing a wire using a soldered joint, (b) crimping terminal clips, (c) completed test light.

REVIEW QUESTIONS

1. For what three reasons will a customer have his automobile serviced?

2. What is the biggest problem the technician faces when he works on automotive electrical circuits?

3. What is the standard distance from a viewing screen for headlight aiming?

4. What are three safety devices used in the electrical system?

5. What three basic electrical circuit problems are usually encountered by the technician?

6. How can a faulty turn signal bulb be identified?

7. What causes a fuse to blow?

8. What limits wire size in automotive wiring?

9. What is the advantage of a test light and a voltmeter when trying to locate an electrical problem?

3

The Automobile Battery

The lead–acid type battery is the primary source of electricity for starting modern engines. It also serves as a reserve source of electricity for the electrical running load of the vehicle. The battery size selected depends upon the use to which it will be subjected. Vehicles with large engines require a greater cranking power and therefore a large battery is used. Large batteries are also used in vehicles with a number of electrically operated accessories. Small batteries are found in vehicles with small engines and light electrical loads.

A properly maintained lead–acid battery of the type used in automobiles will give from three to four years of troublefree service. Proper maintenance involves keeping the battery clean, charged, full of water, and well supported in the battery carrier. When a battery fails to start the engine, the technician must be able to check the battery and the rest of the electrical system to determine the cause of failure in order to properly repair the problem. It is possible that the battery has failed or that other electrical system parts have failed.

3-1 BATTERY OPERATION

A battery is made of different materials. Chemical reactions between different materials involve the movement of electrons in the outer shell of some of their atoms. Electron movement is an electrical reaction. If it results from a chemical reaction, it is called an electrochemical process. Movement of electrons resulting from a chemical reaction may be controlled by controlling the chemical process producing the electrical current. This process can be reversed so that electrical currents cause a chemical reaction.

A lead-acid automotive battery is an *electrochemical* device. It has a voltage and can produce a current as the result of chemical reactions that deplete battery materials. A reverse current forced through the battery can cause chemical reactions that restore battery materials.

Cell Construction. A simple storage battery *element* is made of two dissimilar metal *plates* that are kept from touching each other by a *separator*. This element is submerged in a liquid sulfuric acid *electrolyte* solution. An electrolyte is a material whose atoms become ionized in solution. These ionized atoms, described in Chapter 1, are free to move about in the solution. The acidity of the electrolyte weakens the electron bonds of the plate materials and so the electrons can drift, causing positive and negative ions to be formed in the plate material. The active material on one of the plates is lead dioxide, usually called *lead peroxide* (PbO_2). It is a dark brown, small-grain crystalline material. The crystalline type of structure is very porous and so the electrolyte can freely penetrate the plate.

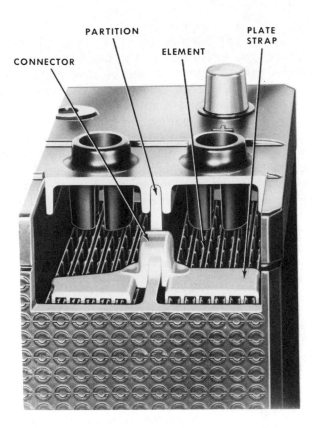

Fig. 3-1 Battery construction showing the connector going through the partition (Chevrolet Motor Division, General Motors Corporation).

The electromotive force between the lead peroxide plate and sponge-lead plate is 2.13 V. Cell voltage is the result of the type of materials used in the plates and not the plate size, shape, or number of plates in a cell.

If a conductor connects the plates outside the cell, electrons can leave the negative plate and flow through the conductor to the positive plate. This process will continue as long as the chemical action within the cell transfers electrons to the negative plate. This process is called *discharging* the cell.

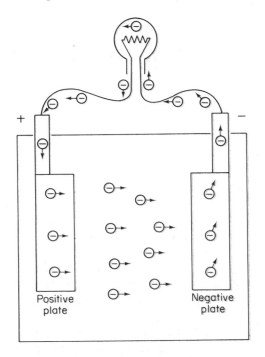

Fig. 3-3 Electron movement when a complete external circuit is connected to the battery posts.

Electrons leave the lead peroxide plate and enter the electrolyte, leaving positive ions behind in the lead peroxide plate.

The active material on the other plate is *porous* or *sponge lead* that is also easily penetrated by electrolyte. Electrons leave the electrolyte and enter the lead, giving the sponge-lead plate excess electrons that produce negative ions in the plate.

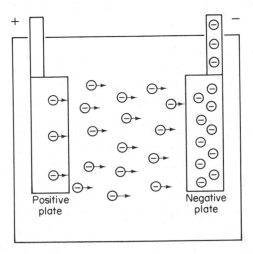

Fig. 3-2 Electron movement within a cell having no external circuit.

Cell Chemical Action. During discharge, excess electrons leave the sponge-lead plate through the exterior conductor, leaving positive lead ions (Pb^{++}) on the plate. Negative sulfate ions (SO_4^-) from the electrolyte are attracted by the positive lead ions. They combine to form neutral lead sulfate ($PbSO_4$) on the negative plate. During this time, the lead peroxide (PbO_2) of the positive plate combines with hydrogen (H^+) from the electrolyte to release electrons as a positive lead ion (Pb^{++}) and water (H_2O) is formed. The positive lead ion from this reaction combines with a negative sulfate ion (SO_4^-) of the electrolyte to form neutral lead sulfate ($PbSO_4$) on the positive plate.

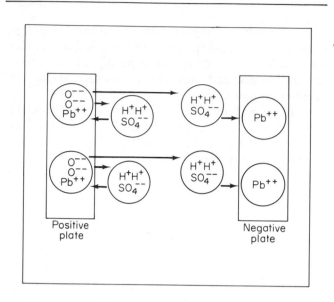

Fig. 3-4 Chemical ion movement in a cell during discharge.

As a cell reaches the fully charged state, hydrogen gas is formed at the negative plate and oxygen gas is formed at the positive plate. This process is called *gassing*. Because of this, care must be exercised to avoid a spark at the cell opening. In the presence of a spark, these gases combine with a sudden explosion that can ruin the cell and throw acid out of the cell. This means all circuits, including a battery charger, should be turned off before leads are connected to or removed from the battery post to avoid sparks that could cause an explosion.

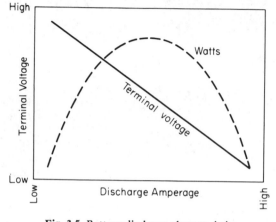

Fig. 3-5 Battery discharge characteristics.

During discharge, this reaction will continue as long as active material remains. In an ideal cell that is completely discharged, the plates will both become lead sulfate and the electrolyte will become water. Fully charged electrolyte has a specific gravity 1.26; that is, it is 1.26 times as heavy as pure water. The specific gravity of water is 1.00. The *specific gravity* of the electrolyte indicates the amount of electrical activity remaining in the cell. A measurement of the cell's specific gravity is called the cells *state-of-charge.*

In the lead-acid battery the electrochemical process is reversible; it is reversible because the lead sulfate is only very slightly soluble and remains on the plates. If a cell is connected to a voltage higher than the cell voltage, electrons will flow backward through the cell. This reverse electrical current causes a reverse chemical action. Sulfate ions leave the plates and re-enter the electrolyte. The plates again become lead and lead peroxide. The cell can only be charged or discharged as fast as the ions form and the electrons move to the negative plate. Forcing the reaction results in the formation of excess hydrogen and oxygen gas that leave the cell through the vent.

In operation, battery cells are continually being slightly charged and discharged. They are seldom fully discharged, but are usually kept near full charge.

Batteries gradually wear out as they are used. This results from warping of internal parts, loosening of active plate material, hardening of plate material, and corrosive action on the separators. As the battery begins to wear out it also begins to lose its ability to form ions and thus the battery is not able to produce as much electrical power as it did when it was new. Electrical power is measured in *watts* (watts = volts x amperes). The electrical power available from an automobile battery is expressed in *ampere-hours,* the voltage being a constant 12 volts. The ampere-hour rating of the battery is based on the twenty-hour rate test described later in this chapter. The electrical power of the battery must be great enough to meet the electrical power needs of the engine. A new battery that has only power enough to meet the engine needs will no longer provide the engine with sufficient electrical power after the battery begins to wear out. If a new battery is large enough so that it has electrical power in excess of the engine requirements it will still be able to function after it begins to wear out, thus providing a longer battery service life.

The electrical power producing characteristic of a battery is important. An equally important battery characteristic is its reaction while being recharged. A battery in a low state-of-charge has a small counter electromotive force as a result of weak chemical action within the cells. This allows the battery to accept a high amperage charging rate at a low charging voltage. As the battery state-of-charge increases its counter electromotive force also increases so the amperage charging rate lowers if charging voltage is held constant. Charging voltage must be increased if the charging amperage is to be kept constant. In a normal automotive charging system the charging amperage gradually decreases and voltage increases until it reaches the maximum voltage allowed by the system voltage regulator. Voltage no longer increases when it reaches regulated voltage so charging amperage will decrease as counter electromotive force increases during battery charging. This provides a desirable high charging rate for a discharged battery and a low charging rate for a fully charged battery.

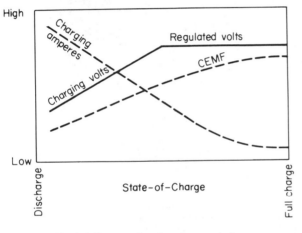

Fig. 3-6 Battery charging characteristics.

Temperature affects the chemical reaction rate within the battery. Low temperature slows the chemical reaction and high temperature speeds the reaction. This is especially important during cold cranking. The chemical reaction in a cold battery produces ions at a slow rate, and so the cold battery does not produce starting current as effectively as a warm battery. If a battery has a low capacity it may fail to start a cold engine. In addition, a cold engine requires more effort to turn it over, and so it demands above-normal cranking amperage. Thus, cold-cranking problems are compounded when an under-capacity battery is used. Temperature compensating devices are used in some voltage regulators, as described in Chapter 7, to raise the charging voltage when the system is

cold. This keeps the charging amperage at its normal range by forcing ions to form rapidly within the cold battery. When the battery and charging system warms up, the regulated voltage is lowered to its normal value to maintain normal charging amperage.

3-2 BATTERY FEATURES

The automotive battery is made of six *cells*. Each cell produces slightly over two volts. The cells are connected end to end, with the negative terminal of one cell attached to the positive terminal of the next cell. This type of connection is called a *series* connection. In a series circuit, the total voltage is the sum of the individual voltages, so that a six-cell battery produces twelve volts.

Within each cell there are a number of plates with separators between them. The *plates* are made from finely cast lead-antimony alloy grids that are filled with active plate material. In each cell, there is always one more negative plate than positive plate. An "eleven plate" battery has five positive plates and six negative plates in each cell. A negative plate is placed on each side of the positive plates to allow the active positive plates to provide maximum battery performance. The plates are connected together within each cell to form a positive group and a negative group. The plate groups are interleaved with *separators* to keep them from touching. This assembly of plates and separators is called an *element*.

The separators are made from resin-impregnated cellulose fiber, microporous rubber, and plastic. They are flat on one side and ribbed on the other. The ribbed side is placed against the

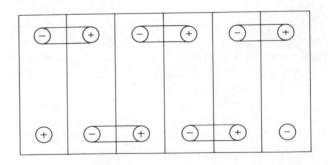

Fig. 3-7 Cell connections in a 12-volt lead acid battery.

positive plate to allow free electrolyte flow along the positive plate. Some batteries use a fiber-glass mat or specially designed separators over the positive plates to help hold the material in place on the grid, thereby reducing loss of active material into the bottom of the case, a phenomenon called *shedding*.

The element is placed in a snug-fitting case surrounded by electrolyte; this assembly is called a *cell*. Four bridges in the bottom of the case support the elements. Sub-feet on the positive plates rest on bridges 1 and 3, while sub-feet on the negative plates rest on bridges 2 and 4. This arrangement supports the plates, at the same time reducing the tendency for them to short-circuit within the cell.

Six cells are connected together to form a twelve-volt automobile battery. The battery case with six compartments is made from hard rubber, polyvinyl chloride plastic, or bituminous composition. It must withstand the acid electrolyte, shock, vibration, and temperature extremes.

The element connecting-post in older batteries came above the case cover where a connector strap was used to connect the element of one cell to the element in the next cell. Current automobile cell connections are below the cell cover. Two methods are used to connect the cells below the cover, over-the-partition and through-the-partition. In over-the-partition types, the cell connector goes up to the underside of the cover where it crosses the cell partition. The connector extends down in the next cell to connect to the plates. This type of connector keeps acid from seeping through the cover, provides a shorter electrical path than the above-the-cover connector, and uses less material. This results in increased battery efficiency at a reduced cost and lower weight. Through-the-partition type connectors further reduce the amount of material used in the battery to further reduce the cost. It also shortens the electrical path to reduce electrical loss to a minimum. When the cell connector goes through the partition, it is critically important to seal the connector at the partition.

The cover is sealed to the case and partitions with bituminous or resin materials. These materials form an acid-tight joint that remains sealed during vibrations and temperature changes. Automotive batteries with one-piece covers are not repairable and must be replaced when they no longer function properly.

Fig. 3-8 Cell construction.

Fig. 3-9 Battery with cell connectors going over the partition (The Prestolite Company).

Each cell must have sufficient electrolyte to cover the plates. As the cell gasses, hydrogen and oxygen separated from the electrolyte by hydrolysis will escape from the cell. This must be replaced with water before the plates are exposed to air and dry out. Openings over the cell are usually designed to show the full electrolyte level. Vent plugs or caps designed to allow gases to escape while retaining liquid electrolyte are fitted in the openings. If the battery is overfilled with water so that the vent hole is plugged, electrolyte will be forced from the cell ahead of the gases. The loss of acid reduces the ability of the battery to function. Spilled acid will corrode parts surrounding the battery as well as provide a potential leak between the battery posts.

Some newly designed automotive batteries are considered to be sealed batteries. They have no openings through which the electrolyte can be checked, so water is never added. They do have vents through which cell gasses can escape to equalize pressure and have baffels that form a liquid/gas separator.

(a)

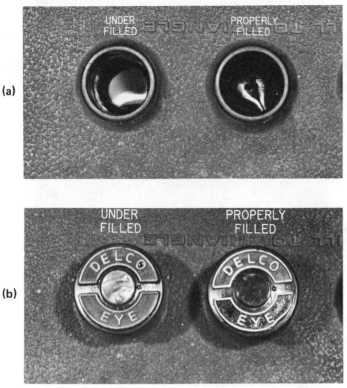

(b)

Fig. 3-10 Electrolyte level. (a) As viewed in the cell opening, (b) as shown by the Delco eye.

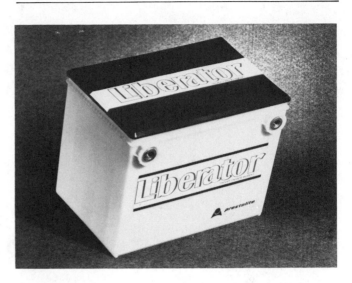

Fig. 3-11 A sealed battery with no cell openings (The Prestolite Company).

In the sealed battery, gassing is reduced by eliminating the antimony metal from the plate grids. This minimizes the electrolyte loss. The plates are enclosed in porous envelopes which keep the plates from shedding. The plates can then be placed on the bottom of the case, providing a large electrolyte reservoir above them. Most of these batteries have a state-of-charge indicator in the cover.

REVIEW QUESTIONS

1. Name the parts of a battery.

2. What is the name of the process that occurs as the electrons move through a conductor from the negative post to the positive post?

3. What limits the charging and discharging rate of the battery?

4. What is the expression used to describe electrical power?

5. What is the result of weak chemical action in the battery?

6. What makes up a battery element?

7. What reduces battery plate shedding?

8. Name two types of cell connectors used in modern batteries.

9. How long should a properly maintained battery last?

10. What is the name of the active material on the positive battery plate?

11. What determines the battery cell voltage?

12. What material does the negative plate become when it is completely discharged?

13. What gas forms at the negative plate while the battery is charging?

14. Why does the charging amperage decrease as the battery becomes fully charged?

15. What is the fully charged voltage of a battery cell?

16. What material is used to resupply electrolytes lost from gassing?

4

Battery Service

In order to start an engine the battery must be in good condition. This will provide electrical power for cranking the engine and also for ignition. To ensure dependable service the battery must be serviced during each tune-up; sometimes more frequent tune-ups are necessary.

During a tune-up the first considerations in checking a battery are its physical condition and proper installation. The battery should be cleaned and should be securely mounted in a carrier with the proper hold-down clamps. The electrical cables must be clean and tight. Pure water should be added to the battery electrolyte, filling it to the indicator level. In many service stations, the battery electrolyte level is checked each time the engine oil level is checked. Only distilled water is recommended for addition to the electrolyte. In some areas drinking water has been satisfactorily used for battery water, but it is not recommended by the battery manufacturers.

If the exterior of the battery is moist and dirty, electricity will bleed across the battery case between the battery posts on which the cables are attached. This will gradually discharge the battery. Leakage can be easily determined by placing voltmeter lead terminals in the moisture on the top of the battery. If leakage is occuring a voltage reading will be observed on the voltmeter.

Fig. 4-1 Electricity bleeding across the battery top as shown on the voltmeter whose leads are touching the cover, not the posts.

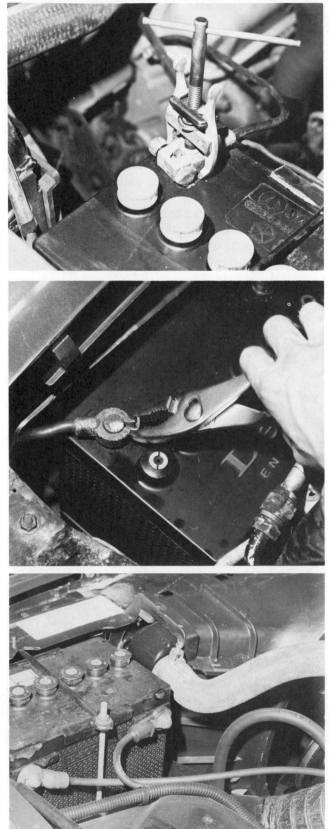

(a)

(b)

(c)

Fig. 4-2 Removing the battery cable. (a) Puller, (b) self clamp, (c) side terminal.

4-1 BATTERY CARE

The battery can best be cleaned by removing it from the vehicle. Gases should be blown from the battery vents in order to help reduce the chance of their being ignited by a spark as the battery cables are removed. All electrical switches should be turned off so there is little likelihood that sparks will occur as the cables are removed. The ground battery cable is removed *first* so that a spark will not occur if the wrench happens to touch the body metal. The cable clamp is loosened and a puller is used to lift the clamp if the terminal is still tight on the battery post. Some clamps can be released with a plier and some cables are held with a cap screw. The insulated battery cable is removed in the same manner. This is followed by the removal of the hold-down clamp to release the battery. The hold-down clamp may go across the top of the battery or it may hold at the bottom of the case. The battery is lifted from the vehicle, by hand or with a battery carrier. Be careful to keep the battery away from clothing. Battery electrolyte is *acid* and it will make holes in cloth and will burn skin. If acid gets on a person or his clothing the acid can be neutralized by putting baking soda or ammonia on the acid, then flushing it with a lot of water. This will minimize the damage caused by acid.

Heavy accumulations of acid on the outside of the battery can be neutralized with baking soda or ammonia. The technician must be careful to keep the soda or ammonia out of the battery cells because these base materials will neutralize the acid electrolyte within the battery and ruin the battery. Flushing the exterior of the battery with hot water while brushing it with a soft brush will usually loosen acid, oil film, and dirt from the battery exterior. The hot water quickly evaporates, leaving the battery clean and dry.

The battery should be given a good visual inspection before the original or a replacement battery is installed. There should be no signs of cracks in the battery case or cover. The battery cover and sides should be smooth and flat. Internal damage will usually cause the battery case to bulge. The battery posts should be in good condition and secure. The battery date code should be checked to determine the battery age. Batteries seldom cause trouble in less than two years and rarely operate longer than four years. The date code is either

Fig. 4-3 Washing a battery.

ONE PIECE CELL COVER   ELECTROLYTE LEVEL INDICATOR

VENT PLUG

HOLD-DOWN SLOT

TOP TERMINAL

Fig. 4-4 Exterior battery features (Chevrolet Motor Division, General Motors Corporation).

stamped on the case or on a post, or a code is punched on a special date tag or warranty card. Date coding usually consists of a number indicating the last digit of the year the battery was put into service, for example, 5 for 1975 and 8 for 1978. This is accompanied by a letter indicating the month, with A for January, B for February, etc.

The battery carrier and clamps in the vehicle should be cleaned in the same manner used to clean the battery. Coating the clean battery carrier and clamp with acid-proof paint will help keep them in good condition.

Battery post and terminal clamps are cleaned with a brush especially designed for this work. The brush is twisted on the post and in the terminal to form a clean, fresh surface that will have minimum electrical resistance.

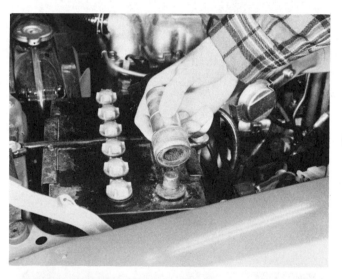

(a)

(b)

Fig. 4-5 Cleaning battery terminals and cable connectors.

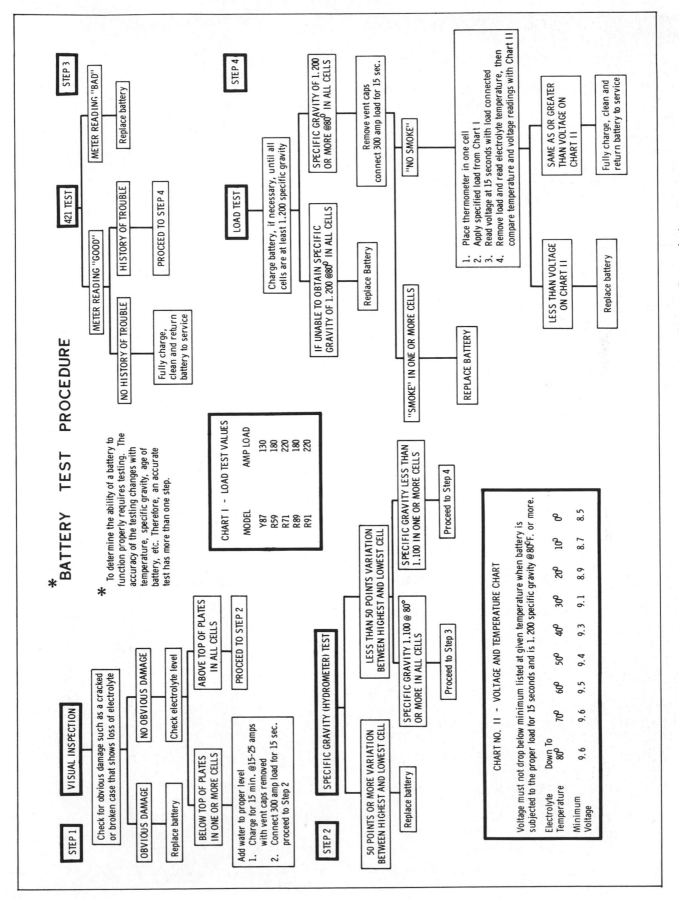

*BATTERY TEST PROCEDURE

* To determine the ability of a battery to function properly requires testing. The accuracy of the testing changes with temperature, specific gravity, age of battery, etc. Therefore, an accurate test has more than one step.

STEP 1

VISUAL INSPECTION

Check for obvious damage such as a cracked or broken case that shows loss of electrolyte

- OBVIOUS DAMAGE → Replace battery
- NO OBVIOUS DAMAGE → Check electrolyte level
  - BELOW TOP OF PLATES IN ONE OR MORE CELLS
    - Add water to proper level
      1. Charge for 15 min. @15-25 amps with vent caps removed
      2. Connect 300 amp load for 15 sec. proceed to Step 2
  - ABOVE TOP OF PLATES IN ALL CELLS → PROCEED TO STEP 2

STEP 2

SPECIFIC GRAVITY (HYDROMETER) TEST

- 50 POINTS OR MORE VARIATION BETWEEN HIGHEST AND LOWEST CELL → Replace battery
- LESS THAN 50 POINTS VARIATION BETWEEN HIGHEST AND LOWEST CELL
  - SPECIFIC GRAVITY 1.100 @ 80° OR MORE IN ALL CELLS → Proceed to Step 3
  - SPECIFIC GRAVITY LESS THAN 1.100 IN ONE OR MORE CELLS → Proceed to Step 4

CHART I - LOAD TEST VALUES

MODEL	AMP LOAD
Y87	130
R59	180
R71	220
R89	180
R91	220

CHART NO. II - VOLTAGE AND TEMPERATURE CHART

Voltage must not drop below minimum listed at given temperature when battery is subjected to the proper load for 15 seconds and is 1.200 specific gravity @80°F. or more.

Electrolyte Temperature Down To	80°	70°	60°	50°	40°	30°	20°	10°	0°
Minimum Voltage	9.6	9.6	9.5	9.4	9.3	9.1	8.9	8.7	8.5

STEP 3

421 TEST

- METER READING "GOOD"
  - NO HISTORY OF TROUBLE → Fully charge, clean and return battery to service
  - HISTORY OF TROUBLE → PROCEED TO STEP 4
- METER READING "BAD" → Replace battery

STEP 4

LOAD TEST

- SPECIFIC GRAVITY OF 1.200 OR MORE @80° IN ALL CELLS
  - Remove vent caps connect 300 amp load for 15 sec.
    - "NO SMOKE"
      1. Place thermometer in one cell
      2. Apply specified load from Chart I
      3. Read voltage at 15 seconds with load connected
      4. Remove load and read electrolyte temperature, then compare temperature and voltage readings with Chart II
        - SAME AS OR GREATER THAN VOLTAGE ON CHART II → Fully charge, clean and return battery to service
        - LESS THAN VOLTAGE ON CHART II → Replace battery
    - "SMOKE" IN ONE OR MORE CELLS → REPLACE BATTERY
- IF UNABLE TO OBTAIN SPECIFIC GRAVITY OF 1.200 @80° IN ALL CELLS → Replace Battery
  - Charge battery, if necessary, until all cells are at least 1.200 specific gravity

Fig. 4-6 Typical battery test procedure (Oldsmobile Division, General Motors Corporation).

41

The battery is mounted and clamped securely, not tightly, and the cables installed and tightened. The insulated cable is installed first, followed by the ground cable. After installation the cable clamp is often covered with grease to keep moisture from the clamp and battery post. Special materials that can be used to coat battery terminals are available in spray cans and can be purchased at automobile accessory stores. Coating the terminal will minimize corrosion that leads to resistance. The alternator belt condition and tension should be checked to insure proper alternator driving speed.

4-2 BATTERY TESTING

Batteries should be tested to help prevent vehicle problems that result from battery failure. The battery is tested to determine its state-of-charge and how well it either produces or accepts current. The voltage a battery produces is tested while a known current flows. If the voltage of a fully charged battery is low while discharging, or if it is either too high of too low while charging, the battery is faulty.

State-Of-Charge. As electricity is drawn from the battery the chemical reaction reduces the acidity of the electrolyte. This causes the electrolyte to thin or reduce its specific gravity. Specific gravity is measured with a *hydrometer*. If the specific gravity is high the electrolyte is thick and the hydrometer will float high. If the specific gravity is low the electrolyte is thin and the hydrometer floats low. The acid concentration in the electrolyte, as indicated by the hydrometer float level, is an indication of the battery's state-of-charge.

A fully charged battery will have a hydrometer reading of 1260 (indicating a specific gravity 1.26 times that of water). A completely discharged battery will have a hydrometer reading of 1070 (indicating a specific gravity of 1.07 times that of water). The use of a hydrometer is the best means of checking battery state-of-charge. Two precautions should be considered when using a hydrometer. If water has just been added to the cell electrolyte it will remain on top of the plates. This will produce a hydrometer reading that is lower than the actual battery state-of-charge. The second precaution has to do with battery temperature. If

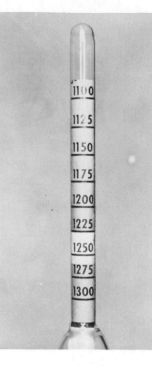

Fig. 4-7 Hydrometer float markings.

Fig. 4-8 Hydrometer thermometer markings, including a correction scale to compensate for differences in temperature.

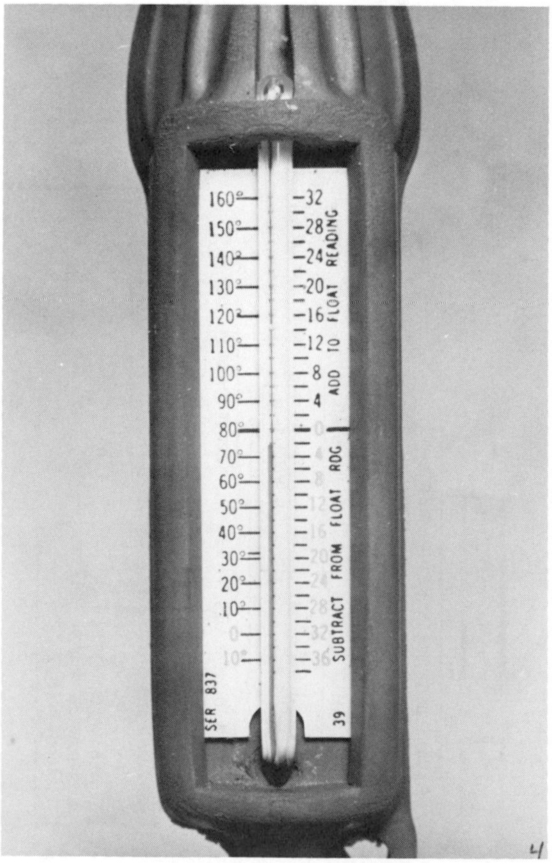

the battery is hot the electrolyte will be thin and the hydrometer will give a false low reading. If the battery is cold the electrolyte will be thick and give the hydrometer a false high reading. Four points are added to the hydrometer reading for each $10°F$ ($5.5°C$) that the electrolyte temperature is above $80°F$ ($27°C$) and four points are subtracted for each $10°F$ ($5.5°C$) that the electrolyte temperature is below $80°F$ ($27°C$). Good battery hydrometers have thermometers built into them with the correction factors indicated on the hydrometer scale. Cells should have their hydrometer readings within 50 points on good batterys.

The battery state-of-charge can also be measured with a voltmeter. A fully charged battery that has been inactive for more than 8 hours will have an open-circuit voltage of 12.6 volts while a completely discharged battery will have a voltage of 11.64 volts. Measuring the state-of-charge by the voltage method requires the use of a voltmeter sensitive in the 11 to 13 volt range. Precautions must be observed when using a voltmeter to measure state-of-charge. The surface charge is the voltage that is measured by a voltmeter at the battery posts when there is no current flowing either into or out of the battery. The voltmeter will indicate a state-of-charge higher than the actual state-of-charge if the battery has just been charged and the surface charge is high. On the other hand, if the battery has just been used to supply a heavy electrical current, such as in cranking the engine, the charge on the surface of the plate indicates a state-of-charge that is lower than the actual battery state-of-charge. For a battery open-circuit voltage to be meaningful, the technician needs to know how the battery has been used just prior to his measuring open-circuit voltage. This principle can be recognized if a voltmeter is attached to the battery posts as the engine is cranked or as the battery is charged.

Some voltmeter-type cell testers have cadmium-tipped probes that are used to measure the difference in voltage from the electrolyte in one cell to the electrolyte in the adjacent cell and between each end cell and post. The sum of these voltages will total the battery open-circuit voltage.

If the state-of-charge from the highest cell reading to the lowest cell reading is more than 50 hydrometer points or is over 0.05 volts when measured with the cadmium-tipped cell tester, the battery is defective and should be replaced. If the cells are within these limits but the hydrometer reading is below 1225 or if the open-circuit battery voltage is below 12.0 volts (and the battery has not

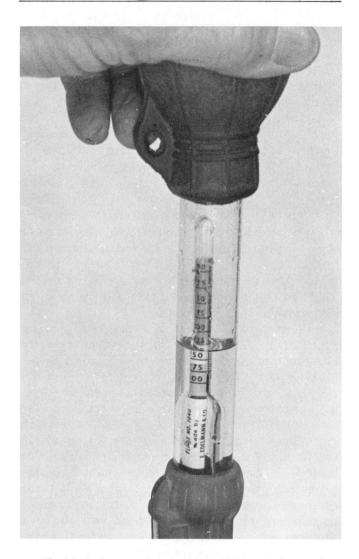

Fig. 4-9 Hydrometer being used to measure the battery state-of-charge.

had a recent heavy current discharge), the battery has a low state-of-charge and should be charged before any further testing can be done properly.

Battery Capacity. The voltage between the positive and negative plates in a healthy full-charged lead-acid battery is always the same, no matter how the battery is designed or built. Its ability to produce current, however, is the result of its construction. A number of different battery rating tests have been devised by the battery manufacturers. These are standardized by the Society of Automotive Engineers (SAE) and appear in the *SAE Handbook*.

A *twenty-hour rate test* has been used for many years to rate batteries. It measures the amount of steady current draw, in amperes, that will reduce the voltage of a 12 V battery to 10.5 V in 20 hours while the battery is at 80°F (27°C). This capacity is expressed in *ampere-hours* (AH). Battery manufacturers use this rating to indicate battery size. The twenty-hour rate measures the amount of available reserve electrical power remaining in the battery to handle light accessory loads.

The *150- and 300-ampere rate tests* are run at 0°F after the battery is subjected to a 24-hour cold soak. Terminal voltage is recorded at the end of a specific time period (5 to 15 seconds). The time period differs with different type and size batteries. This test is designed to indicate the ability of the battery to crank a cold engine.

There are a number of other tests that rate battery capacity and design; these tests include *charging-rate acceptance, cycling life,* and *vibration* tests.

The maximum current that can be drawn from a battery is proportional to the plate surface area exposed to electrolyte. The length of time the current can be drawn from a battery is proportional to the amount of active material available in the battery. A battery with a large number of thin plates can produce high current for a short period of time. If a few thick heavy plates are used, the battery cannot produce a high current, but it can produce a low current for a long period of time. Batteries are designed to produce the type of current that is required by each application.

The main function of the automobile battery is to provide electrical energy to crank the engine and, at the same time, to supply current for the ignition system. After the engine has started, the charging system provides the electrical energy required for most of the running requirements of the vehicle, and so the battery supplies no current. Automotive batteries are designed to produce high discharge rates that are required for starting. A battery with a high ampere-hour rating will usually have a higher service life than a battery that just barely meets the vehicle needs because it will still be able to supply adequate electrical power even after its capacity decreases. One way of expressing the battery power is in watts. Watts of a battery equal the battery voltage times the battery ampere-hour rating.

One test of a battery, called the battery *capacity test* (or *load test*), measures the battery's ability to rapidly convert chemical energy into electrical energy. This is done by drawing a heavy current from the battery while observing the terminal voltage at the battery posts. When current is drawn from the battery faster than the chemical action can occur within the battery, the battery terminal voltage is lowered. In the battery capacity test an *open* carbon pile variable resistor is connected in series with the fully charged battery and with an ammeter that can carry a large enough current to complete an electrical circuit across the battery. The ammeter and carbon pile are usually contained within a battery-starter test unit. A voltmeter is also connected across the battery posts or terminals. The voltmeter is included as part of a battery-starter tester. Voltage is noted 15 seconds after the carbon pile is adjusted to produce a current that is three times the ampere-hour capacity of the battery. It should be remembered that ampere-hour capacity is a battery rating used to indicate the maximum electrical potential power or size of the battery and is marked either on the battery or in a specification book. For a healthy full-charged battery at 80°F (27°C) or above, the battery terminal voltage should not drop below 9.5 volts at the end of 15 seconds while the current is still flowing. When the battery is at 30°F (−1°C) the minimum battery voltage needed for this test is only 9.0 volts. If the test is performed on a battery with a state-of-charge below 1225, the terminal voltage at the end of the capacity test will be very low. This voltage reading serves no useful purpose

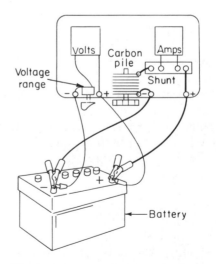

Fig. 4-10 Battery capacity test hook-up.

in determining the battery condition, because the capacity test is only valid when performed on a battery that has a state-of-charge above 1225. A battery with a low state-of-charge should be recharged before a capacity test is performed.

4-3 BATTERY CHARGING

A battery will charge when a voltage higher than the battery post terminal voltage is applied to the battery. This forces electricity through the battery in the reverse direction to produce a reverse chemical action within the battery. Charging will store energy in the battery. The higher the terminal voltage while charging, the faster the battery internal chemical action will occur. Excess charging voltage, however, will force chemical action to occur so fast that the battery will gas excessively, the plates will buckle, active material will break loose, and the battery will be destroyed. To minimize damage, battery temperature during charging should never be allowed to exceed 110°F (49°C). At higher temperatures the battery quickly loses its resistance to an external voltage, allowing the charging rate to go very high at a normal charging voltage; the battery will heat rapidly and will be ruined.

A battery charger should be turned off when it is connected or disconnected from a battery. If the charger is on a spark may occur when the charging cable clips are attached to or removed from the battery posts. This spark can ignite the gases in the battery cell and cause an explosion. Check that the electrolyte is at the proper level, and then connect the red charger cable clip to the positive battery post. The positive post is always the larger of the two battery posts and it is usually marked with a (+) sign or red paint. The black charger cable is attached to the negative post. The charger is always turned to the lowest charging rate first, then the rate can be increased to the desired charging rate. This avoids excess voltage surges that could damage the battery.

A normal battery can be fully charged by using a charger that will force from 3 to 5 amperes through the battery. Chargers are equipped with ammeters that show the charging rate. A battery will be fully charged when three successive hydrometer readings taken at one hour intervals show no increase in readings.

A battery that has a hydrometer reading below 1225 will accept a much higher charging rate than a battery that is near full charge. A fast

charger can be used for as long as 30 minutes at rates as high as 50 amperes on a partially charged 12-volt battery. A fast charger should only be used long enough to recharge the battery sufficiently for engine starting. A normally operating vehicle charging system will finish charging the battery after the engine is running. If the vehicle charging system does not recharge the battery the charging system will have to be repaired to provide satisfactory electrical operation.

It is helpful in understanding battery operation if one connects a voltmeter across the battery to watch terminal voltage during both charging and discharging. The terminal voltage will be near 14.0 volts during slow-charging and it will be over 14.5 volts during fast-charging. After the charger is turned off the voltage will gradually drop to normal battery voltage as the high voltage surface-charge soaks into the plates. During discharge the voltage drops below normal open-circuit battery voltage. The higher the discharge rate the lower the terminal voltage. After a heavy discharge the terminal voltage will remain temporarily low. When the battery is allowed to stand, the terminal voltage will gradually increase because the surface of the plate is reactivated as the charge within the plates works to the surface to produce normal terminal voltage.

4-4 SPECIALIZED BATTERY TESTS

Basic battery testing involves a measurement of the battery state-of-charge (hydrometer or cell voltage) and the battery capacity test. A fully-charged battery that passes the capacity test is considered to be normal. A number of additional tests have been developed to check the battery condition when it is not fully charged.

Three-Minute-Charge-Test. If a battery is partly charged the capacity test will not indicate the true battery condition. A three-minute-charge-test was developed to measure the condition of a partly-charged battery. It is based on the principle that a healthy partly-charged battery requires a known voltage to charge the battery at a specified amperage charging rate.

The three-minute-charge-test charges the battery with a fast charger for three minutes at 40 amperes, or as close to 40 amperes as it is possible to set the charger. At the end of three minutes with the charger still charging at 40 amperes the battery terminal voltage should be less than 15.5 volts and the difference in cell voltage, using the cadmium-prod cell tester, should be less than 0.1 volts. If the battery voltage is over 15.5 volts the plates are deteriorated or sulfated. If the cell voltage difference is greater than 0.1 volts the low-voltage cell may be partly shorted or the high-voltage cell may be sulfated. The battery is defective and should be replaced whenever the battery voltage is over 15.5 volts or whenever there is more than 0.1 volts between cells at the end of the three minute test. If the battery is within these limits it is a healthy battery and is only discharged. It should be fully charged by the slow-charging process, then placed back in service.

Other Battery Tests. Many tests have been devised to make quick battery checks to determine battery condition using special test equipment. These tests generally have had a short life, as servicemen and automobile companies have gone back to the battery tests previously discussed.

One battery test that has been recommended by battery manufacturers is called the *light load test.* This test starts with a three-second engine cranking to remove any plate surface charge; then the headlights are turned on low beam to produce a 10 ampere current draw on the battery. After one minute the cadmium-tip tester is used in the electrolyte between cells. A good battery has less than 0.05 volts difference between cells and each cell should be above 1.99 volts while the battery produces 10 amperes through the headlights. If the adjacent cells are within 0.05 volts of each other but they are all below 1.95 volts the battery requires a 1000 ampere-minute boost charge (50 amperes for 20 minutes, for example) to properly condition the battery; then the light load test is repeated. If the battery still fails the boost charge should be repeated. An alternate method is to slow charge the battery until it is fully charged before running the light load test. The test requires quite a bit of time and consequently servicemen seldom use it.

A second test developed for quick battery testing is the *421 test.* This test requires the use of a special piece of test equipment that automatically

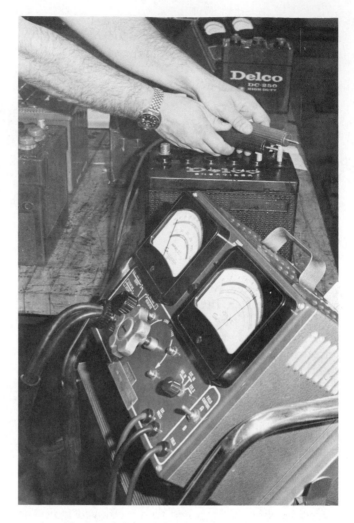

Fig. 4-11 Using cad tips to measure cell voltage.

cycles through a test sequence. A load cycle places a 50 ampere drain on the battery for 15 seconds then delays for 5 seconds before battery terminal voltage is read. The 421 test unit has a single load cycle and a load cycle that repeats three times before the voltage is read. A good battery will end the test with a high voltage. If the voltage is too low at the end of three cycles the battery is given another automatic test that consists of a 20 ampere test charge for 45 seconds with a 10 second delay before the voltage is read. Excessive voltage after this charge indicates high battery resistance that may be caused by sulfation. A reading below normal indicates a worn-out battery. The actual voltage to be used as the normal range is marked on the instrument face scale. The specific scale to be read is selected by the voltage results obtained during the load test. Directions for using the 421 test are printed on the front of the equipment. A battery that passes the 421 test may be charged to bring it to a normal full-charge condition.

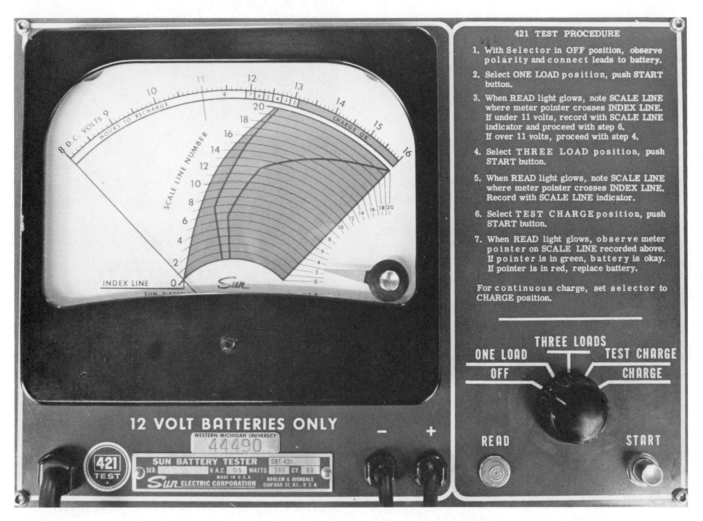

Fig. 4-12 Typical 421 battery tester with instructions.

4-5 BATTERY FAILURE

The most frequent reason for service calls is battery failure. This actually means that the battery will not crank the engine, not necessarily that the battery is not good or that it must be replaced. When the automobile battery does not crank the engine, jumper wires are connected from the battery of the service car to the battery of the stalled car so that the stalled engine can be cranked by using the service car battery.

Jumper wires must be installed correctly to avoid damage. First the red jumper wire should be connected between the positive post of the battery in the stalled vehicle and the positive post of the service car battery. The black jumper wire should

then be connected between good clean metal of both engines to avoid sparks at the battery. The service car engine should be brought up to a fast idle to increase its alternator output to the maximum charging rate. The stalled car can then be cranked. After starting the charging system of the stalled car will charge the battery if the problem was caused by leaving a light or electrical item turned on until the battery ran down. If some other problem caused the battery to fail the automobile should be taken directly to a service garage where the specific problem that caused failure can be identified and corrected.

A battery will often self-discharge while a vehicle is standing in a shop awaiting repairs. A procedure generally practiced, although it is not

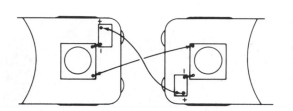

Fig. 4-13 Jumper connections for starting a car with a dead battery.

recommended by battery manufacturers, is to connect a fast charger to the battery in the vehicle, red lead to the positive post and black to the negative post. The battery output plus the high output of the fast charger will usually produce enough electricity to crank the engine. After the engine is running the fast charger is turned off and removed. The engine charging system will take over to fully charge the battery.

Failed batteries require replacement. The battery salesman must first determine the vehicle battery requirement. The original equipment battery has the lowest ampere-hour rating that will produce satisfactory service when all components are in excellent condition. A battery with a higher ampere-hour rating will give a longer period of useful service life. A battery with a lower ampere-hour rating will be unsatisfactory. The battery selected must have its terminals or posts located in the correct position on the cover or case to match the vehicle cables and must have dimensions that will fit in the battery carrier. It is installed in the same manner as the cleaned battery previously discussed.

Batteries are available in two forms, wet-charge and dry-charge. Wet-charge batteries are delivered from the manufacturer to the customer filled with electrolyte and fully charged. If there is any delay in shipment or delivery the battery may have to be recharged several times during storage. Most batteries available to automobile owners after the original battery fails, called the *after-market,* are dry-charged batteries.

Dry-charged batteries are fully charged after manufacture, then are emptied and baked to thoroughly evaporate all moisture. The openings are sealed with a plastic seal. In this manner the battery can be stored indefinitely without deterioration. When a dry-charged battery is to be put into service the plastic seals are pushed into the battery cell space above the electrolyte where they remain

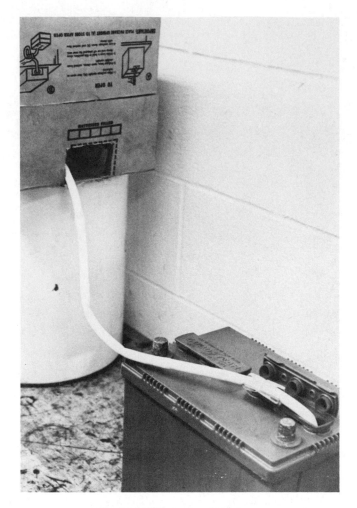

Fig. 4-14 Filling a dry charge battery.

and do not affect battery performance. Electrolyte, purchased in separate containers, is poured into each cell to fill it to the normal electrolyte level. Some of the electrolyte will soak into the plates so the cells will have to be topped off with electrolyte.

The battery will immediately be able to crank the engine for starting, but a 30 ampere charge for at least 10 minutes is recommended to properly condition the battery before use. A dry-charged battery properly filled and charged will have a longer service life than a wet-charged battery that has been subjected to storage.

Summary. The automotive storage battery must be fully charged and must have adequate capacity in order to supply enough electricity to start the engine. It is always the *first* item to be checked when electrical problems exist or when a tune-up is to be done. The vehicle will not function in a satisfactory or dependable manner with a faulty battery.

REVIEW QUESTIONS

1. Why should a battery be kept clean?

2. Why is it a standard practice to make sure all switches are turned off before removing a battery cable?

3. Why should the ground battery cable be removed first?

4. How is spilled acid neutralized?

5. How should the exterior of a battery be cleaned?

6. Why is it a normal practice to clean battery terminals during battery service?

7. Why is grease applied to a battery terminal and post?

8. What are the test indications of a defective battery?

9. What test measures the amount of available reserve electrical power to handle light accessory loads?

10. What test indicates the ability of a battery to crank a cold engine?

11. What battery feature controls the length of time current can be drawn from a battery?

12. Why is it necessary to limit battery temperature while the battery is being charged?

13. Why should sparks at the battery post be avoided?

14. How does one know that a battery is fully charged?

15. What is the most frequent reason for service calls?

16. What is a dry-charged battery?

17. How is a dry charged battery properly conditioned before it is put into service?

5

Motors and Starters

Electric motors are used in automobiles to drive blowers in heaters, defoggers, and air conditioners. They operate power seats, window lifts, power antennas, headlight doors, windshield wipers, windshield washers, electric fuel pumps, and many other units. Most of these motors are built in an inexpensive manner and are not repaired when they malfunction. It is fortunate, however, that the motors seldom fail during the useful life of the automobile.

The electric motor uses electricity to produce a rotary mechanical motion, usually driving through a gear train to operate a mechanism. Electric motors used in automobiles may be one-speed motors, two-speed motors, or variable-speed motors. They can also be designed to run in either direction or in both directions. Some are designed to produce a high turning force while others are designed to operate at a constant speed. The difference in motors is primarily the difference in the design of the magnetic field and in the method of switching.

One motor used on all vehicles is the cranking motor. It is a one-speed motor turning in one direction. It has a starter drive assembly that causes its rotating member to engage the teeth on the outer edge of the engine ring gear. This provides a gear train that will produce high turning force. The ring gear is on the flywheel or drive plate which is bolted to and rotates with the engine crankshaft.

The starter drive mechanism is engaged with the ring gear while the engine is being cranked. When the engine starts to run, the ring gear rotates faster than the starter drive, the starter drive disengages from the ring gear, and the starter stops rotating.

Small motors are usually connected to electrical power directly through a switch. Motors requiring high current, such as cranking motors, are connected to electrical power through a relay. A relay is a remotely controlled electrical switch. Within the relay an activated electromagnet pulls an armature bar to close a heavy set of electrical contacts that supply current to the motor. A spring opens the contacts when the electromagnet coil is deactivated. The electromagnet coil is activated and deactivated by a switch located within easy reach of the driver.

5-1 MOTOR PRINCIPLES

One of the simplest electric motor designs is a permanent-magnet motor. It has no field windings. The field pole shoes are very strong permanent magnets fastened inside the motor case. An armature supported by end bearings rotates within the pole shoes.

The armature consists of a stack of stamped soft iron pieces, called laminations fitted on the

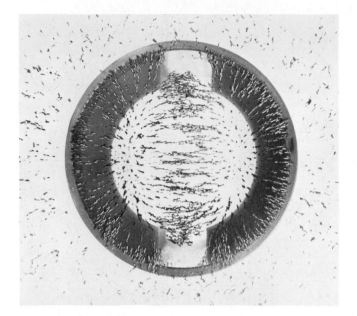

Fig. 5-1 Magnetic field surrounding field pole shoes.

contact the following commutator bar. This starts a new turning sequence to keep the motor rotating. As each winding completes its share of the turning effort it is replaced by a new set of windings located at a position to most effectively use the magnetic fields to produce rotation.

Fig. 5-3 Armature positioned in the field.

armature shaft. Insulated wire is wound through matching slots in the iron laminations and soldered or welded to commutator bars. The commutator bars are insulated from the rest of the armature assembly. Electric current is applied to the armature windings through brushes contacting the armature commutator bars. Current flowing through the armature windings produces magnetism in the armature. This magnetism reacts with the magnetism of the permanent magnet to force rotation of the armature.

As the armature turns the commutator bars move from under the brush and the brush will

Fig. 5-2 Wiper motor with the field frame removed to show the remaining parts.

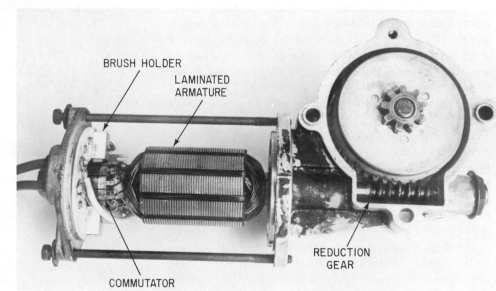

BRUSH HOLDER

LAMINATED ARMATURE

COMMUTATOR

REDUCTION GEAR

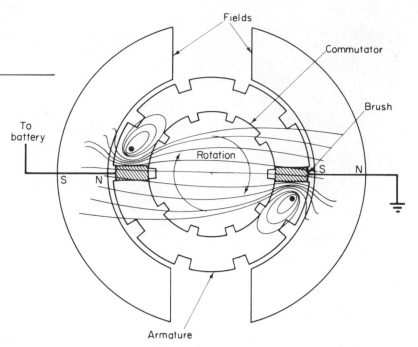

Fig. 5-4 Armature movement in the magnetic field.

The magnetic field can be considered to be made of two thin slices of a large bar magnet bent to the pole shoe shape. This makes the inner surface of one pole shoe a north magnetic pole and the inner surface of the other pole shoe a south magnetic pole. The iron armature core, which almost touches both pole shoes, becomes a magnetic bridge between the field poles to concentrate the magnet lines of force between the pole shoes when no current is flowing in the armature windings. Reluctance, it may be recalled, is the resistance to form a magnetic path; iron has low reluctance, and has the ability to carry magnetic lines of force. The iron case forms the field frame and provides a path to complete the magnetic lines of force between the field pole shoes.

When voltage from one side of the vehicle electrical system is applied to one motor brush, which is contacting the commutator bars, current is carried from one commutator bar to a set of windings which lead to another commutator bar being contacted by the second brush. The second brush is connected to the other side of the vehicle's electrical system. Current flowing through the armature winding produces a magnetic field in the armature core. This magnetic field reacts with the magnetic field of the pole shoes. When both fields have the same polarity they oppose each other, and when they have the opposite polarity they attract each other. The magnetized section of the armature is repelled by one pole shoe and attracted by the other. This produces a force that turns the armature.

As the armature rotates, the brushes slide onto another pair of commutator bars which magnetize another portion of the armature that is now located in the most effective part of the magnetic field of the pole shoe. This action keeps repeating, thereby forcing continued armature rotation as the brushes keep switching commutator bars to keep the armature magnetism in the most effective part of the magnetic field pole shoe.

The motor speed and turning force, called torque, are controlled by the magnetic strength of the pole shoes and the armature windings. This book is not intended to be a guide to electric motor

Fig. 5-5 Brushes on the motor commutator. A circuit breaker is located on the top of the brush holder.

design, but it is important to know several design considerations in order to understand how motor speed and direction are controlled. An understanding of these principles becomes important when diagnosing motor problems.

The first design consideration is that the stronger the pole and armature magnetic field strength becomes the slower the motor will rotate. The second consideration is that the slower an armature turns the more current it will draw and the more turning torque will be produced by the motor. Both of these considerations are based on the electromagnetic self-induction principle described in Chapter 1. To briefly review: the armature is rotating within a magnetic field produced by the pole shoes. This forces the armature windings, which are conductors, to cut across the pole shoe lines of magnetic force and this, in turn, develops an electromotive force within the armature windings. The electromotive force produced in this manner opposes the voltage being supplied to the motor from the automobile electrical system. It is therefore called counter electromotive force. The faster the armature rotates the more counter electromotive force is produced and this effectively restricts current flow through the armature windings. This type of opposition to the applied voltage is called *inductance*. With this principle in mind one can see how the electric motor design considerations can affect motor operation. If the motor is slowed as it drives a heavy load more current will flow in the armature to increase the turning force to handle the increased load. When the load is lowered motor speed increases and this increases CEMF to reduce current flow.

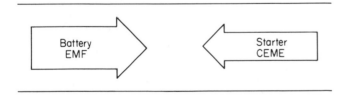

Battery EMF

Starter CEMF

Fig. 5-6 Starter counter electromotive force reducing the effect of electromotive force of the battery.

The permanent-magnet type of motor just described has a number of applications in the automobile as a motor to drive accessories. It can be made to turn forward or backward merely by reversing the direction of current flow through the armature by using external switches. Window-lift and power-seat adjusters are examples of this type of motor.

Permanent-magnet type motors may also be designed to operate at two speeds in applications such as windshield wipers. Two-speed permanent magnet wiper motors have three insulated brushes. The brushes directly across the commutator from each other provide low speed operation when fed through a resistor and provide reversing action when the polarity is reversed. The third brush is fed directly through the insulated motor-feed circuit to provide high speed operation.

Fig. 5-7 Electromagnetic fields on a motor.

Most automotive electric motors have electromagnetic fields rather than permanent magnetic fields, but the two types of motors operate in the same manner. Each electromagnetic field consist of a wire coil wound around a laminated soft iron pole shoe. Low-speed high-torque motors have the field coils in series with the brushes and armature. The motors can be operated in the opposite direction by reversing the direction of current flow through the fields while still maintaining the same brush polarity. Field current reversal is done by contacts designed into the switch.

Electric motor speed can be made to increase by weakening the *effective* field strength. This reduces the retarding effect of the motor counter electromotive force which in turn allows a higher armature rotating speed before counter electromotive force is high enough to balance system voltage. The effective field strength of multiple-speed

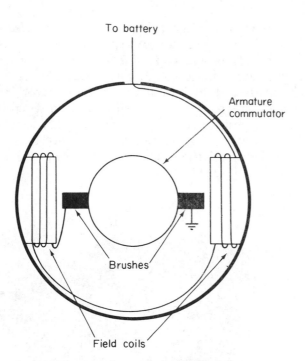

Fig. 5-8 Series wound motor. The field and armature are connected in series through the brushes.

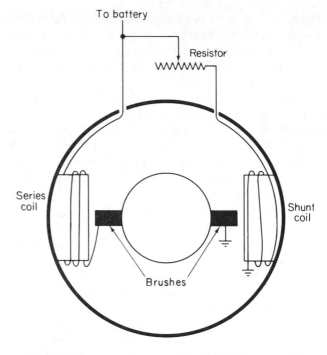

Fig. 5-9 Shunt wound motor. One field is in series with the armature while the other goes directly to ground.

5-2 CRANKING MOTOR

In automotive applications the cranking motor is usually referred to as the *starter* because it is used to start an engine. The cranking motor is a specialized electric motor designed to produce a high turning effort, called *starting torque*, at high speeds for a short period of time. It has a drive mechanism to connect the motor armature to the engine ring gear while cranking and to disconnect it when the engine starts.

Cranking Motor Designs. The armature of the cranking motor is similar to the armature of the small motors previously described. Its major difference lies in its size and armature shaft design. The armature is supported in a sleeve bearing or bushing in a *drive end frame* on the engine end. The other end of the armature is supported in a sleeve bearing in the *brush end frame.* A housing, called a *field frame,* holds the field windings and pole shoes close to the armature windings to take maximum advantage of the magnetic lines of force. The field frame also supports the end frames.

Most automotive starters have four fields and four brushes. This makes more effective use of the space available for the starter. The polarity of the pole pieces alternates, first a north, then a south, then a north, then a south pole.

and variable-speed small automotive electric motors can be controlled by using different field coil windings on each pole shoe. Heavy windings on one pole shoe are connected in series through the brushes and armature so that all of the current going through the field also goes through the armature. A winding of a large number of turns of smaller wire is wound in the opposite direction on the other pole shoes and it is connected to ground. This connection actually couples the small wire winding in parallel across the brushes. This type of motor winding is called a *shunt* winding. When the motor operates, current is fed through the series coil. When the speed needs to be increased current is also sent through the shunt winding. It is fed through a resistor while the series windings continue to be fed directly by the electrical system. Fixed resistors located in the switch are used to feed the shunt winding for step speeds. A variable resistor is used in the shunt circuit to provide variable speeds. As the flow of current is increased in the shunt winding it forms an opposing magnetic field that causes the effective electromagnetic field strength of the motor to weaken. This weakened field allows the motor armature to operate at higher speed.

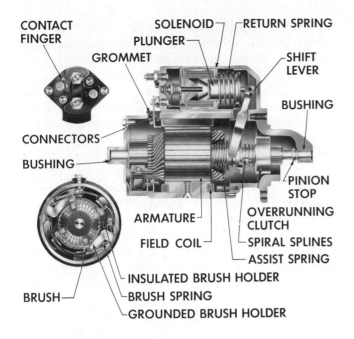

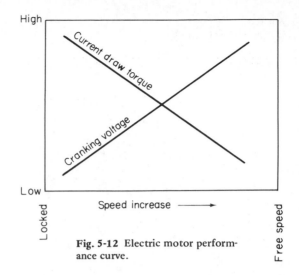

Fig. 5-12 Electric motor performance curve.

Fig. 5-10 Section view of a typical direct drive starter motor (Delco-Remy Division, General Motors Corporation).

Fig. 5-11 Pointer indicates the location of the soldered junction between the windings and commutator bars on a starter armature.

The conductors in the cranking motor, both armature and fields, are copper bars. These are required to give the starter minimum resistance so that a large current can flow. Starter turning effort or torque is directly proportional to the current flow. When the cranking motor is locked so that it cannot turn it will draw the most current and provide maximum torque. Under these conditions the starter resistance may be as low as 0.01 ohm. As the mechanical load on the armature is reduced the

speed of the armature will increase. This will increase counter electromotive force which, in turn, reduces current flow through the starter. When the starter load is completely removed the starter will achieve maximum speed. This is called *free speed*, when counter electromotive force will be highest and current draw will be lowest.

Torque and free speed characteristics of a cranking motor are controlled by the design of its field coils. Field coils may all be series wound; they may have three coils series wound and one coil shunt wound; or they may have two pairs of coils in parallel with each other and both pairs in series with the armature. Parallel field windings have a larger number of coil turns using smaller wires than series field windings.

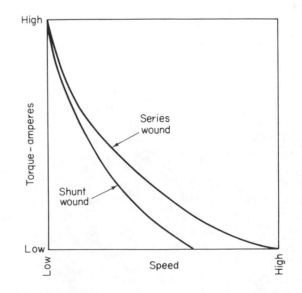

Fig. 5-13 Speed and torque characteristics of series and shunt wound motors.

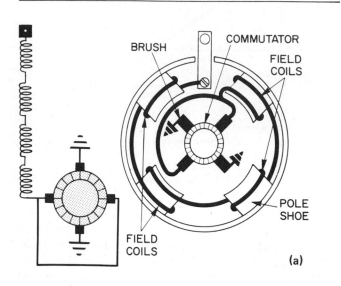

(a)

Series-wound motors have very high free speeds. As the counter electromotive force builds up, motor current draw is reduced and this reduces field strength which allows an increase in speed. Very high operating speeds can occur immediately after the engine starts, before the operator releases the "start" switch. A shunt winding helps to limit maximum speed to safe speeds. One end of the shunt winding is connected directly to ground. Its field strength is based on cranking-circuit voltage, and not counter electromotive force, and so its magnetic field remains strong. The strong field increases counter electromotive force at high armature speeds. This helps provide maximum torque at low speeds but still limits excess starter speeds. The accompanying illustrations show schematic drawings of a number of different field-wiring combinations used in current passenger-car cranking motors.

Fig. 5-14 Starter motor field wiring combinations. (a) Series, (b) 3 series and 1 shunt, (c) series-parallel, (d) 2 series, 2 parallel, (e) series-parallel with movable core that acts as a solenoid. (a, b, c, d, Oldsmobile Division, General Motors Corporation).

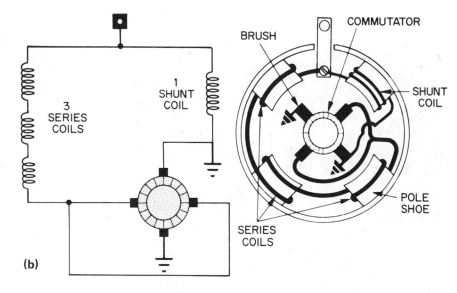

(b)

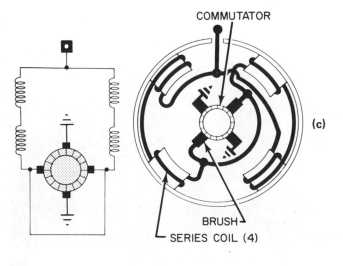

(c)

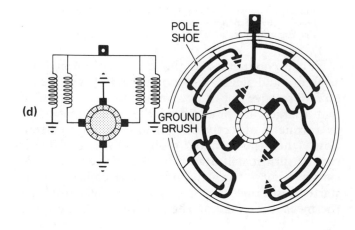

(d)

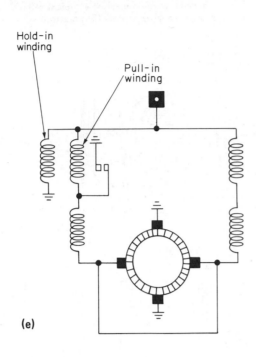

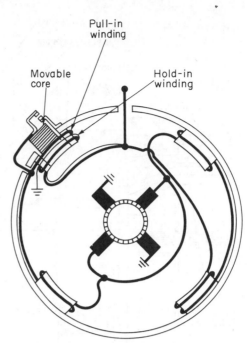

(e)

The cranking motor armature, like the series fields, has copper bar conductor windings to carry high amperage. Windings are wound to provide low resistance and to provide four electrical paths when four field poles are used. Each complete winding loop from a commutator segment is completed at an adjacent commutator segment. This is done all around the armature so all windings are interconnected. The ends of two windings are soldered to junctions on each commutator segment bar.

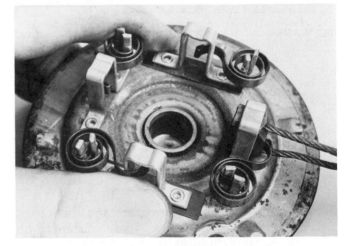

Fig 5-16 Brush holder types.

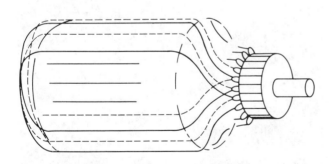

Fig 5-15 Typical armature winding.

Brushes are supported by a brush holder and held against the commutator by a brush spring. The brushes are usually angled slightly to provide good contact, minimum arcing, and long service life. Two opposite brushes are insulated from the frame. The other two brushes are grounded to the frame.

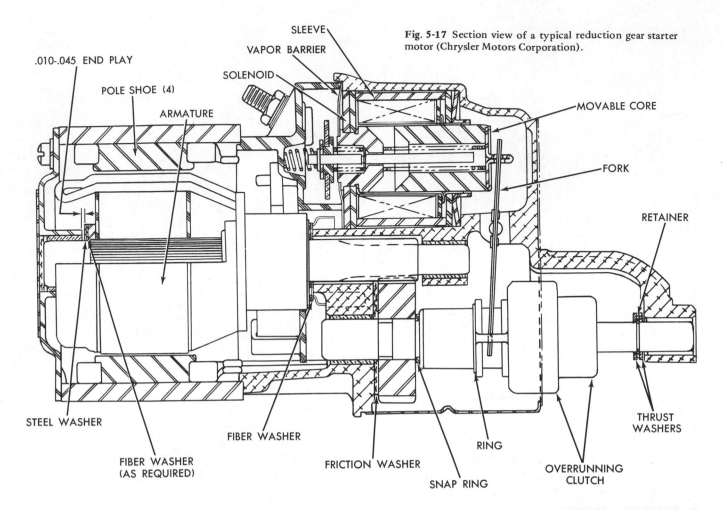

.010-.045 END PLAY

POLE SHOE (4)

ARMATURE

SLEEVE

VAPOR BARRIER

SOLENOID

MOVABLE CORE

FORK

RETAINER

STEEL WASHER

FIBER WASHER (AS REQUIRED)

FIBER WASHER

FRICTION WASHER

SNAP RING

RING

OVERRUNNING CLUTCH

THRUST WASHERS

Fig. 5-17 Section view of a typical reduction gear starter motor (Chrysler Motors Corporation).

Drive Mechanisms. Starter armatures are designed to turn at relatively high speeds to minimize amperage draw. To do this they are geared down to the crankshaft. Starter drive ratios run from 15:1 to 20:1. Some starters have a built-in 3.5:1 reduction gear between the armature and the starter pinion drive gear. This allows these starters to be built somewhat lighter and to use a smaller crankshaft ring gear. The small starter pinion drive gear meshes with a large ring gear mounted on the flywheel or torque converter drive plate to produce the required torque multiplication ratio required to crank the engine.

Fig. 5-18 Starter pinion engaged with the ring gear.

(a)

(b)

Fig. 5-19 Starter pinion position.
(a) Retracted position, (b) engaged position.

The starter drive must be able to engage while the ring gear is not turning and be able to release from the ring gear when the engine starts. Starter drives have evolved to one basic type of drive mechanism used on the majority of starters. This is the overrunning clutch drive. Some small engines still use the so called Bendix drive.

Fig. 5-20 Exploded view of a starter with a movable field core solenoid (American Motors Corporation).

The overrunning clutch is an assembly made of rollers or balls that wedge between a hub and outer race when the assembly is turned in one direction and release when it turns in the opposite direction. The overrunning clutch assembly is splined to the armature shaft. The starter solenoid pushes the entire overrunning clutch assembly toward the ring gear until the drive gear is in full mesh with the ring gear. As the armature turns, the armature splines drive the overrunning clutch hub. Hub rotation forces the rollers up a ramp, jamming them between the hub and outer race. This pulls the outer race along, turning the starter drive gear. When the engine starts, the ring gear spins the drive pinion gear faster than the starter will turn, and the outer clutch race moves ahead of the drive rollers, causing them to roll down the ramp to release the clutch hub. The starter-drive pinion gear will spin freely while being driven by the ring gear, causing no damage to the armature. This continues until the driver releases the starter switch, allowing the solenoid return spring to pull the starter pinion gear from the ring gear.

Fig. 5-22 Bendix-type starter drive.

drive until it slides free of the ring gear. This releases the starter drive mechanism. A locking mechanism is provided to prevent premature pinion release before the engine is fully started.

Other types of drive assemblies are in use on heavy duty gasoline and diesel engines but they are beyond the scope of this book.

Starter Switches. The starter draws a large current. This requires low-resistance wires that are large and short. An electrical relay switch in the starter circuit allows the operator to control starter

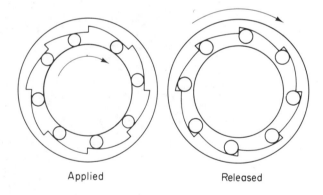

Applied   Released

Fig. 5-21 Overrunning clutch operation.

(a)

Fig. 5-23 Starter relays. (a) External view, (b) schematic.

The Bendix drive consists of a spring-driven pinion gear on a spiral helix. When the operator closes the starter switch the armature suddenly begins to rotate. The inertia of the stationary pinion gear allows the spinning armature to force the drive pinion gear along the spiral helix into engagement with the engine ring gear. Upon engagement the starter armature drives the pinion gear through the drive spring, often called a Bendix spring. When the engine starts the ring gear spins the starter pinion gear faster than the armature shaft so the pinion gear moves back down the helix

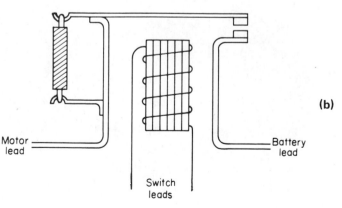

(b)

Motor lead   Battery lead

Switch leads

operation from the ignition switch and still maintain low starter-circuit resistance.

Essentially, the relay is a set of heavy-duty contacts closed by an electromagnet and opened by a spring. The electromagnetic circuit is fed through contacts in the ignition switch. When the operator turns the ignition switch to the start position, current flows through the magnet coil of the relay. This produces sufficient magnetism to close the switch contacts and engage the starter circuit. The starter motor will crank as long as the coil is energized. When the operator releases the start switch the relay loses its magnetism and the relay spring opens the heavy-duty contacts to stop the cranking motor operation. This type of starter switch is used on Bendix drive starters and on starters engaged by the magnetic attraction of the starter field on an engaging lever.

(a)

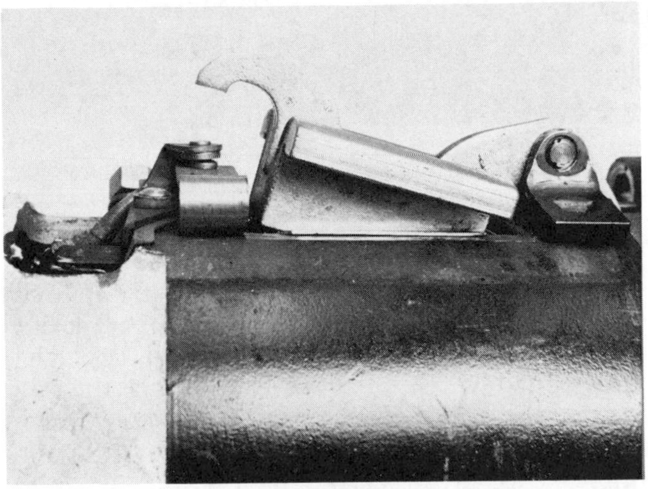

(b)

Fig. 5-24 Starter engagement by the magnetic attraction of the movable field core connected to an engaging lever. (a) Released position, (b) held in the engaged position.

The solenoid used with overrunning clutch-type starter drive is somewhat more complicated. When the starter switch is closed an electromagnet is energized. This pulls an iron core or plunger end wise toward the center of the wire coil. A shift linkage attached to the plunger moves the starter drive pinion gear into engagement with the ring gear. As the core plunger reaches its limit it closes a switch contact disc against heavy contact terminals in the relay portion of the solenoid to close the cranking circuit.

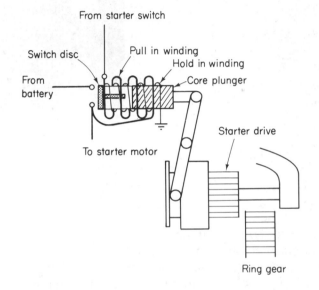

Fig. 5-25 Schematic of a starter solenoid.

The solenoid coil has two windings, a heavy series winding consisting of a few turns of large wire and a shunt winding made of many turns of fine wire. The series winding is connected between the solenoid switch terminal and the heavy terminal connected to the cranking motor. The shunt windings are connected between the solenoid switch terminal and ground.

When the operator turns the ignition switch to the start position the switch circuit is complete between both solenoid windings and the battery. This produces a strong magnetic field that pulls the core plunger, shift lever, and moves the drive pinion into engagement with the ring gear. When the switch disc contacts the heavy terminals to crank the engine it equalizes voltage on both ends of the heavy series coil winding so current will stop flowing in that winding. The magnetism created by the

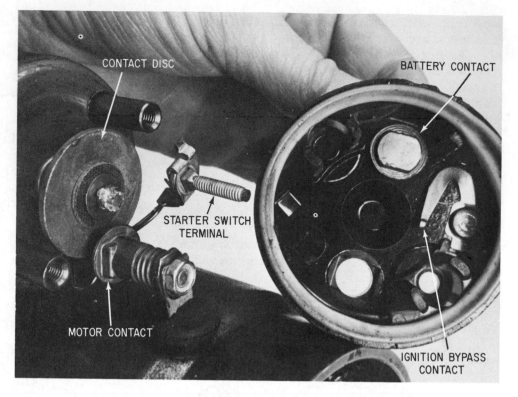

Fig. 5-26 Contacts of a starter solenoid.

shunt winding is all that holds the core plunger in the engaged position. The series winding is therefore called a *pull-in* winding and the shunt winding is called a *hold-in* winding.

When the operator releases the start switch there is no current flow through the solenoid and no magnetism remains. A spring pushes the core plunger from the solenoid. This action through the shift linkage will pull the starter drive pinion from the ring gear to its rest position.

Fig. 5-27 Solenoid return spring and plunger.

5-3 CRANKING MOTOR CIRCUITS

Half of the main cranking motor electrical circuit consists of a heavy cable connecting the positive battery post to the starter terminal through a heavy-duty switch, relay, or solenoid. In the other half of the circuit the negative battery post is connected to the engine block through a battery ground cable. This circuit carries high current while the engine is being cranked so it must have minimum resistance.

The rest of the vehicle electrical system is connected to the battery-starter insulated circuit at a junction between the battery and starter relay or solenoid. This junction might be the battery cable clamp, the battery junction of the solenoid, or a special junction block. The ignition switch is also fed from this junction. When the ignition switch is turned to the start position it energizes the relay or solenoid to operate the starter and crank the engine. This part of the electrical system is called the *starter switch circuit*.

For safety, automatic transmission equipped vehicles are prevented from cranking while the transmission selector is in a gear range. A *neutral safety switch* or *neutral start switch* is used to allow cranking only while the selector is in neutral or park. It is located electrically between the ignition start terminal and the solenoid or relay to

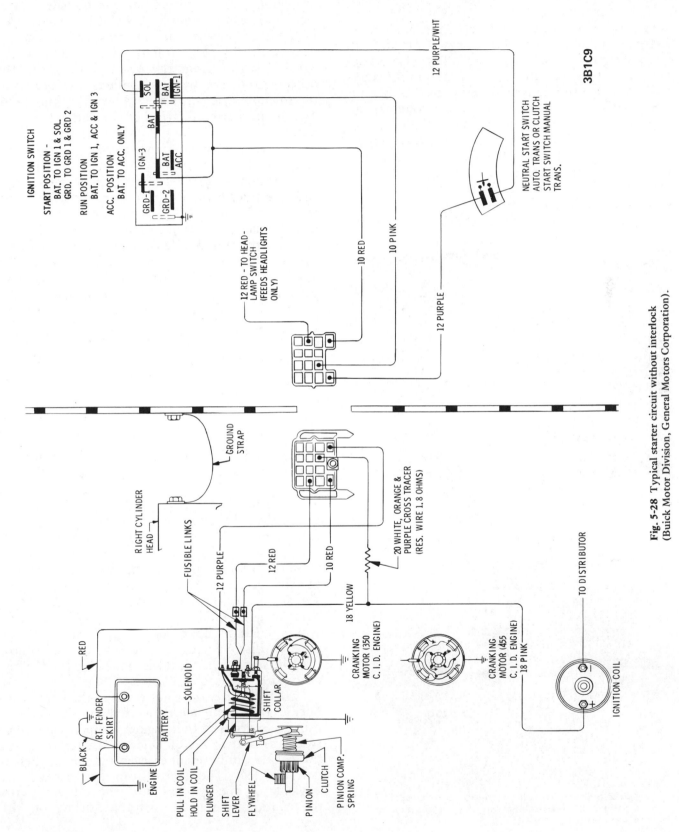

Fig. 5-28 Typical starter circuit without interlock (Buick Motor Division, General Motors Corporation).

keep the circuit open while the transmission selector is in any gear position. Chrysler automobiles use a starter relay and a solenoid. The relay is connected through a neutral safety switch in the transmission. When the transmission is in park or neutral the relay will be closed. The starter solenoid can then be actuated as previously described.

Some vehicles have used a vacuum safety switch in the starter switch circuit when the starter switch was located below the clutch pedal, accelerator pedal, or transmission shift control. These switches have been eliminated since the ignition start position was placed in the ignition switch.

(a)

(b)

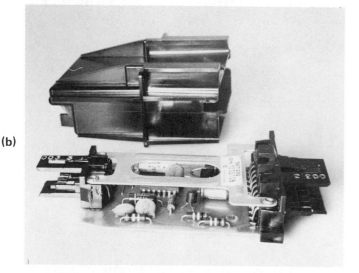

Fig. 5-29 Starter–seat belt interlock. (a) Under dash installation, (b) disassembled view showing the type of components used.

Ignition current fed through its normal circuit including the ignition resistor will not provide enough voltage for ignition while the engine is being cranked. An ignition resistor *by-pass* is provided while the starter is being cranked. Two methods are used to provide this by-pass. In one system the by-pass contacts are located in the ignition switch from the *ign 2* terminal. In the other system the by-pass contacts are located at the solenoid disc contact, as shown in Figure 5-26. The by-pass wire is attached to the solenoid *R* terminal.

When automatic transmissions were first introduced the neutral safety switch was included as a safety item to prevent accidental engine starting with the transmission in gear. During the 1974 and the first part of the 1975 model years automobile manufacturers were required by Federal regulations to equip the automobile with an interlock between the seat belt and the starter switch circuit. The interlock was a safety item designed to force all front-seat occupants to fasten themselves in the automobile with their seat belts. The heart of this system is a solid-state interlock control unit module mounted under the dash or under the seat. It blocks an electrical connection between the solenoid terminal on the ignition switch and the solenoid terminal on the starter motor until the occupants have been seated and their belts buckled. It prevents the engine from being cranked if the belt is not buckled or if the belt is buckled before a passenger sits on the seat. The module also turns on a *fasten your seat belt* light and activates a buzzer signal.

Sensors in the seat and switches in the seat belt, either in the take-up end or in the buckle, are connected to the module. Diodes, transistors, resistors, condensers, and a logic module sense the weight of the occupant on the seat and sense belt-switch operation to allow cranking after correct sequencing. If the starter cranks without proper sequencing it could be the result of a disconnected sensor junctions under an occupied seat. With the junction disconnected the module does not know that the seat is occupied. Disconnecting the module deactivates the interlock system.

If the starter does not crank in the normal sit-buckle-crank sequence the system can be bypassed using a switch in the engine compartment. The switch is marked START. Once the switch is pushed the engine can be cranked even though the belt is not buckled. The starter can be cranked for servicing if one reaches into the car and turns the ignition switch key without sitting on the seat.

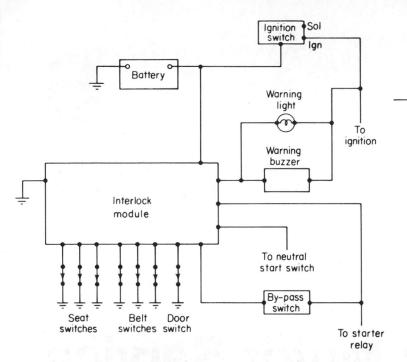

Fig. 5-30 Schematic of a typical starter-seat belt interlock circuit.

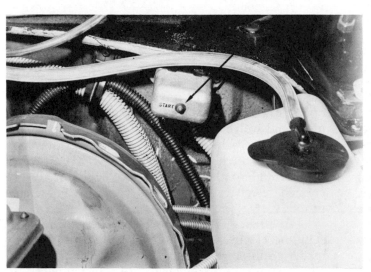

(a)   Fig. 5-31 Typical starter-seat belt interlock bypass switch.   (b)

REVIEW QUESTIONS

1. What controls motor speed and turning force?

2. What must be done to the motor to increase its torque?

3. How is the rotation direction controlled on a motor with electromagnetic fields?

4. How is the motor rotation controlled on a motor with permanent-magnet fields?

5. What is the approximate gear reduction between the starter armature and the engine crankshaft?

6. What must be done to a motor to increase its speed?

7. How is the rotating speed decreased in a shunt-wound motor?

8. When does the starter produce the greatest torque?

9. Under what condition does the starter draw the least current?

10. What is installed on automatic transmissions to prevent cranking when the selector is in gear?

6

Electric Motor Service

When an automotive electric motor fails to operate, the system must be checked to identify the specific fault. Electric motor and starter system service consists of checking the electrical system voltage, the condition of the conductor, and the operating units. Conductors must complete the electrical circuit, maintaining minimum resistance. The insulated circuit must make no contact with vehicle metal. Switches must open and close the circuit at the operator's command with no effective resistance. Motors must run at the proper speeds drawing minimum electrical current. If the circuit is tested using correct procedures, malfunctioning units can be identified. They must be either repaired or replaced, and then the system should be retested to make sure that the repair has properly corrected the problem.

Heavy electrical cables are used in the starter circuit to carry the large electrical current that is required by the starter. In automotive applications the negative battery post is connected to the engine block. The engine block forms a path for current to flow to the starter motor. The circuit is completed through the heavy switch contacts located in the starter relay or solenoid and through a cable connecting to the positive battery post. The automotive electrical system is called a single-wire system because almost all of the electrical units use a single wire for the insulated half of the circuit and the vehicle metal for the grounded half.

The size of the battery cable is very important. An oversize cable will not affect the starter circuit operation. It is only objectionable because it costs more and weighs more than the correct size cable. An undersize cable will cause problems. It has high resistance which reduces the flow of electrical current and so the starter motor will not receive enough electrical power to crank the engine properly.

An analogy may be helpful as an aid to understanding electrical flow sufficiently to enable the reader to intelligently check the operation of electrical circuits with electrical test instruments. In this analogy the flow of electricity will be compared to the flow of air in the shop air supply system.

The air compressor pushes air into an air tank. This crowds air into the tank, building up air pressure when the tank outlets are closed or restricted.

A valve installed on the air tank outlet can be gradually closed to increase the outlet restriction. With the compressor working, the more the air tank outlet is restricted the more the pressure will be built up in the air tank. When the valve is closed completely the compressor can put its full amount of pressure in the tank. *The outlet must be restricted in order to have pressure.*

If there were no outlet valve on the air tank and a 1-inch pipe opening were open to the atmosphere, the compressor would pump air but very little pressure would be built up. If a 20-foot piece

66

of 1-inch pipe were put in the tank opening, a higher pressure would be built up in the tank because the air could not move through the pipe as freely as it could before the pipe was installed. If the pipe length were increased to 200 feet the compressor would build up still more pressure because the added pipe would tend to restrict the air flow. *Resistance increases as the conductor length increases.*

If a bushing were placed in the tank opening and a 10-foot piece of $\frac{1}{2}$ inch pipe were placed in the bushing the compressor would build a higher pressure than in the preceeding example because the air could not get out of the $\frac{1}{2}$ inch pipe, which forms a restriction, as fast as it could get out of the original 1-inch pipe opening. *Resistance increases as the size (cross-section) of the conductor decreases.*

Different size pipes or hoses lead from the air tank to the shop air outlets. If a pressure gauge were put on any one of the shop outlets it would read the same pressure as the pressure gauge on the air tank when no air is being used. When air is drawn from the outlet, to operate a spray gun, for example, the pressure indicated on the outlet gauge will be lower than the pressure indicated on the air tank pressure gauge. The difference between the pressure in the air tank and the pressure at the shop outlet is called *pressure drop. Pressure drop only occurs when air is flowing in the system.* The amount of pressure drop will increase as the rate of air flow increases. For example, if two spray guns were operated from the same air outlet, they would use a larger amount of air than one spray gun alone. The pressure reading at the outlet gauge feeding air to the two spray guns would be lower than it was when only one spray gun was being used. Using more air produces a greater pressure drop.

In an air system the amount of pressure drop from the air supply tank to the operating unit increases as the volume of air flow increases, as the length of the line between the tank and operating unit increases, and as the size of the airconducting pipe or hose is reduced.

To complete the analogy, in electrical systems the battery takes the place of the air tank and the generator takes the place of the compressor. Air lines are replaced by wires and cables to carry electricity. Shut-off valves are replaced by electrical switches.

To restate the example in electrical terms, electrical pressure is measured with a voltmeter. The flow of electricity through a conductor is measured with an ammeter. Increasing the elec-

trical resistance in the conductor reduces the amperage flow and this increases the system voltage between the battery and the resistance. Reducing the resistance allows more amperage to flow and this lowers the system voltage. When the resistance is constant, increases in voltage will force more amperage to flow and decreases in voltage will result in less amperage flow.

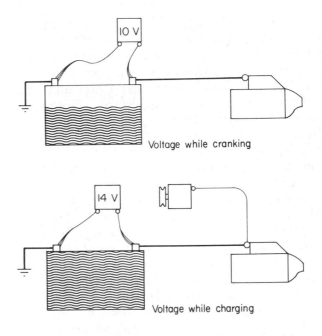

Fig. 6-1 Battery voltage while cranking and while charging.

In most of the automotive electrical systems the resistance is very low and therefore it is difficult to measure directly. Instead, these resistances are determined by measuring *voltage drop* while a specified amount of current is flowing in the circuit. If the current flows easily there is little voltage drop and consequently there is little resistance. If it is difficult for the current to flow because of high resistances a large voltage drop will be observed. *Current will only flow when there is a voltage drop.*

6-1 STARTER CIRCUIT TESTING

Starter circuit testing uses the voltage drop method to determine if excessive resistances exist in the circuit. In a normally cranking engine at room temperature a standard amount of current is required to crank an engine of a given engine size. The typical small V-8 engine requires about 160 amperes to crank the engine. Automotive engines under 200 cubic inch displacement will require less than 150 amperes while engines larger than 400 cubic inch displacement may require more than 220 amperes to crank the engine.

Cranking Voltage. The starting system can be given an overall check by measuring the cranking voltage. To keep the engine from starting during this test, the coil secondary cable can be removed from the distributor cap center tower and placed against the engine block. An alternate method is to connect a jumper wire from the *distributor side* of the coil primary to ground. The negative voltmeter lead is connected to the engine metal for ground. The positive voltmeter lead is connected to the battery cable terminal of the starter. As the engine is cranked with the ignition key the cranking voltage should be above 9.5 volts when the starter is cranking at normal speeds with a fully charged battery. Cranking should be limited to the shortest cranking period necessary to get a stable voltage reading. The positive voltmeter lead can also be connected to the switch side of the coil, an alternate location that is more accessible. The minimum cranking voltage at the coil should be 9.0 volts. In some cases cranking voltage is measured across the battery posts. With this connection cranking voltage should be above 9.6 volts. Manufacturer's

(a)

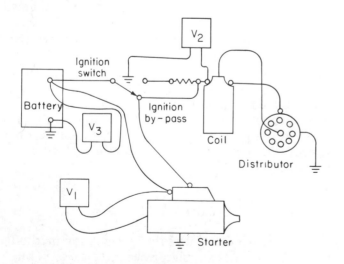

Fig. 6-2 Starter cranking voltage test connections.

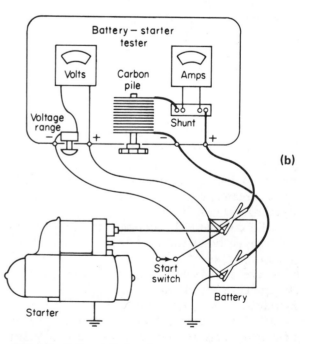

(b)

Fig. 6-3 Carbon pile in a battery starter tester. (a) Photo of internal parts, (b) schematic of test connections.

specifications should always be followed. In a normal warmed-up engine in good condition the cranking voltage will usually be 10 volts or more. A technician should make a habit of placing the transmission in *neutral* and setting the *parking brake* when cranking the engine, especially when he is using a remote-control starter switch.

Cranking voltages lower than 9 volts indicate problems with battery cables and their connections or with the starter itself.

Starter Amperage Draw. The starter can be checked by running a cranking voltage test with the voltmeter connected directly to the battery posts. While the starter is cranking, the voltage of the battery is the voltage available to the ignition system to start the engine. To measure starter amperage draw, a large carbon-pile-type rheostat with an ammeter is placed across the battery so that current can be drawn off through the carbon pile at a rate that will produce exactly the same voltage reading as the cranking voltage. The rate of current flow observed on the ammeter during this test is the same as the current used by the starter. This observed amperage value is called the *starter amperage draw*. The test should only be run for the few seconds required to set the correct voltage and observe the amperage.

High amperage draw occurs when the starter turns abnormally slow. This may be the result of the mechanical condition of the engine, abnormally thick oil, a problem within the starter motor, or circuit resistance as shown in Figure 6-4.

A general idea of the amperage draw can be determined without test instruments when the battery is known to be in good condition. The engine is cranked while headlight brightness is observed. If the lights dim considerably while the starter cranks slowly the amperage draw is excessive. If the lights do not dim while the starter cranks slowly there is resistance in the circuit. If the lights go out and the starter does not crank at all when the starter switch is engaged, the battery cable connections on the battery post are probably loose or corroded. If the lights do not dim at all and the starter does not crank the starter circuit has an open condition.

Voltage Drop. The starting circuit is tested by checking the voltage drop of the circuit. The engine can be cranked with a remote-control starter switch. To repeat a safety precaution, any time a remote-control starter switch is used the technician should make a habit of placing the transmission in *neutral* and setting the *parking brake*.

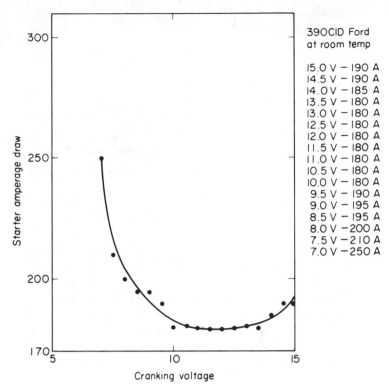

390CID Ford at room temp

15.0 V – 190 A
14.5 V – 190 A
14.0 V – 185 A
13.5 V – 180 A
13.0 V – 180 A
12.5 V – 180 A
12.0 V – 180 A
11.5 V – 180 A
11.0 V – 180 A
10.5 V – 180 A
10.0 V – 180 A
9.5 V – 190 A
9.0 V – 195 A
8.5 V – 195 A
8.0 V – 200 A
7.5 V – 210 A
7.0 V – 250 A

Fig. 6-4 Starter amperage draw at various cranking voltages.

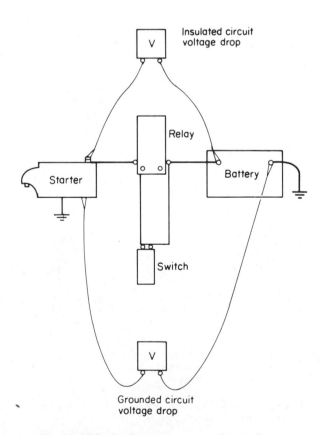

Fig. 6-5 Voltage drop test connections with a relay operated starter circuit.

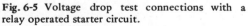

69

The remote-control starter switch is merely a heavy-duty push-button switch with two leads, each lead having a clip at its end. One clip is connected to the relay or solenoid switch terminal and the other clip is connected to a terminal with battery voltage or ground, depending on the type of starter solenoid or relay switch used on the engine. When the remote control switch is closed, the engine will crank. A special safety precaution should be observed when the remote control switch is used for cranking the engine with the spark plugs installed. Some starting solenoids have a built-in by-pass ignition system that operates while cranking, even if the ignition switch is turned off. One way to be sure that the engine will not fire is to ground the ignition system on the *distributor side* of the coil. The simplest way to prevent engine starting is to remove the coil cable from the center of the distributor cap and lay it against the engine metal.

With the voltmeter set on the 16-volt or 20-volt range the positive voltmeter lead should be attached to the positive battery post and the negative lead placed on the large starter motor terminal. While the cranking motor is operating, switch the voltmeter range to the 1-volt or 2-volt range and

observe the voltage. Immediately return the voltmeter scale to the 16-volt or 20-volt range before the starter remote switch is released. The voltage drop of this insulated portion of the starting circuit should be less than 0.5 volts. If it is, no further testing of the circuit is necessary.

If the voltage drop is greater than 0.5 volts the individual parts of the circuit will have to be checked. This is done by leaving the positive voltmeter lead on the battery post and moving the negative lead to the battery side of the solenoid. The voltage drop reading taken at this point shows the resistance in the insulated circuit to the solenoid. If it is higher than 0.2 volts the problem is in the insulated battery cable or in its connections. A general rule allows a maximum voltage drop of 0.2 volts for each normal battery cable, and each switch. Voltages slightly higher than this indicate that a problem is developing.

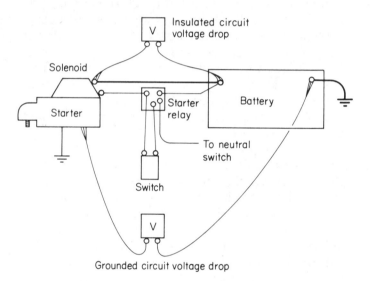

Fig. 6-7 Voltage drop test connections with a combination relay-solenoid operated starter circuit.

The grounded side of the system is just as important as the insulated side. It is checked by placing the negative voltmeter lead on the negative battery post and positive lead on the starter frame. With the starter cranking the maximum allowable voltage drop of 0.1 volt is normal. A larger voltage drop indicates a resistance that can be located by bringing the positive voltmeter lead toward the negative post, a junction at a time, and operating the starter as the positive voltmeter lead is held at each point, first on the engine block, then on the engine end of the battery ground cable, and finally on the negative battery clamp.

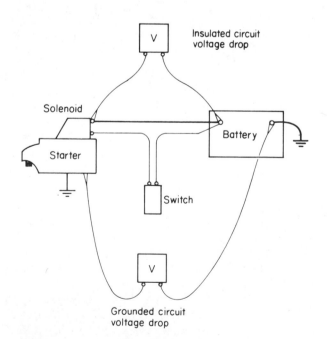

Fig. 6-6 Voltage drop test connections with a solenoid operated starter circuit.

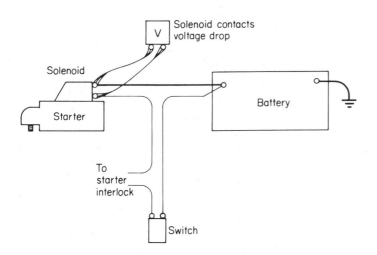

Fig. 6-8 Test connections to measure solenoid voltage drop.

Most starter problems occur because resistances develop in the battery cables, cable junctions, and electrical contacts within the solenoid. They may look bad and still function normally. The starting circuit can be accurately checked using the voltage drop procedure just described.

Fig. 6-9 Burned relay contacts.

Switch Circuit. The starter switch circuit uses contacts in the ignition switch to energize a coil in the starter relay or solenoid that, in turn, connects the starter to the battery with heavy electrical switch contacts. If the solenoid does not engage it may be the result of faulty ignition switch contacts, or faulty relay or solenoid connecting wiring. The operation of these items can be checked by placing the negative voltmeter lead on a good ground and the positive lead on the small relay or solenoid terminal. In a normally operating starter switch circuit, cranking voltage should be observed on the voltmeter when one attempts to crank the starter. If the starter does not crank and no voltage is observed the switch circuit is at fault. If battery voltage is observed the solenoid is open. If a very low voltage is noted the solenoid is shorted.

Fig. 6-10 One type of solenoid adjustment.

Solenoid switch repair kits are available. They contain new switch contacts and a disc. The solenoid is removed and the switch disassembled. New parts are installed and the switch reassembled. Where sealing is required, it should be done carefully because the starter is mounted under the engine where it gets road splash that can corrode the switch contacts. Some starter solenoid shifting forks require adjustment anytime the solenoid is serviced to give the correct pinion clearance. With the solenoid fully engaged the pinion should not touch the starter-drive end housing. Adjustments are made on the solenoid plunger attachment or on the solenoid mounting bracket.

STARTING CIRCUIT DIAGNOSIS

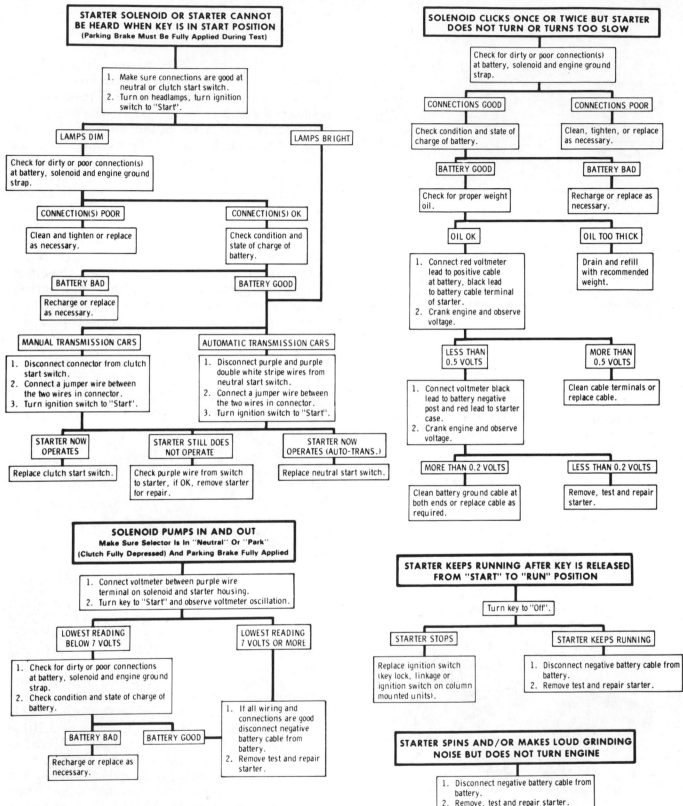

STARTER SOLENOID OR STARTER CANNOT BE HEARD WHEN KEY IS IN START POSITION
(Parking Brake Must Be Fully Applied During Test)

1. Make sure connections are good at neutral or clutch start switch.
2. Turn on headlamps, turn ignition switch to "Start".

LAMPS DIM

Check for dirty or poor connection(s) at battery, solenoid and engine ground strap.

LAMPS BRIGHT

CONNECTION(S) POOR

Clean and tighten or replace as necessary.

CONNECTION(S) OK

Check condition and state of charge of battery.

BATTERY BAD

Recharge or replace as necessary.

BATTERY GOOD

MANUAL TRANSMISSION CARS

1. Disconnect connector from clutch start switch.
2. Connect a jumper wire between the two wires in connector.
3. Turn ignition switch to "Start".

AUTOMATIC TRANSMISSION CARS

1. Disconnect purple and purple double white stripe wires from neutral start switch.
2. Connect a jumper wire between the two wires in connector.
3. Turn ignition switch to "Start".

STARTER NOW OPERATES

Replace clutch start switch.

STARTER STILL DOES NOT OPERATE

Check purple wire from switch to starter, if OK, remove starter for repair.

STARTER NOW OPERATES (AUTO-TRANS.)

Replace neutral start switch.

SOLENOID PUMPS IN AND OUT
Make Sure Selector Is In "Neutral" Or "Park"
(Clutch Fully Depressed) And Parking Brake Fully Applied

1. Connect voltmeter between purple wire terminal on solenoid and starter housing.
2. Turn key to "Start" and observe voltmeter oscillation.

LOWEST READING BELOW 7 VOLTS

1. Check for dirty or poor connections at battery, solenoid and engine ground strap.
2. Check condition and state of charge of battery.

LOWEST READING 7 VOLTS OR MORE

BATTERY BAD

BATTERY GOOD

Recharge or replace as necessary.

1. If all wiring and connections are good disconnect negative battery cable from battery.
2. Remove test and repair starter.

SOLENOID CLICKS ONCE OR TWICE BUT STARTER DOES NOT TURN OR TURNS TOO SLOW

Check for dirty or poor connection(s) at battery, solenoid and engine ground strap.

CONNECTIONS GOOD

Check condition and state of charge of battery.

CONNECTIONS POOR

Clean, tighten, or replace as necessary.

BATTERY GOOD

Check for proper weight oil.

BATTERY BAD

Recharge or replace as necessary.

OIL OK

1. Connect red voltmeter lead to positive cable at battery, black lead to battery cable terminal of starter.
2. Crank engine and observe voltage.

OIL TOO THICK

Drain and refill with recommended weight.

LESS THAN 0.5 VOLTS

1. Connect voltmeter black lead to battery negative post and red lead to starter case.
2. Crank engine and observe voltage.

MORE THAN 0.5 VOLTS

Clean cable terminals or replace cable.

MORE THAN 0.2 VOLTS

Clean battery ground cable at both ends or replace cable as required.

LESS THAN 0.2 VOLTS

Remove, test and repair starter.

STARTER KEEPS RUNNING AFTER KEY IS RELEASED FROM "START" TO "RUN" POSITION

Turn key to "Off".

STARTER STOPS

Replace ignition switch (key lock, linkage or ignition switch on column mounted units).

STARTER KEEPS RUNNING

1. Disconnect negative battery cable from battery.
2. Remove test and repair starter.

STARTER SPINS AND/OR MAKES LOUD GRINDING NOISE BUT DOES NOT TURN ENGINE

1. Disconnect negative battery cable from battery.
2. Remove, test and repair starter.
3. Examine ring gear for damage.

When electrical checks of the starting system indicate that the cranking motor is faulty, it will have to be removed. The ground cable is first removed from the battery to prevent accidental shorts that could produce dangerous sparks. The vehicle should be placed on jack stands or on a hoist if it is necessary to work under the vehicle. The starter wires are removed and the two or three mounting bolts removed. The starter can then be slid straight forward to remove it from the engine.

When the starter is on the bench it can be rechecked using a battery with starter-cable-size jumpers to run a *no-load* test. The starter should be held or clamped securely because it has a lot of turning torque when it first starts to rotate. With experience, the technician can judge whether the approximate turning speed is normal or low. Accurate measurement of the starter speed can be made with a hand-held tachometer, and the amperage draw can be determined using an ammeter while the starter is operating at a specific voltage, usually in the 9 to 11 volt range. If the starter does not meet the operational specifications as given in the applicable service manual it will have to be disassembled and repaired. To make this operational test, jumper wires are connected between the battery posts and the starter, negative to the starter frame and positive through a test ammeter and a large variable carbon pile to the starter cable terminal, usually a battery-starter tester. A small jumper can connect the switch terminal to the positive battery terminal to operate the starter solenoid. The carbon pile is tightened to produce the specified amperage and the free speed is observed.

Some manufacturers recommend a test to measure the starter electrical current draw when the starter pinion is held. In some cases a special link and spring scale are used to hold the pinion as the starter switch is closed to measure the locked turning torque of the starter. This test is called a *locked resistance* test or a *starter stall* test. For this test the starter should be held securely but not tightly in a vise and the pinion should be locked, so it cannot turn. A 12-volt battery is connected to the starter through a test ammeter and a variable carbon pile in the same manner as in the no-load test. A voltmeter is connected to the starter terminal and ground to observe operating voltage. Usually a battery-starter-tester that includes all necessary test components is used for this test. The carbon pile is adjusted to give a specified voltage and the amperage is observed. The spring scale is also observed when measuring stall torque. The starter is

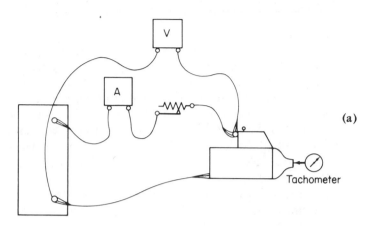

(a)

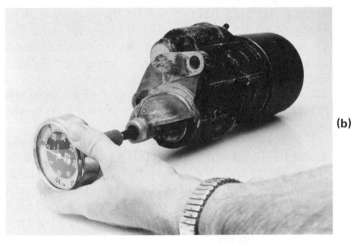

(b)

Fig. 6-12 Starter motor free speed test. (a) Test connections, (b) tachometer.

Fig. 6-13 Holding the pinion for the lock-torque test.

faulty if it does not meet the minimum test operating specifications shown in the applicable specification book.

A visual check of the starter solenoid will show if the solenoid has to be removed before the starter is disassembled. Some solenoids can have their shift forks disconnected and some require that their electrical terminals be disconnected before starter disassembly.

The direct-drive starter is disassembled by removing two long assembly through-bolts from the brushing end plate. The end plate and field frame can then be removed. In the reduction-gear-type of starter the field frame must be lifted only slightly from the drive end frame until the terminal screw can be removed and the shunt field wire unsoldered, and then the field frame can be lifted off. Following this, the shift lever mechanism and solenoid are removed to free the drive end plate from the armature. Each part can be inspected and tested for proper operation, then repaired as required.

The starter electrical parts should *not* be soaked in or flushed with cleaning solvents. Cleaning solvents will deteriorate the protective insulating varnish and the solvents may remain in the part to become a fire hazard after the starter is put back into use. Electrical parts should be wiped with a

clean rag. Stubborn surface oil can be removed with a rag damp with cleaning solvent, then wiped again with a clean dry cloth. Mechanical parts, with the exception of the overrunning clutch, can be cleaned with solvent in the normal manner used in parts cleaning. The overrunning clutch has a sealed-in lubricant that will wash out if the clutch is soaked in cleaning solvent.

The shift levers and forks are mechanical. They should operate freely without binding or sticking. They should not be bent or show signs of wear. The overrunning clutch and pinion assembly of the starter drive is the part most likely to require replacement. The overrunning clutch slips when it becomes worn and the teeth of the starter pinion become worn or broken. The assembly is not repairable but is replaced as a complete unit when it is faulty.

Each part of the starter can be bench tested. The simplest test is to check the parts with a 110-volt test light for continuity and electrical grounds. If an electrical system is insulated for 110 volts it can keep 12 volts from leaking to ground. The test light probes are connected to the commutator bars and armature metal core. If the light comes on the armature is grounded. The test probes are then placed on both ends of the field windings. If the bulb does not light the field is open. One probe is then switched to the field frame, while the other probe is kept on one end of the field winding. If the light comes on with the series field winding starter the field is grounded. The shunt winding is

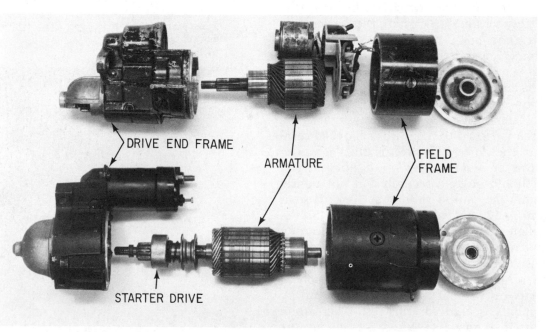

Fig. 6-14 Major starter parts.

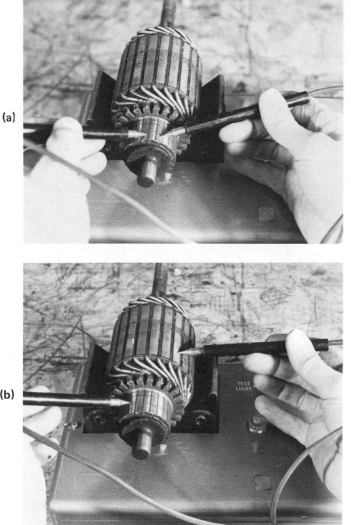

(a)

(b)

Fig. 6-15 Testing the armature. (a) Continuity, (b) grounds with a test light.

Fig. 6-16 Testing the armature for shorts on a growler.

Opens are difficult to find on a starter armature. The windings are so heavy and so few that they will not produce measurable amounts of voltage while in the growler field; that is, they will not produce voltage that can be measured with automotive service-type test equipment. However, starter armature opens can usually be seen during a visual inspection. They occur where the windings are soldered to the commutator. If the starter is overheated the solder will melt and be thrown into the frame. When this occurs the joints between the windings and commutator will loosen to produce an open. Vibration may cause a soldered joint to harden and break. Sometimes starter opens can be resoldered with rosin core solder to repair the armature.

connected to ground; this will cause the test lamp to light, so it must be disconnected for this test.

The brush holders can be checked by placing one test light probe on the frame and touching the other probe to the brush holder. Two opposing holders cause the bulb to light (grounded brush holders) while the other two should not (insulated brush holders). If the insulated holders allow the bulb to light the insulated brush holders are grounded.

Armature shorts can be checked by placing the armature in a growler, which is a device that puts a 60-cycle alternating magnetic field across the armature. A blade is laid across the armature as the armature is turned by hand on the growler. A shorted armature will cause the blade to vibrate at some point.

Fig. 6-17 Solder thrown from an overheated starter motor into the field frame.

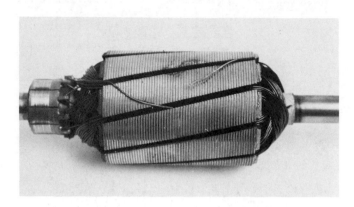

Fig 6-18 Winding thrown from a windshield wiper motor.

Starter brushes slide on the commutator, causing wear and scarring. If the brush pressure is not great enough the brush will tend to float slightly, producing a slight arc between the brush and commutator. This will burn the commutator surface.

Fig. 6-19 Scored commutator.

Brush pressure is caused by the force of the brush spring. Brush pressure can become weak when the brush wears down more than one-half its original length or if the brush spring becomes weak. Brush wear is visible. Spring tension can be measured using a pull scale. The end of the scale is hooked into the brush spring and it is pulled to its normal operating position.

Fig. 6-20 Measuring brush spring tension.

6-3 STARTER RECONDITIONING

During the bench test the visual inspection and electrical test will indicate the parts that are faulty. In general, electrical starter parts that have opens, shorts, or grounds can be exchanged for new or rebuilt parts, that are readily available. Service manuals show how to replace starter fields, for example, but parts departments seldom stock these parts. Many servicemen run the no-load test on a questionable starter. If the starter does not seem to operate properly, and if the serviceman does not understand starter servicing or does not have starter servicing equipment, he will exchange the starter for a rebuilt starter to get the customer's automobile on the road as soon as possible.

Fig. 6-21 Turning a commutator.

Starter servicing generally includes replacing faulty parts, providing new brushes, and turning the commutator. The armature is set up in a lathe or a special armature turning tool. Light cuts are taken across the commutator until it has a smooth surface. The insulation between the commutator bars should be under cut about $\frac{1}{16}$ inch so there is no chance of its holding the brush away from the commutator bars. Undercutting is best done with a small cutting wheel on a motor drive. After the undercutting procedure is finished, the grooves should be checked to see that no metal particles remain in them. Particles of metal can short the armature and reduce turning torque.

Fig. 6-23 Soldering new brushes in a starter.

Fig. 6-22 Undercutting a commutator.

Brush spring tension should be checked. Spring tension that is too light will allow the brush to float causing an arc that will burn the commutator. Too much spring tension will cause excessive brush and commutator wear. Weak brush springs should be replaced.

Insulated brushes in most starters are soldered to the field. These junctions must be heated enough to loosen the solder and release the old brush lead. New brushes are soldered in place with rosin core solder. Ground brushes are usually bolted or riveted in place. In some cases the brush is bolted to a spring-loaded arm. These brushes can be replaced by merely bolting a new brush in place.

The new brush may not correctly fit the commutator arc so the brushes should be seated. This is done by placing sandpaper around the commutator, sand side out. The brushes are installed in their holder and placed against the sandpaper. The commutator and sandpaper are rotated back and forth until the correct arc is formed on the brush face.

Some manufacturers recommend the replacement of shaft bushings in the drive end plate. The bushing bore opening goes clear through the end plate and so the old bushing can be pressed out and a new one pressed in. Brush end frame bushings are only open at one end and so the usual procedure is to replace the end frame with a new one that has a new bushing already installed.

The only parts of the starter that should be lubricated are the bushings and the shifting fork linkages. The solenoid plunger, armature, commutator, brushes, and fields operate without lubricants.

The drive assembly and shifting forks should now be assembled. In starters having the solenoid mounted on the drive end frame, the solenoid must be attached at the same time the fork is assembled. In starters with the solenoid mounted on the field frame, the solenoid is installed after the rest of the starter is assembled.

The bearing journal ends of the armature are lubricated with high-melting-point grease and the armature is installed in the drive end bushing. In geared starters the armature must be fitted through the brush holder; the serviceman should carefully seat the brushes on the commutator. The field frame is then fitted over the armature. Many direct-drive starter brushes are in the field frame so they must be fitted over the commutator. In some starters, electrical attachments are made at this time by bolting or soldering. Field frames are proprerly positioned over alignment pins.

The brush end frame is finally installed making sure it is aligned on the pins. Some brush end frames hold the brushes. These are the most difficult to install because the four brushes must be held back against the springs while the frame is slipped over the commutator. This can be done by pulling the brush out of the holder far enough so that it can be jammed with the brush spring. A bent piece of a wire clothes hanger makes a useful tool for this. Pushing the brush against the commutator after assembly will seat the brush spring in its normal position.

The whole starter is held together by installing the long assembly bolts and tightening them securely. Where required, the solenoid is installed. The pinion clearance is checked and adjusted as necessary.

After assembly the starter is rechecked with the no-load test and locked-resistance or locked-torque test when recommended. If the starter meets these tests after service it is ready to be installed on the engine.

Fig. 6-24 Locking a starter brush for assembly.

The starter is installed by slipping the drive end into the bell housing and installing the mounting screws. Tightening torque specifications are usually given for the cap screws. The battery lead, switch lead, and ignition by-pass, where used, are installed on the solenoid connections. When this is complete the battery ground cable can be installed and the starter system operated to make sure that it cranks the engine satisfactorily.

REVIEW QUESTIONS

1. What is necessary to build up pump pressure?

2. What is necessary to produce an electric current flow?

3. What amperage draw should be expected from a normal starting system cranking a cold engine?

4. What does high cranking voltage indicate when the starter is cranking rapidly?

5. What does a high cranking voltage indicate when the starter is cranking slowly?

6. What problem exists when a starter turns slowly with a high cranking voltage?

7. What is the general rule regarding starter system cable voltage drop?

8. Where do most starter system problems occur?

9. What part of the starter drive mechanism is most likely to fail?

10. What tests are made on an assembled starter that is not made on an engine?

11. How is a starter armature short determined?

12. Why should the technician avoid soaking starter parts in clean solvent?

13. Why are commutators undercut?

14. What holds the starter components together?

15. What checks are run after starter assembly?

7

The Charging System

When the automobile engine is running, the charging system is designed to supply all of the current required by the electrical load and to charge the battery. The battery will supply any occasional extra electrical demand that exceeds the capacity of the charging system. This condition will usually occur at idle speed when a large number of accessories and lights are turned on.

The charging system consists of a belt-driven generator, a regulator to limit maximum voltage, and the necessary electrical wiring and switches to connect these units into the automobile electrical system.

In 1960 diode-rectified alternators rather than commutator-rectified generators were installed on some domestic automobiles as standard equipment. By the mid-1960's all domestic automobiles were using alternators. The installation of the alternator charging systems did not change the design of the rest of the automotive electrical system. It produced the same type of pulsing direct current that the older generator had produced. The alternator, however, produced electrical current at lower engine speeds, had lighter-weight construction, would safely operate at higher speeds, and was less expensive. All of these were good reasons to use the alternator in place of the traditional generator.

7-1 GENERATING PRINCIPLES

The generator makes use of electromagnetic induction principles described in Chapter 1. Relative motion between magnetic lines of force and a conductor causes the electrons in the conductor to drift in one direction. This forced drift produces an electromotive force or voltage in the conductor. The strength of this induced voltage is based on the number of magnetic lines of force cutting the conductor each second.

More magnetic lines of force can be made to cut a conductor in three ways. First, by increasing the *rate* at which the magnetic lines of force cut the conductor. Second, by increasing the *number of windings* in the conductor. Third, by increasing the *magnetic field strength.* The generator is belt-driven and so its speed is dependent on the engine speed; consequently, the rate at which the magnetic lines of force cuts the conductor cannot be used to control the automotive charging system. The number of generator conductor windings is part of the generator design and so it cannot be used to control the generator output while the generator is in operation. Generator output is very effectively controlled in automotive charging systems by changing the magnetic strength of the generator field. Generators are designed so that they will produce maximum output when maximum electrical system voltage is placed across the terminals of the generator field. This causes maximum current to flow in the field. Maximum field strength will produce far more voltage than is normally required by the electrical system so the regulator is designed to reduce the magnetic strength of the generator field to the level that allows the generator to produce the voltage that is needed by the electrical system during each operating condition.

Alternator Operation. The alternator produces electricity as the belt drive turns the rotor so that its magnetic lines of force cut across the stator windings. This relative motion of the lines of magnetic force cutting stator produces a voltage in the windings. The voltage produced pushes current through the charging system when all connections are complete and properly insulated.

The electrical problems that can occur are reviewed here to help the reader keep them in mind. A broken wire, called an *open*, will stop the electri-

cal current flow. If the insulation is broken and the wire touches the engine or body sheetmetal the electrical current can go directly to the alternator frame. This failure is called a *ground*. If the insulation on two adjacent wires breaks down and the wires touch each other the electrical current can take a short cut back to the alternator so this type of failure is called a *short*. One other system failure is a *partial open*. This provides less conductor for the electrical current to flow through, so it resists current flow and becomes warm. A partial open is the most common type of electrical failure in atuomobiles and is called a *resistance*.

The alternator speed is changed according to the engine speed demanded by the driver, and so speed cannot be used to control maximum alternator output. Maximum output is controlled by adjusting the magnetic strength of the rotor field. This is done by changing the amount of current flowing in the rotor coil windings. The regulator increases and decreases the current flowing in the field by switching the field voltage on and off to provide the required field current amperage. The longer it is on compared to being off the stronger the average field current will be. The timing of the on-off cycle is changed by the regulator to limit maximum charging system voltage produced by the alternator.

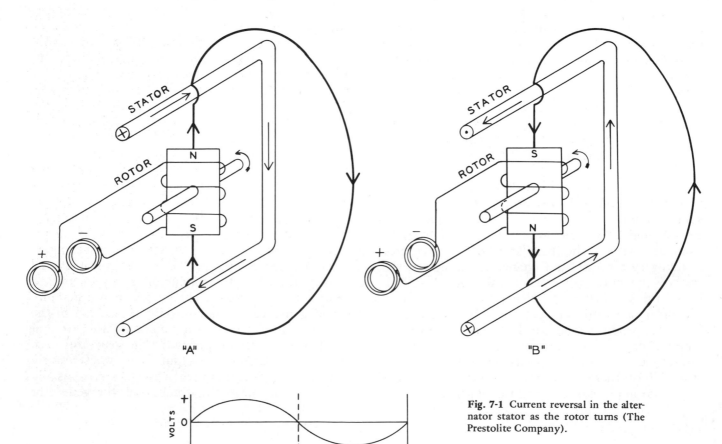

Fig. 7-1 Current reversal in the alternator stator as the rotor turns (The Prestolite Company).

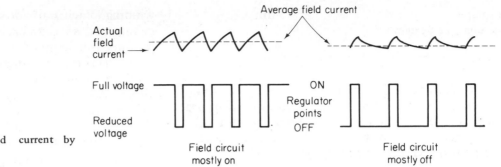

Average field current

Actual field current

Full voltage

Reduced voltage

ON
Regulator points
OFF

Field circuit mostly on

Field circuit mostly off

Fig. 7-2 Regulator provides field current by switching on and off.

7-2 ALTERNATOR COMPONENTS

Modern automotive generators are rectified with diodes. A diode is an electronic device that passes current in only one direction. Diode-rectified generators are usually called alternators. The diodes rectify the alternating stator current to form a pulsating direct current used in the automobile electrical system.

In the alternator, the main conductor is wound on a frame, and the assembly is called a *stator*. A field winding is wound around a hub that is supported on a shaft and bearings. Pole shoes, to concentrate the magnetic field, are placed over the field windings. This field assembly is called a *rotor*. The rotor turns inside the stator, forcing the magnetic lines of force to cut the stator windings.

Each end of the rotating field coil is brought to a copper ring that is insulated from the shaft.

Carbon brushes ride against and slip on these rings, called brush *slip rings*, to connect the field windings to the regulator circuit.

In operation, the regulator controls current flow through the field windings located in the rotor. This current produces a magnetic field that magnetizes the pole shoes, one-half north pole and the other half south pole. As the rotor turns, the magnetism that surrounds the pole shoes cuts across the conductor windings of the stator. This

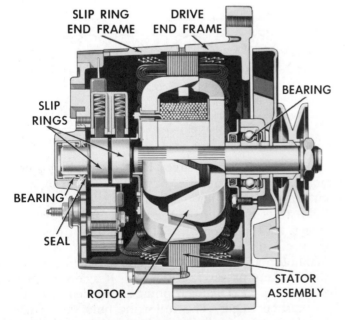

SLIP RING END FRAME   DRIVE END FRAME

SLIP RINGS

BEARING

BEARING

SEAL

ROTOR

STATOR ASSEMBLY

Fig. 7-3 Section view of a typical alternator (Delco-Remy Division, General Motors Corporation).

Fig. 7-4 Typical alternator field brush holders.

induces voltage in the stator windings. Current will flow in the stator if the stator is connected into a completed electrical circuit, whenever stator voltage is greater than the vehicle electrical-system voltage produced by the battery.

Stator. Alternator stators are made with three separate windings. Within each of these windings are a number of separate coils wound in series. They are spaced so that the magnetic field polarity is the same on each of the coils within a

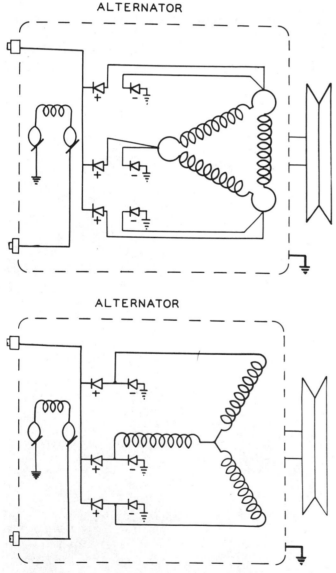

Fig. 7-5 Delta and Y alternator stator connections (The Prestolite Company).

winding. Each coil adds to the voltage of the preceding coil so that each stator winding is able to produce the designed voltage.

All three windings are connected together. The most common connection used in automobile alternators is a *Y* connection; however, some applications use a *delta* connection. Both operate in a similar manner. The following discussion of alternators will cover the Y-connection type stator.

The three windings in a Y connection are fastened together at the Y junction. The other end of each winding goes to a pair of diodes, one positive and one negative. The diodes are connected to the charging system, positive to the battery and negative to ground.

Rotor. The field pole shoe fingers of the alternator rotor are alternately spaced, north-south-north-south, etc., around the rotor. Alternate magnetic fields from the rotor pole shoes cut the stator windings as the rotor turns. This causes the electrons in the stator windings to be forced one way, then back the other way as the alternate magnetic fields cross the stator winding. This produces an alternating voltage in the stator. If the stator were connected directly to an outside circuit, the alternating voltage would produce an *alternating current* (AC). Automotive electrical systems, however, require the voltage and current to be in one direction. This is called *direct current* (DC). Alternating current produced in the stator needs to be *rectified* to become direct current for use in the automotive electrical system.

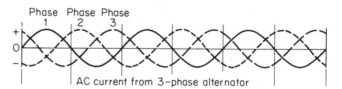

Fig. 7-6 Alternating current from three phase windings (The Prestolite Company).

The voltage produced by each winding is proportional to the number of magnetic lines of force cutting the winding each second. The magnetic field starts from zero at the center of the pole shoe finger. As the rotor turns, the number of magnetic lines of force cutting the winding increases to a maximum as a point equidistant between the pole shoe fingers passes the winding. It again drops to zero at the next neutral point at the center of the rotor shoe finger. The following pole shoe finger has the opposite polarity and so, in effect, the magnetic field direction changes. This changes the direction of the voltage produced in the winding. The continual buildup, first in one direction and then in another, produces a *sine wave* voltage. The name comes from the trigonometric function called sine. If a single conductor and a single two-pole magnet were used, the voltage would be proportional to the trigonometric sine of the angle of the magnet in relation to the conductor. Three stationary windings are equally spaced and their voltages produce three sine waves as the rotor turns. The current produced by these voltages is called a *three-phase alternating current.*

Older-type generators had a stationary field and a rotating armature, similar to the starter. The conductors in the rotating armature cut the magnetic lines of force surrounding the stationary field. Current from the armature flows through commutator segments and brushes to the automotive electrical system.

7-3 RECTIFICATION

The current from each of the three-phase alternating voltages produced by the stator is fed through diodes, which are one-way electrical check valves. The diodes are connected so that they will stop the reverse half of the current, while allowing the forward half to flow normally in the circuit. This is called *half-wave rectification.* In alternators, half-wave rectification would reduce the output current by half, so *full-wave rectification* is used. Full-wave rectification reverses the effective polarity of one-half of the sine wave, so that the whole wave is in the same direction. The electrical circuit only senses maximum voltage which results in a direct-current voltage ripple. The alternating current in a generator armature is rectified by commutator bars, while the current produced in the alternator stator is rectified by diodes. Current is the flow of electrons.

Fig. 7-7 Full wave rectification (The Prestolite Company).

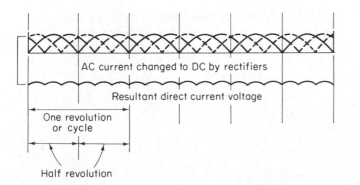

In operation, the voltage in each coil builds in the positive direction, then collapses. Then it immediately builds in the negative direction and again collapsing, operating in a continuous cycle. Each of the phase windings are equally spaced and take turns building and collapsing. To help understand diode rectification in each of the accompanying illustrations, the action will be stopped when one of the phases is at zero as it is reversing its polarity.

Figure 7-8 shows the first rectifying stage as electrons flow from phase winding 1 to phase winding 2 (phase winding 3 is momentarily at zero).

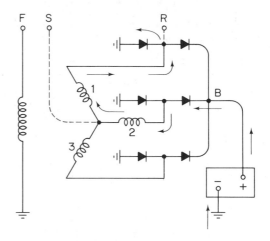

Fig. 7-8 Phase 1 to Phase 2 rectification.

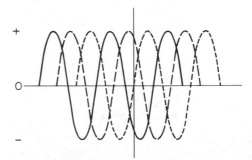

Electrons flow from the phase 1 winding, out the grounded diode and into the grounded side of the battery. This reverses the electron flow through the battery to cause battery charging. Electrons then flow to phase winding 2 through its positive diode, through the Y connections and on to the phase winding 1 to complete the circuit.

The second rectifying stage is shown in Figure 7-9. With phase winding 3 neutral, the electrons flow from phase winding 2 through the grounded diode, then on to the negative battery post through the positive diode of the phase winding 1. The circuit is completed through the Y connection.

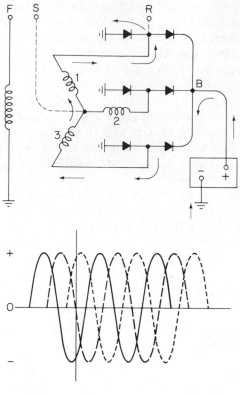

Fig. 7-10 Phase 1 to Phase 3 rectification.

Fig. 7-11 Phase 3 to Phase 1 rectification.

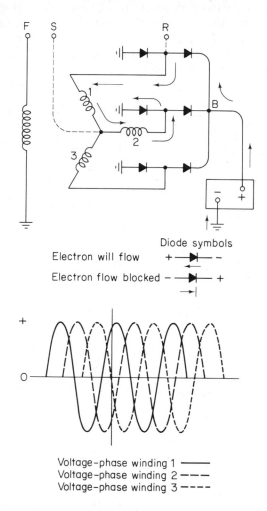

Diode symbols

Electron will flow   + ▶▎ –

Electron flow blocked – ▶▎ + →▎

Voltage-phase winding 1 ———
Voltage-phase winding 2 – – –
Voltage-phase winding 3 - - - -

Fig. 7-9 Phase 2 to Phase 1 rectification.

Phase winding 2 is momentarily at zero during the rectifying stage three in Figure 7-10. Electrons flow from phase winding 1 through the grounded diode to the grounded battery post. The flow continues to the positive diode of phase winding 3 and the Y connection to complete the circuit.

During rectifying stage four, phase winding 2 is neutral. Electrons leave phase winding 3 through

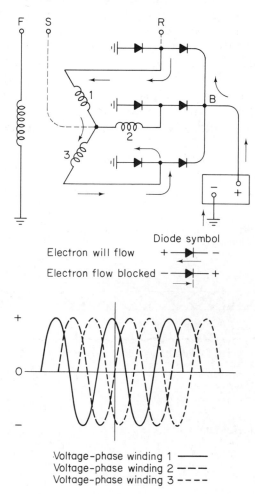

Diode symbol

Electron will flow   + ▶▎ – ←

Electron flow blocked – ▶▎ + →

Voltage-phase winding 1 ———
Voltage-phase winding 2 – – –
Voltage-phase winding 3 - - - -

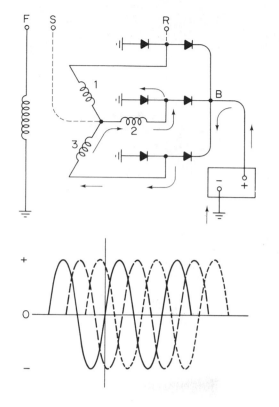

Fig. 7-12 Phase 2 to Phase 3 rectification.

Fig. 7-13 Phase 3 to Phase 2 rectification.

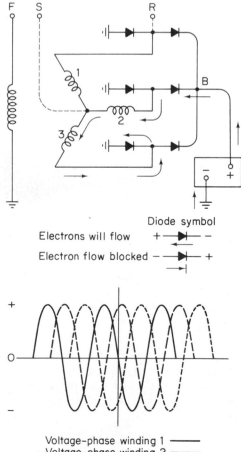

Diode symbol

Electrons will flow + ▸▸▮ –

Electron flow blocked – ▸▸▮ +

Voltage-phase winding 1 ——
Voltage-phase winding 2 ———
Voltage-phase winding 3 ————

its negative diode to flow to the battery. The phase winding 1 positive diode carries the electrons from the positive battery post through the winding and Y connection.

Rectifying stage five is timed to show the electron flow while phase winding 1 is at zero as it is changing polarity. Electrons flow from phase winding 2 through the grounded diode and the battery, then on into phase winding 3 through its positive diode. The circuit is completed through the Y connection.

The sixth rectifying stage is the reverse of stage five. Electrons from phase winding 3 go to the battery through the grounded diode. From the positive battery post, the electrons flow through the positive diode and into phase winding 2. The Y connection completes the circuit to phase winding 3.

It should be noted that as the electron flow reverses within the phase windings, the outside circuit from the alternator ground and to the alternator battery (BAT) terminal is always in the same direction. The entire external voltage of an alternator is a pulsating voltage in one direction, just as the voltage from the generator is pulsating in one direction. This one-way voltage is the force that moves a direct current when the circuit is completed.

Each free end of the three stator windings is connected to the leads of one negative diode and one positive diode. The three negative diodes are pressed into the alternator case or placed in a diode plate where they can make a good electrical connection through the engine and ground wire to the battery. The three positive diodes are pressed into or fastened in a block of aluminum or heavy sheet metal called a *heat sink*, which is insulated from the alternator frame and is exposed to an air flow to keep the diodes cool. The insulated heat sink is connected to the insulated or positive side of the battery.

Battery current will not flow through the diodes because they are connected in a manner that causes the battery to put a reverse bias voltage on each of the diodes. When the operating alternator voltage increases above battery voltage, a forward bias voltage is placed on the diodes and they conduct current to charge the battery and to supply current to operate accessories.

Fig. 7-14 Typical diode installations in alternators.

7-4 CHARGING SYSTEM CIRCUITS

The alternator is the source of electrical energy used to operate all of the electrical devices on the automobile while the engine is running. In addition, the alternator has extra capacity to recharge the battery. The charging circuit consists of wiring that interconnects the alternator, the regulator, the battery, and the vehicle electrical system.

The main portion of the insulated circuit consists of a wire between the alternator BAT terminal and a junction where the alternator can feed both the vehicle electrical system and the battery. A second wire between this junction and the battery completes the insulated portion of the charging circuit. The battery uses this second wire to feed the vehicle electrical system when the alternator does not supply adequate electrical power by itself. Vehicle manufacturers use a number of different junction points. The junction may be the BAT terminal of the starter solenoid, a junction block on the radiator support or inner fender pan, or the BAT terminal of the horn relay. The ground portion of the charging circuit is the metal-to-metal contact between the alternator case and the engine. The engine is connected to the negative battery post by the battery ground cable that completes the main charging circuit.

The voltage regulator is an important part of the charging system. It is connected in series with the alternator rotor field winding to control electrical current going through the field, thereby controlling alternator maximum voltage. When mechanical regulators are used one end of the regulator field-circuit is connected to the insulated circuit through a switch and the other end is connected to ground. Solid state regulators are usually connected in the field circuit between the alternator field and ground.

The switch in the regulator field-circuit is necessary to open the circuit when the engine is not running and to close the circuit when the engine operates. The ignition switch serves this function. Some vehicles use a heavy-duty ignition switch to directly feed electrical power into the regulator field-circuit while others use a standard-duty ignition switch to signal a field relay located in the same case with the voltage regulator. The relay connects the regulator field-circuit to the charging circuit.

The charging circuit includes an indicator—either an ammeter or an indicator lamp—to show battery charge or discharge. The ammeter, as used in Chrysler charging systems, is connected in the charging circuit between the junction and the battery. It will show *charge* when the alternator is producing an excess output that will charge the battery. It shows *discharge* when the alternator cannot supply enough electrical current by itself so that some of the current is also coming from the battery to help supply the electrical demands of the vehicle.

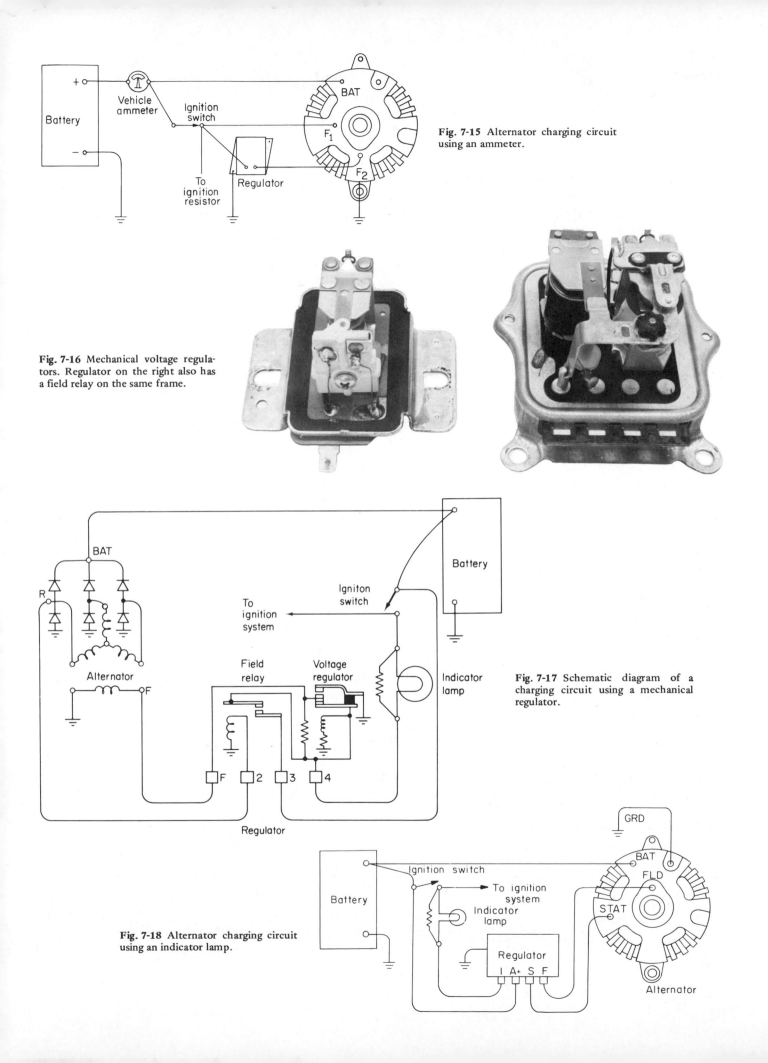

Fig. 7-15 Alternator charging circuit using an ammeter.

Fig. 7-16 Mechanical voltage regulators. Regulator on the right also has a field relay on the same frame.

Fig. 7-17 Schematic diagram of a charging circuit using a mechanical regulator.

Fig. 7-18 Alternator charging circuit using an indicator lamp.

The indicator lamp is connected parallel to a resistor in the circuit between the ignition switch, the Delco number 4 or Ford number I regulator terminal, and the alternator field windings. When the ignition switch is turned on alternator field current is supplied through the parallel-wired resistor and indicator lamp. If the indicator lamp bulb burns out the system will still be fed through the resistor to prevent complete failure. When the alternator starts to charge, the Delco alternator R or Ford alternator S terminal feeds a small amount of current to the field relay winding through the Delco number 2 or Ford number S regulator terminal. This energizes the field relay coil which in turn attracts the relay armature. This attraction closes the relay contact points. The points connect the Delco number 3 and 4 terminals or the Ford I and A+ terminals that connect to the insulated side of the charging circuit. The closed field relay points effectively connect both sides of the indicator lamp electrically so the voltage is equal on both lamp terminals; therefore no current will flow through the lamp bulb and the light goes out. It stays out as long as the alternator is charging, even when part of the electrical power is being taken from the battery.

7-5 CHARGING SYSTEM REGULATION

The battery regulates voltage in the charging system at all voltages below a maximum voltage which is limited by the voltage regulator. The maximum amount of current produced by the alternator is limited by inductance built into the alternator

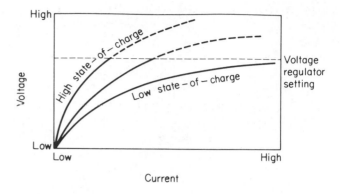

Fig. 7-19 When the voltage is limited by the regulator, the charging current reduces as the battery's state-of-charge increases.

design. Maximum current in a commutator-rectified generator is limited by a current regulator.

Battery Regulation. The battery supplies electrical power to crank and start the engine. If the start is not immediate, quite a bit of electrical energy is withdrawn from the battery. This results in a slight decrease in battery terminal voltage. As soon as the engine starts, the charging system comes into operation to supply the electrical load of the vehicle and recharge the battery. The charging system voltage increases as the battery counter electromotive force increases. While the battery counter electromotive force is low, the charging system supplies high current to the battery. As the battery becomes charged, battery counter electromotive force increases, decreasing the charging amperage rate. This change is accompanied by an increase in the voltage of the entire charging system. When battery counter electromotive force reaches the regulator voltage setting, the regulator begins to take control to limit the voltage level.

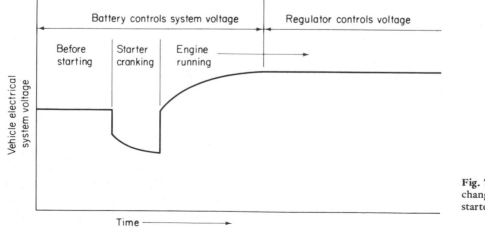

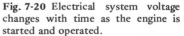

Fig. 7-20 Electrical system voltage changes with time as the engine is started and operated.

Mechanical Voltage Regulator Operation. The mechanical voltage regulator consists of breaker points mounted on an armature above a voltage-sensitive coil, with associated supporting mechanical and electrical components. The voltage regulator points are connected in series with the alternator or generator field. The points are *normally closed* to allow full current flow in the field which will provide maximum magnetic field strength. When charging system voltage reaches the voltage setting, the regulator points open, breaking the field circuit. This stops field current and the magnetic field decays, reducing alternator or generator output voltage. When voltage drops, the regulator points close, reestablishing field current and the magnetic field. This cycle happens very rapidly, as shown on the oscilloscope in Figure 7-21, keeping an essentially constant charging system voltage as shown on a voltmeter.

The normally closed voltage regulator points are held closed with an adjustable calibrated spring.

(a)

(b)

Fig. 7-22 Voltage regulators. (a) Lower points normally closed, (b) upper points normally closed.

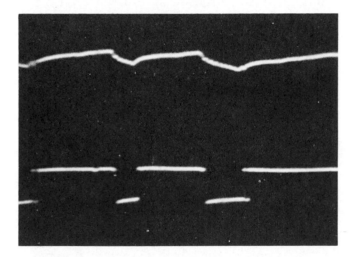

Fig. 7-21 Oscilloscope trace of field current (upper trace) and field voltage (lower trace).

An electromagnetic force pulls the regulator armature down to open the points when system voltage reaches the voltage setting.

The electromagnet of a voltage regulator is made from a great number of fine wire turns wrapped around a soft iron core. This wire has high resistance because it is long and has a small diameter. Its high resistance will only allow a very small current to flow even though it is connected across the charging system from the insulated side through a ballast to ground. The amount of current flowing through the fixed resistance of the regulator coil is determined by charging system voltage. As the charging system voltage increases, the current flow

through the regulator coil increases which, in turn, increases the magnetic field strength of the coil.

The magnetic strength of a coil may be measured in *ampere turns*. The voltage regulator coil uses low amperage with a large number of turns. Amperage or current flow in the regulator coil is greatest at a high charging system voltage. The strong magnetism produced in the regulator coil pulls on the spring-held regulator armature with moveable contact point attached. This separates the normally closed points to break field current flow. A weakened alternator field causes a reduction in the charging system voltage. The reduced charging system voltage weakens the magnetism of the regulator coil and so the armature spring closes the points. This cycle repeats whenever the regulator is controlling system voltage.

A resistor is used across the regulator points to form a by-pass for some of the field current. This keeps the magnetic field of the rotor from decaying completely when the points are open, but the resistor will weaken the magnetic field to give a voltage level close to nominal battery voltage. This results in a rapid regulator response that provides proper voltage control. Other resistors and ballasts may be used in the voltage regulator to reduce point burning and to aid in maintaining smooth voltage control.

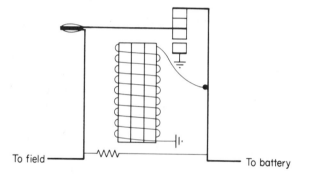

Fig. 7-23 Mechanical voltage regulator schematic diagram.

The resistor across the points in some charging systems allows somewhat more current to flow through the field during the time that the regulator points are open. With field current being fed through the resistor and the charging system running under light electrical loads at moderate speeds, the generator voltage matches the electrical

load. When this happens, the points *float* and do not touch. Any increase in speed or any reduction in electrical load would result in excess system voltage.

To prevent excessive voltage from occurring at higher speeds on alternators and on some high output generators, a second *normally open* contact point is added to the voltage regulators. This second point is grounded. As the electrical system voltage increases, more current flows through the voltage regulator coil winding, increasing the magnetism and pulling the armature further, which causes the normally-open voltage regulator points to contact the grounded point. All of the current flowing through the resistor is then directed to ground and so no current flows through the alternator field. This causes magnetic field of the alternator rotor to decay, lowering system voltage which, in turn, reduces the magnetic field strength of the voltage regulator coil. When the system voltage decreases, the spring opens the normally open grounding points, allowing current to again flow through the resistor to the field coil, building up the rotor magnetic field and increasing system voltage. This action repeats itself, and causes the points to vibrate on the normally open grounded point.

Magnetism attracts the regulator armature through an air gap. The effectiveness of a magnet reduces as the square of the distance through which the magnetism must act. The magnetism would be only one-quarter as effective at twice the air gap. The air gaps between the regulator coil core and armature are critical for correct regulator operation and they must be within specifications. Mechanical regulator voltage settings are adjusted by changing the tension of the armature return spring. Increasing spring tension increases the amount of regulator coil magnetic strength that is required to move the regulator armature. The coil magnetic strength increases as system voltage increases, and so increasing spring tension increases system voltage.

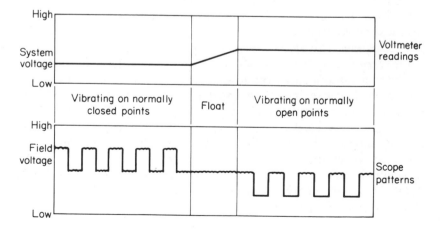

Fig. 7-24 System voltage and field voltage in different regulating modes.

Most voltage regulators are temperature compensated. When they are cold they regulate at higher voltage levels than when they are warm. The temperature compensation of the regulator is matched to the charging amperage acceptance rate of the battery at different temperatures. When a battery is cold the chemical action is slow and so a high voltage is required to force current through the battery for charging. When the battery is warm the chemical action is more rapid so less voltage is required to force the same current through it.

Fig. 7-25 Mechanical voltage regulator temperature compensating devices.

The regulator has two means of temperature compensation. One method uses a thermostatic bimetallic hinge spring. It provides extra spring tension when cold so that the regulator coil will use a stronger magnetism to operate it. Stronger regulator magnetism can only come from a higher charging system voltage. The second compensation device is a magnetic shunt. The shunt is placed across the top of the regulator coil. When the shunt is cold it has a low reluctance so it shunts or bypasses some of the coil magnetism to the regulator frame. This leaves a smaller amount of effective magnetism to pull the regulator armature. The coil must have a greater total magnetism so enough remains to force the regulator to operate. The magnetic shunt reluctance increases as it becomes warm so less magnetism is by-passed. This leaves a larger percentage of the coil magnetism to attract the regulator armature and causes the regulator to control at a lower voltage, which is desirable for a warm battery.

Some voltage regulators are made with a resistor connected across the voltage regulator coil windings, one end at the coil pick-up junction and the other end grounded. The resistor becomes a ballast for the coil. When the resistor is cold it

carries current so the coil gets slightly less current to reduce its magnetic strength. When the ballast gets hot it has higher resistance, allowing more current to flow through the coil to increase its magnetic strength. In this way, the resistor reduces the effect of temperature on the operation of the voltage regulator.

Current Regulation. The current flowing in the alternator stator reverses itself, increasing and decreasing as it alternates in the same manner as the voltage. As the current flow increases in a stator, it forms a magnetic field around the winding. This newly-formed field cuts across adjacent conductors within the stator coil winding. This produces a counter voltage in the adjacent conductors (as described in Chapter 1) which opposes the initial voltage induced by the rotor field. The principle of inducing a counter voltage in a coil wire that is carrying an increasing or a decreasing current is called *inductance*. Maximum alternator current output is limited by the induced counter voltage. As counter voltage approaches the output voltage, the alternator output stabilizes at a maximum safe amperage.

Current regulation of commutator-rectified generators is similar to voltage regulation except that the current regulator coil design is different. Normally closed single contact current regulator points are connected in series with the voltage regulator points and the generator field. Whenever the current regulator points open, field current is lowered to the amount of current that will flow through a resistor. The current regulator coil is made of a few turns of heavy wire which carries all of the current produced by the generator. When the generator is producing maximum regulated current, the current regulator coil has enough ampere-turns to produce a magnetic attraction which will open the current regulator points. This drops field current, reducing generator field strength, which in turn, lowers generator output. The current regulator coil strength decreases as generator output current drops and this allows the armature spring to close the points, reestablishing field current in the generator. The current regulator points vibrate to control field current, which, in turn, will limit generator current output.

The voltage regulator and current regulator do not control the generator output at the same

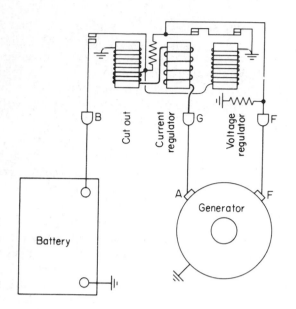

Fig. 7-26 Schematic of a commutator rectified generator charging system.

time. When there is a large amperage flow, electrical pressure cannot build up. When current flow is restricted, voltage will increase.

Voltage limitation is required to protect the battery and accessories. If too much voltage were to be impressed on them, it would force them to carry excess current. This, in turn, would result in overheating and a short service life. Current limitation protects the alternator or generator. If they were allowed to produce more than their design current, they, too, would overheat and fail.

Reverse Current. Commutator-rectified generators are provided with a *cut-out* that disconnects the battery from the charging system when the generator is not charging. The cut-out is located in the same box with the voltage and current regulators. When the engine starts, generator voltage builds up forcing current to flow through the series windings and shunt windings of the cut-out coil. When the magnetic strength produced by the ampere-turns in this circuit becomes strong enough, coil magnetism will pull the normally open points into the closed position, completing the battery-to-generator connection. The points remain closed as long as the engine is running.

Current flows backward between the battery and generator as the engine is stopped. This reverse current splits at the cut-out coil, part going through

the cut-out shunt winding in its normal direction and part going through the cut-out series winding in a reverse direction. The magnetic fields of the two cut-out windings oppose and neutralize each other, releasing the cut-out armature so the spring can pull the points open to disconnect the battery from the generator.

Reverse current requires no switching in diode-rectified generators (alternators). It was shown in Section 7-3 how diodes prevent battery current from leaking through the alternator.

Solid-State Regulation. Mechanical regulators are being replaced by solid-state regulators. The solid state regulators are constructed with no moving parts and make use of semiconductors, resistors, capacitors, and conductors. Some solid-state regulators are assembled from individual parts. This fabrication technique is called *discrete.* Some of the units may be encapsuled into groups. These groups are assembled into an operating unit and the fabricating method is called *hybrid.* A more advanced fabrication method used to produce a single integrated circuit is called *monolithic.* Discrete and hybrid fabricating techniques are used in applications where the regulator is separate from the alternator. Monolithic techniques are used in most applications that have the regulator built into the alternator case. The solid-state regulator parts work in the same manner regardless of the fabricating technique that is used.

The advantage of solid-state regulators over mechanical regulators is their ability to control higher field currents with improved durability and reliability. They provide an almost foolproof regulator system, while at the same time they have a small unit size and can be mass-produced at low cost.

Transistor Regulation. Solid-state regulators are based on the same basic principle as mechanical regulators. They control alternator voltage by controlling the alternator field strength. Instead of breaker points, the solid-state regulator uses a power transistor to do the required field current switching. The operation of the power transistor is controlled by other transistors, diodes, and resistors. Regulators built in a discrete or hybrid form may be repaired in some cases, but the entire regulator is usually replaced when faulty. Monolithic regulators cannot be repaired. It is important to understand the operation of transistor regulation in order to understand the methods used to test transistor regulators.

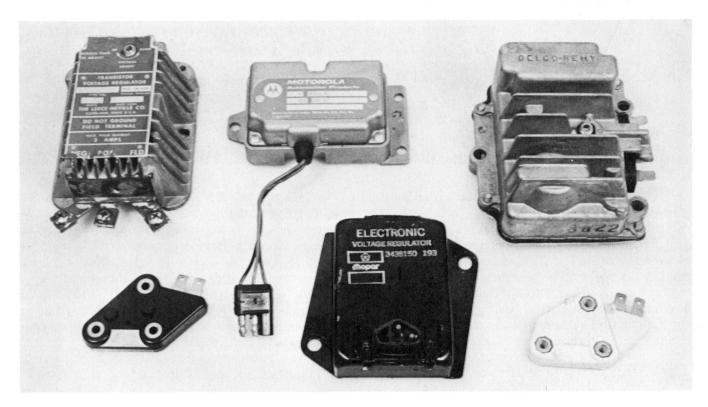

Fig. 7-27 Typical solid-state semi-conductor voltage regulators.

A simplified transistor regulator circuit is shown in Figure 7-28. Using the hole movement method described in Chapter 1 to explain the circuit, holes or electricity comes from the battery to transistor T_1 emitter. The base of T_1 is connected to the ground through R_1 so it conducts. With the base conducting, current can go from the T_1 emitter to the T_1 collector and on to the alternator field to supply full alternator field current. Transistor T_1 is called the power transistor.

Battery voltage is also impressed on the emitter of transistor T_2. The base of T_2 is connected to the Zener diode D_z which is reverse biased so that no base current will flow through D_z and transistor T_2 is turned off so that it will not conduct. Voltage also is impressed on resistors R_2 and R_4, variable resistor R_3, and thermal resistor R_t, allowing a very small current to flow to ground. A voltage drop exists across each resistor as current flows.

The Zener diode D_z is the voltage sensing device in the solid-state regulator. It is used to control maximum circuit voltage. When the reverse bias voltage across the Zener diode reaches its

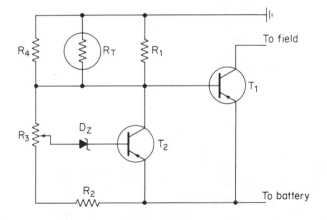

Fig. 7-28 Basic transistor solid-state regulator circuit schematic diagram.

breakdown point, the diode will conduct current in the reverse direction. The reverse bias voltage is equal to the voltage drop across R_2 and part of R_3. Changing the connection point of the Zener diode on variable resistance R_3 is used to change regulator settings when they are designed to be adjustable.

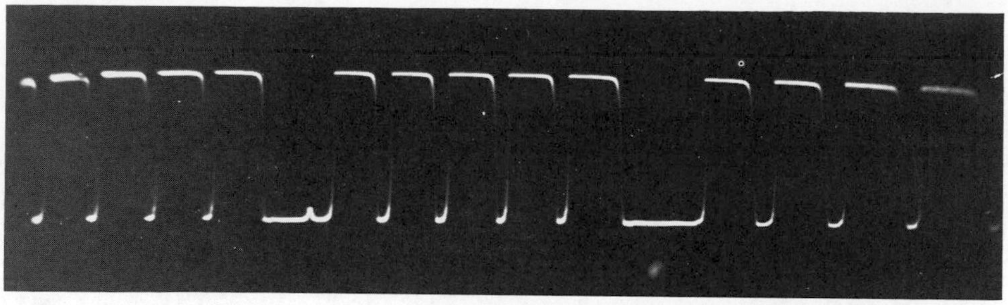

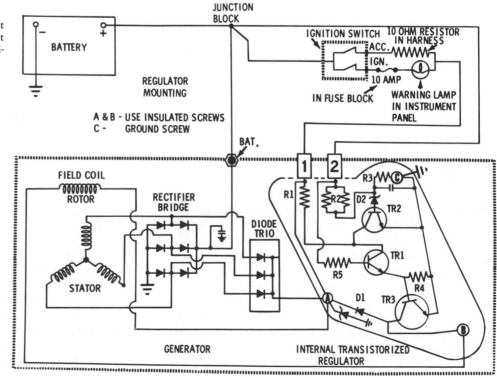

Fig. 7-29 Scope pattern of a transistor regulator's field voltage while regulating.

When the Zener diode conducts, the base of transistor T_2 is turned on and T_2 conducts from the collector to ground through R_4. The collector of T_2 then places the same voltage on the T_1 base as the emitter of T_1. With the voltage the same on the emitter and on the base, transistor T_1 is effectively turned off, stopping field current to the alternator. The alternator voltage falls off when the field current stops, and the Zener diode stops conduction in reverse bias which, in turn, stops the base current of T_2, turning it off. This allows the base current of T_1 to restart conduction through R_1 and begin to supply field current to the alternator. This cycle is repeated very rapidly, controlling the alternator voltage.

The resistor R_t is sensitive to temperature. At low temperatures, it has high resistance. This reduces current flow through the series resistances. A high circuit voltage is required at low temperatures to force the Zener diode to conduct in a reverse bias. This causes the charging system to operate at higher voltages when cold and at lower voltages when warm, to be compatible with battery operation characteristics just as temperature-compensated mechanical regulators are.

The basic transistor regulator circuit operation is smoothed out and is speeded up using resistors and capacitors. Transient voltages and leakage are controlled with additional diodes, resistors, and capacitors.

Fig. 7-30 Complete charging circuit with the transistor regulator built into the alternator. (Oldsmobile Division, General Motors Corporation).

REVIEW QUESTIONS

1. In what three ways can more magnetic lines of force cut a conductor?

2. What means is used to control generator output?

3. When does a generator deliver its maximum output?

4. How is alternator output voltage controlled?

5. What is the most common type of electrical system failure?

6. What type of current is produced in the stator?

7. What type of current does the alternator provide to the electrical system?

8. What is used to rectify current in an alternator?

9. What is the name given to a heavy metal part that helps to cool diodes?

10. How does the field circuit connect to the alternator rotor?

11. When does the alternator begin to charge?

12. What is the term that is used to indicate that the voltage is backward across a diode?

13. To what does the term "ampere-turns" refer?

14. What does the vehicle ammeter indicate?

15. When does the vehicle ammeter indicate discharge?

16. What does a temperate compensation device do to regulated voltage as the regulator warms?

17. What condition exists in the regulator when the alternator is producing maximum output current?

18. What condition exists in the regulator when the alternator is producing maximum voltage?

19. What is the main advantage of solid-state regulators?

20. What prevents the battery from discharging through the alternator?

8

Charging System Service

Many mechanics and technicians have difficulty in understanding charging system operation. This is the main reason technicians find it difficult to intelligently test and diagnose charging system problems. Therefore, they are likely to start changing parts until the charging system works satisfactorily and then they expect the customer to pay the bill. For one who understands the charging system and the application of diagnostic equipment required to test it, it will take very little time to test a charging system to pinpoint the faulty unit. Further checking of the faulty electrical unit will disclose the specific part or junction producing the problem.

The battery is an integral part of the charging system. In addition to supplying electrical power when the alternator is not providing enough output, the battery acts as an electrical reservoir. Excess alternator output is absorbed by the battery to charge the battery. As the battery becomes charged its voltage increases so it begins to resist further charging. This causes the alternator charging rate to drop. The resistance to current flow into the battery is measured in volts and may be called the *battery counter voltage*. The charging system works in much the same way as an air compressor system where the compressor fills an air tank while it also supplies air to operate a spray gun. As the air is forced into the tank the pressure builds up. The air compressor is therefore unable to put air into the tank as fast when the pressure is high as it can

when the air tank pressure is low, so the air pumping rate drops at high pressure.

In a compressed air system the maximum amount of air compressed is based on the compressor size and its operating speed. In an alternator, the maximum output is based on the alternator size and the rotating speed. In a charging system the alternator speed depends upon the engine operating speed, and the alternator design limits maximum output.

A compressed air system is fitted with a pressure switch that turns the air compressor off when the air pressure has reached a safe maximum limit. The charging system is equipped with a voltage regulator to limit maximum charging system voltage, which is the electrical equivalent of pressure. Like the air pressure switch, the voltage regulator does not affect output until voltage reaches the voltage regulator setting. Voltage regulator setting has no effect on maximum alternator output amperage. Its purpose is to keep voltage below a safe limit to protect electrical operating units, especially the battery. Excess voltage will shorten the life of the battery, ignition points, light bulbs, radios, electrical motors, etc. It is best to have the voltage regulator set just high enough to fully charge the battery without overcharging it.

Voltage of the charging system is controlled by the battery counter voltage whenever the system voltage is below the regulator voltage setting. A charging system operating with a partly charged battery will have low voltage. As the battery becomes fully charged the charging system voltage will rise until it reaches regulated voltage, at which time the regulator will prevent any further increase in charging system voltage.

8-1 CHARGING SYSTEM MAINTENANCE

Even with minimum maintenance the charging system will provide long useful service. Keeping all electrical junctions clean and tight is of primary importance in maintaining the charging system. The wires should be kept clean and should be properly supported to minimize the chance of their becoming shorted or broken. The battery must be kept clean and the cells filled with pure water.

Fig. 8-1 One type of gauge used to check belt tension.

The charging system component that deteriorates the most rapidly is the drive belt. Its condition should be checked at each oil change and the belt tension should be readjusted any time it seems to be loose or when it becomes shiny as a result of possible slippage.

Belt tension is adjusted by first loosening the alternator mount bolt and the cap screw in the slotted adjuster. A pry bar should be placed against the alternator drive end frame to tighten the belt. Correct tension is best determined with a belt tension gauge. When proper tension is reached the adjuster cap screw is tightened, then the alternator mount bolt is secured to complete the belt adjustment procedure.

The alternator has two parts that wear in operation, the field brushes and the bearings. Excessively worn brushes usually show up as intermittent faulty alternator operation and sometimes as noise in the automobile radio that changes frequency as the engine speed is changed. In some alternators the field brushes can be replaced without disassembling the alternator. However, it may be necessary to remove the alternator from the engine to reach the brush attachment screws. When the brushes are faulty in other alternator types, the alternator must be disassembled for brush replacement.

Faulty alternator bearings either rumble or whine. The pitch of the noise changes as the engine speed changes and the sound persists whether the alternator is charging or not. To positively identify an alternator bearing problem, alternator charge can easily be stopped by removing the connecting wire junction from the regulator. It is necessary to disassemble the alternator to replace the bearing. Details of this repair procedure are given in a later section.

8-2 TESTING THE CHARGING SYSTEM

Failure of a charging system will be indicated to the driver by a red warning light or by the vehicle ammeter discharge. An impending failure can be determined by a technician while he is checking the electrical system. Many technicians check the charging system as a routine service operation during a tune-up. The fan belt should be checked first to be sure that belt slippage is not the cause of improper charging.

A simplified method of determining charging system operation can be made with a voltmeter connected across the battery posts. Battery voltage is noted before starting the engine. After starting, the engine speed is increased and held at 1500 rpm. When all electrical systems are off, the voltage should increase and hold at about 14.0 to 14.5 volts. When all of the electrical systems are turned on the voltage should be about 13.0 to 13.5 volts. If these voltages are not reached or if they are exceeded the charging system requires a thorough diagnosis to determine the problem. Details of these procedures are described in the following paragraphs.

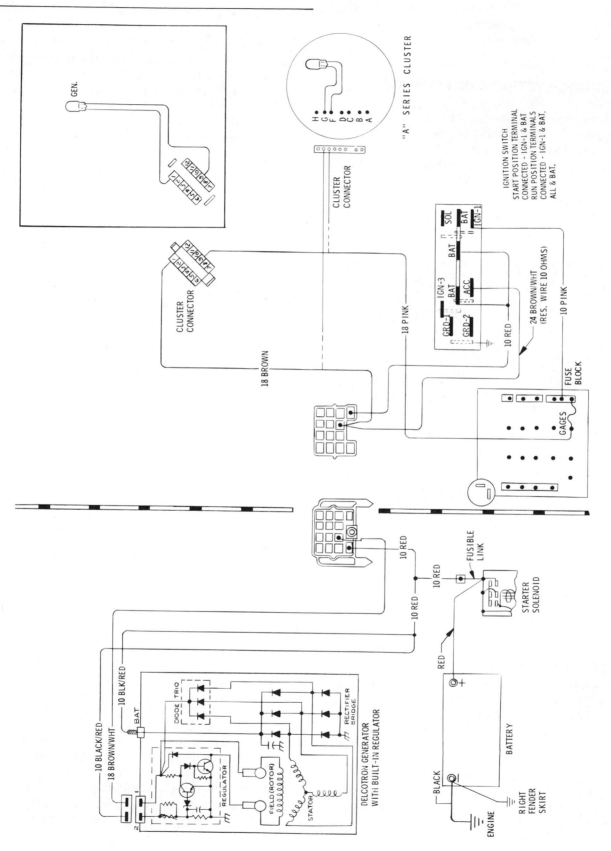

Fig. 8-2 Typical charging circuit schematic diagram (Buick Motor Division, General Motors Corporation).

A test ammeter is connected in the charging circuit when the circuit is tested. The ammeter is required for most tests and will not interfere with test results in test sequences where it is not required. Test equipment manufacturers have designed diagnostic equipment to connect into different parts of the charging system. Connecting the test ammeter on the alternator battery (BAT) terminal will give the most accurate measurement, but good connections on the alternator BAT terminal are difficult to make. One of the most popular ammeter connection methods is to use a special high capacity knife switch or special test lead on the insulated battery post. The test ammeter is connected across the knife switch. When the switch is closed current can flow across the switch, allowing the large starter current draw that is required for engine cranking. When charging circuit amperage readings are to be measured the knife switch is opened. This forces all of the current going into the battery to also flow through the ammeter. The amount of current flow can then be observed on the ammeter dial. After the required amperage reading is taken the knife switch should

be closed to prevent damage that could occur if one tried to start the engine by drawing starter current through the ammeter.

By connecting the ammeter at the alternator BAT terminal, one can measure all of the current produced by the alternator. This type of connection is used to measure alternator rated output. When the ammeter is connected at the battery it only measures the current going into the battery. It takes about 5 amperes of the alternator output to run the ignition system. This amount of current will not be measured across a battery post adapter knife switch. If one of the vehicle doors is open and the interior lights are on, this will further reduce the observed output on the ammeter connected at the battery. When the ammeter is used across a battery post adapter knife switch the normal alternator output readings will be from 5 to 10 amperes less than if they were to be measured at the alternator BAT terminal.

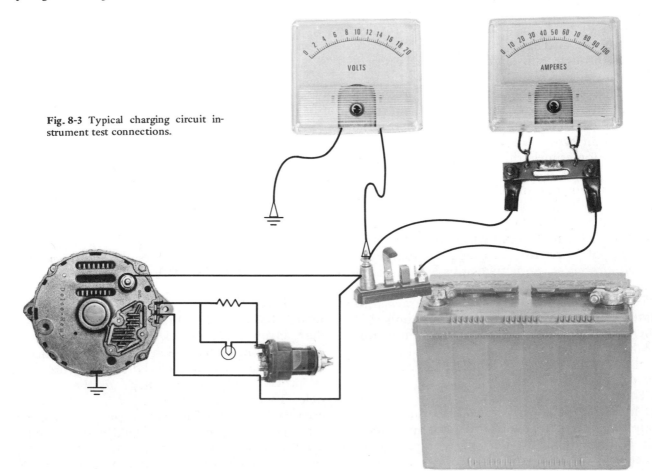

Fig. 8-3 Typical charging circuit instrument test connections.

As in all electrical testing, the battery must be healthy and close to full charge. The battery condition can be checked following the procedures given in Chapter 4. If the battery is not in good condition and fully charged it should be recharged or replaced with a good fully charged battery before meaningful testing can be done on a charging system.

Output Test. Charging system failure can result from any one of a great number of small electrical faults. First, the alternator itself should be checked. If it does not produce its normal output it will have to be repaired before any other testing of the charging system can be done. The output test is used to check the proper functioning of an alternator or generator.

Magnetic rotor field strength is used to control alternator output. Increasing magnetic field strength to maximum will cause the alternator to produce its maximum output. This is done by connecting the field directly to the full system voltage. Three types of field wiring are used in alternators. In one type of alternator, one end of the field is connected through an insulated brush and regulator to the insulated circuit. The other end of the field is connected to ground at the alternator ground brush. An alternator with this field wiring method is called an *internally grounded alternator.* It is the most common type used with mechanical voltage regulators. Sometimes this is called a *B* circuit. A second type of alternator has one end of the field connected through an insulated brush to the regulator where it is grounded. The other end of the field is connected through a second insulated brush to the insulated circuit within the alternator. This type of alternator is called an *externally grounded alternator.* Sometimes this is called an *A* circuit. A third type of alternator has both ends of the field insulated from the case and attached to insulated brushes. One end of the field is connected to the charging circuit outside of the alternator. The other end of the field goes to ground through a regulator. This system is called an *isolated-field alternator.*

The technician must know the type of alternator field wiring he is working with so that he can provide the alternator with full system voltage which will produce full field current. Generally the mechanically regulated alternators have internally grounded fields and transistor-regulated sys-

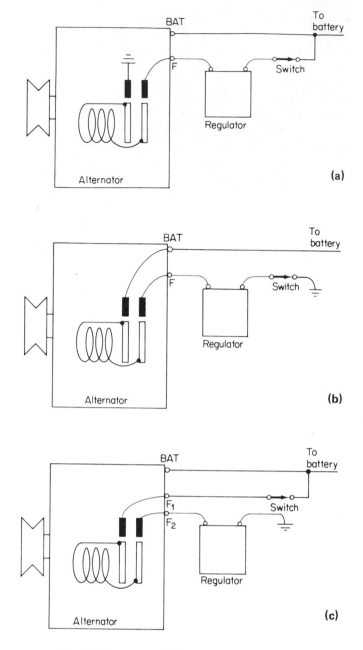

Fig. 8-4 Alternator field circuits. (a) Internal ground, (b) external ground, (c) isolated ground.

tems have externally grounded fields or isolated fields. Basically, the alternator output test procedure involves making electrical connections that have the same effect as that which occurs when the normally closed points of the regulator are closed to provide full system voltage to the alternator field. There are a number of methods that can be used to do this. The manufacturer of each alternator type has a preferred method and each equipment manufacturer has developed a test method with special adapters to make the test as quick and as easy as possible.

Fig. 8-5 Jumper connection to provide full field current for an internal grounded field alternator.

For charging systems with mechanical regulators, the output test method that uses the least amount of test equipment involves the removal of the regulator field lead from the alternator field (F) terminal. This takes the regulator out of service so that it cannot be damaged while alternator output is tested. To test alternators with internally grounded fields a jumper wire is connected from the field (F) terminal to the alternator battery (BAT) terminal to give the field full battery voltage. This will cause maximum current to flow through the alternator field. With a test ammeter in the charging circuit and voltmeter leads connected to the alternator side of the knife switch the engine is started, the knife switch is opened and the speed is brought up to approximately 2500 rpm only long enough to stabilize the ammeter reading. The test ammeter should indicate the alternator rated output or about 5 amperes less if the test ammeter is connected across the knife switch at the battery post.

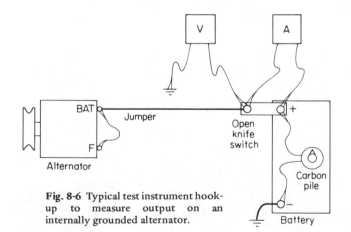

Fig. 8-6 Typical test instrument hook-up to measure output on an internally grounded alternator.

If the battery is fully charged the alternator charge voltage may be too high (above 16 volts), resulting in a low alternator output. To compensate for this, a heavy carbon pile rheostat, like the one used for battery and starter testing, is placed across the battery *posts*. While the alternator is operating, the carbon pile is adjusted to keep the system voltage between 15 and 16 volts, allowing maximum alternator output.

In a modification of this test procedure, a field rheostat (25 watt, 25 ohm) is used in place of the jumper wire. With the rheostat on full resistance (open) no spark will occur during the hook-up, which adds to shop safety. With the engine running at 2500 rpm the rheostat resistance is gradually reduced by turning the knob clockwise, allowing current to flow to the alternator field. The rheostat is adjusted until all the resistance is eliminated allowing the alternator to produce rated output.

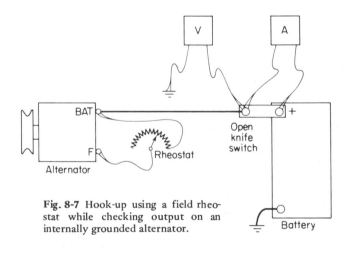

Fig. 8-7 Hook-up using a field rheostat while checking output on an internally grounded alternator.

Sometimes it is difficult to get connectors on the alternator terminals to attach the ammeter, especially on engines loaded with power equipment. On these charging systems the alternator regulator connector junction is disconnected from the regulator and the jumper or rheostat is connected between the appropriate terminals in the connector (Delco F and 3, Ford F and A+ or Chrysler F and BAT for mechanical regulators). Equipment manufacturers have jumpers with special adapters for this test. If they are not available, jumpers can be readily made using repair-type terminal ends attached to a short wire.

If the alternator has an externally grounded field it will show no charge when the preceding test

Fig. 8-8 Jumper connecting the battery voltage directly to the field at the regulator connector junction.

(a)

(b)

Fig. 8-9 Tab in an alternator with an internal regulator. The tab is used to by-pass the regulator for full field current by inserting a screwdriver and touching the tab while holding the screwdriver against the edge of the hole. (a) External view, (b) internal view.

procedure is followed. Both ends of the field would be indirectly connected to the same battery post so no current would flow through the field. In these alternators the jumper or rheostat will have to be connected between the alternator F terminal and ground to provide maximum field current. The rest of the test is run in the same manner.

Isolated-field alternators have two field leads. The one field terminal connected to the regulator is disconnected. The output test is run in the same manner as an external-grounded field type alternator.

Alternators with regulators built inside the alternator case have their fields connected like an externally grounded system. The technician can by-pass the regulator by inserting a screwdriver through a hole in the alternator case so that the screwdriver blade touches a tab on the internal regulator at the same time that it touches the edge of the hole. This completes the field circuit to ground to give maximum field current.

Some service manuals do not recommend the use of an ammeter to check alternator output; they recommend instead that the charging system be checked while it is fully connected in its normal manner. If the ammeter connection should separate during an output test it would send a high voltage surge through the electrical system that could damage solid-state control units used in other systems. When an ammeter is not used, alternator out-

put is checked by measuring the system voltage while all electrical accessories are turned on and the engine is run at a specified speed. Applicable service manuals should be consulted for details of the recommended output test procedures.

If the alternator produces rated output the rest of the charging circuit can be checked. If the alternator output is appreciably low it will require service before the rest of the charging system can be properly checked. Alternator servicing instructions are given in section 8-3.

An alternator with no output may have to be removed and disassembled; and the components checked. The problem is likely to be excessively worn field brushes. These can be removed and replaced in some alternators without disassembling the alternator, while other alternators have to be disassembled to replace the brushes.

When alternator output is low, an engine oscilloscope is very useful in identifying the cause of the low alternator output. Alternator output may be 10% greater than or less than specifications, and the alternator still may be considered to be operating properly. If an alternator output is measured at the battery knife switch, which normally indicates 5 amperes low, and the alternator has a normal output 10% below specifications, the observed output could be as much as 10 amperes below specifications, even though the alternator is operating correctly. The oscilloscope will indicate normal or faulty operation. The oscilloscope primary leads are connected, one to the alternator BAT terminal and one to ground. With the generator charging, the normal scope pattern will resemble Figure 8-10. If the battery is near full charge, the alternator pattern can be made more distinct by placing a carbon pile load between the battery posts and adjusting it to give the most distinct alternator pattern. Alternator service is much quicker and much more accurate when the specific cause of the malfunction is identified on the scope before alternator disassembly. Then the problem can be easily corrected during alternator overhaul before final charging system testing is done.

Fig. 8-10 Oscilloscope trace of a normally operating alternator.

If no further testing is to be done the knife switch, ammeter, jumper, and carbon pile can be removed and the regulator can be reconnected in its normal manner. If further testing is required the test connections can remain in the system and testing can proceed with the charging circuit voltage drop tests.

Charging Circuit Voltage Drop. Deterioration in the condition of the electrical wiring, especially in the connections and junctions, will cause most of the problems that occur in the elec-

trical system. This deterioration increases resistance to electrical current flow. As previously discussed, an increase in charging system resistance will cause the charging system voltage to increase until it reaches the regulated voltage. One of the best examples of this phenomenon in the charging circuit occurs when there is resistance in the charging circuit while the battery remains in a low state-of-charge. The resistance in the charging circuit plus the battery internal resistance (CEMF) tends to slow the current flow. This total resistance causes charging circuit voltage to increase until regulated voltage is reached. The voltage reaching the battery is not high enough to push current through the battery so the battery remains discharged. For proper charging system operation there must be no abnormal resistance in the charging circuit. During charging system service all abnormal resistance should be located and eliminated.

Charging circuit resistance can best be located using the voltage drop test procedure previously described for starter circuits in Chapter 6. While using the same ammeter and jumper connections which were used to make the output test, adjust engine speed to give a 20-ampere alternator output. This adjustment is easier to make with a variable field rheostat used in place of the jumper. Using this procedure causes a known current (20 amperes) to flow through the circuit so voltage drop will be a direct indication of the system resistance according to Ohm's Law ($R = V/A$).

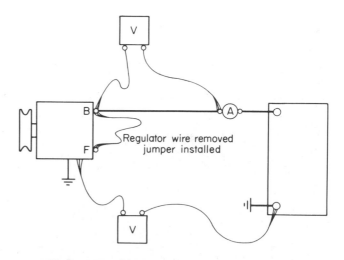

Fig. 8-11 Test instrument hook-up method on an internally grounded field alternator for measuring the charging system voltage drop.

A voltmeter connection that may cause confusion should be identified at this point. While charging, the alternator voltage is higher than battery voltage forcing current to flow *backward* into the battery. On systems with a negative battery ground the positive voltmeter lead will go to the alternator BAT terminal (to the battery side of the test ammeter if it is used at the alternator BAT terminal location) and the negative lead will go to the battery positive post (to the alternator side of the knife switch if the test ammeter is used at the knife switch location) with the rest of the charging circuit leads connected in their normal manner. In systems with a battery having a positive ground the voltmeter leads will be reversed. Voltage drop of the entire insulated circuit will be observed on the voltmeter using these connections while twenty amperes is flowing in the charging circuit. Maximum voltage drop with 20 amperes flowing should be less than 0.7 volts if the vehicle uses an ammeter and less than 0.3 volts if it uses a charge-indicator lamp, sometimes improperly called an "Idiot Light." If the voltage drop is excessive one of the voltmeter leads should be moved along the circuit towards the other lead, from one junction to the next junction until the amount of voltage drop shows a large change. The excess resistance is at this point of a large change in voltage drop.

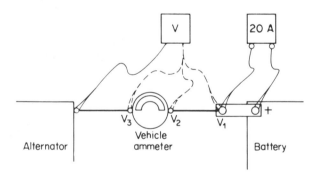

Fig. 8-12 Method used to move voltmeter test lead to locate a point causing high resistance when excessive voltage drop is found in the overall insulated charging circuit.

With the alternator output held at 20 amperes the voltmeter leads are switched to the grounded side of the system. Here again they are used in reverse when compared to battery polarity because the current is being forced backward through the battery by the alternator. In a system with a

negative-grounded battery the negative voltmeter lead is attached to the alternator frame and the positive voltmeter lead is connected to the battery negative post. Voltage drop with 20 amperes flowing should not exceed 0.05 volts for the grounded side of the circuit. When it does the negative lead should be moved to the engine frame. If this causes the voltage to change appreciably the electrical connection between the alternator and engine is poor. To improve the contact will require removing the alternator and cleaning the mounting bracket. If excess voltage drop still exists the battery ground cable or connections are faulty.

When the alternator functions properly and no excess resistance is found in the charging circuit the jumper wire can be removed and the regulator connected so that the regulator operation can be checked.

Regulator Tests. A high voltage-regulator adjustment is indicated by excess use of battery water. This is usually accompanied by a noticeable increase in headlight "flare," or increase in brightness, as the engine is accelerated from idle. Low voltage-regulator settings usually result in low state-of-charge of the battery. Voltage regulator settings should always be checked when servicing the charging system.

The voltage regulator must be warmed up to normal operating temperature before its settings can be properly checked. This is necessary because both current flow through the regulator wires and resistors and the magnetic effect of its voltage-sensing coil on the contact-point armature are affected by changes in temperature. If the regulator temperature were not normalized the observed operating voltage would be incorrect when compared to the specifications. Manufacturers of temperature-compensated regulators give their specifications at different regulator temperatures. The regulator temperature can be determined by placing a thermometer within $\frac{1}{4}$ inch (0.5 çm) of the regulator cover. A cool regulator will control at a higher voltage than will a warm regulator, as described in Chapter 7.

The reader should be reminded that voltage will not increase unless current flow is restricted. When the regulator is checked all accessories must be turned off and the battery should be fully charged. The only place for current to go is to the ignition, with a small current flow through the battery to keep it fully charged. With this small current flow, the charging voltage will increase until the voltage regulator begins to limit the increase when its voltage setting is reached.

(a)

(b)

Fig. 8-13 Temperature measurement of the regulator ambient temperature. (a) With a glass thermometer, (b) with a special mechanical thermometer.

A voltmeter connected from the alternator BAT terminal to ground will indicate the regulated voltage. Some manufacturers suggest placing the voltmeter leads between the battery side of the ignition resistor and ground to measure charging system regulated voltage. Others suggest measuring regulated voltage across the alternator side of the knife switch and the negative battery post. Each

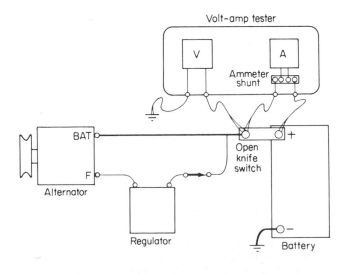

Fig. 8-14 Basic hook-up for measuring the charging system voltage regulator setting.

location should give the same voltage indications. During this test, the test ammeter is usually in the same location in the charging circuit as it was in the preceding charging system tests. The alternator, however, must be connected to the regulator in the normal operating manner.

After the regulator temperature is normalized the alternator is cycled. *Cycling* is dropping the alternator output to zero then bringing it back up to full voltage. This is easily done by disconnecting and reconnecting the regulator, which can be done by removing and replacing the regulator connector. Some test equipment companies recommend using a rheostat in the alternator field circuit to cycle the charging circuit. In this way there will be no arcing at the regulator connector.

At this point the engine speed is adjusted and the voltage observed. The different alternator manufacturers and test equipment companies recommend a number of different approaches to setting engine speeds and using voltage connections. Several approaches are described. Any one of them can be used to give a "ballpark" quick check of the voltage regulator settings. It is always advisable to carefully follow the specific procedures recommended by the system manufacturer or test equipment company to obtain accurate regulator setting values.

One approach is to connect the voltmeter across the battery before the engine is started for the test. The open circuit battery voltage is observed. The engine is then started and run at fast idle for 15 minutes. At the end of this time with the engine running battery voltage is again checked. It should be from 1 to 2.5 volts higher than the original observed reading. If it is within these limits the headlights and heater motor are turned on while the engine is running. This should lower the voltage less than 0.5 volts if the regulator is working correctly.

Another method is to bring the engine speed up to 1250 rpm. The system charging rate should be 15 amperes. If the amperage is not high enough, the accessories should be turned on or a carbon pile load, such as the battery-starter tester unit, should be placed across the battery posts and adjusted to give 15 amperes flow in the charging circuit. The voltmeter will then indicate the voltage regulator setting on the normally-closed contact points that control voltage at moderate speeds when amperage flow is relatively high.

Normally-open contact points control the system voltage at higher engine speeds when the amperage flow is low. They can be checked by increasing engine speed to 2200 rpm, turning off all accessories, and opening the carbon pile. If the alternator output is still above 5 amperes the battery is not providing enough resistance and so the resistance of the charging circuit is increased by inserting a $\frac{1}{4}$-ohm 25-watt resistor in the circuit. Watts are units of electrical power calculated by multiplying volts times amperes ($W = V \times A$). Inserting the resistor can easily be done by positioning a switch to a fixed resistance position on most volt-amp testers designed for testing the charging system. The normally-open points will control the voltage about 0.5 volts higher than the normally-closed points.

Automotive engine oscilloscopes having primary ignition pattern connections can be used to watch mechanical regulator point operation so that the technician can be sure which part of the regulator is functioning. The positive scope primary lead is connected to the regulator field terminal and the negative lead is connected to ground. The scope pattern as illustrated in Chapter 7 will form a high rippled line that shows normal alternator voltage until the normally-closed points begin to

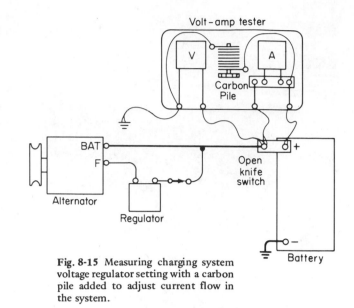

Fig. 8-15 Measuring charging system voltage regulator setting with a carbon pile added to adjust current flow in the system.

vibrate. Their vibration will be indicated as vertical lines downward. As the alternator speed is increased the vertical lines form rippled bottoms and less top until the bottom forms a complete rippled line. This occurs when the contact points float, touching neither normally-closed or normally-open points. Further increases in speed will cause the normally-open points to vibrate. This is shown on the scope pattern by a second series of vertical downward lines. These have a straight bottom line because the alternator field voltage is momentarily stopped.

The most common method used by test equipment manufacturers to measure voltage regulator setting is to put a $\frac{1}{4}$-ohm resistor in series with the

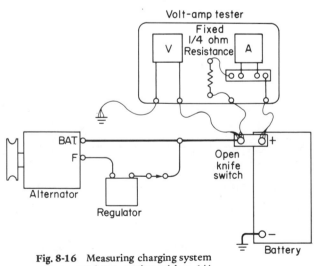

Fig. 8-16 Measuring charging system voltage regulator setting with a 1/4 ohm resistance to restrict current flow in the system.

Fig. 8-17 Methods used to adjust regulator settings. On the left the spring hanger is bent with an adjusting tool. On the right the spring hanger is bent using a screw.

tioning a switch. This makes it quick and easy for the technician to check the alternator output, circuit voltage drop, and voltage regulator setting with minimum changes in hook-up of electrical system test equipment.

When the voltage regulator is controlling at the wrong voltage it will have to be adjusted or replaced. Mechanical voltage regulators can be adjusted while the regulator is operating by removing the cover and moving the spring hanger. This can be done with a bending tool or by tightening a screw. If the screw method is used and the voltage is too high the screw must be loosened and the hanger bent up by hand to loosen the spring. The hanger can be retightened to give the correct voltage settings.

Installation of the regulator cover will usually affect the voltage setting and so final regulator settings must be rechecked after the cover is installed.

Some early model solid-state regulators can be adjusted with an internal hex wrench. Adjustments are made with the regulator operating. Late model solid-state regulators must be replaced if they do not regulate correctly because they cannot be adjusted.

charging circuit. This resistance is enough to restrict the charging current and thus to force the voltage to increase to the regulated voltage, even when the battery is only partly charged. This amount of resistance is not excessive even when the battery is fully charged. A few manufacturers of inexpensive alternator test equipment use an external separate $\frac{1}{4}$-ohm resistance. Most manufacturers of automotive test equipment build the $\frac{1}{4}$-ohm resistance into the volt-amp test unit so that the resistance can be placed in the circuit by posi-

Fig. 8-18 Fusable wires used in alternators to protect the contacts.

FUSE WIRES

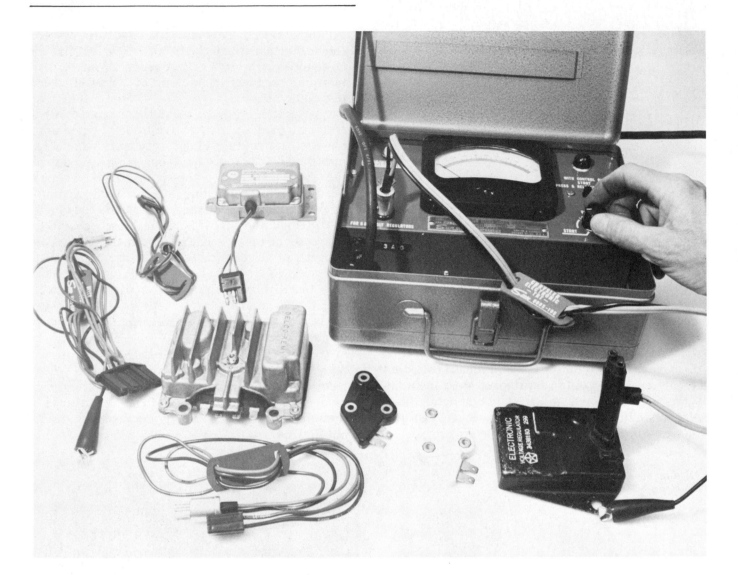

Fig. 8-19 A tester that can be used to test solid-state regulator voltage settings while the regulator is on the bench.

Some regulators are provided with internal fuse wires. If the connectors are inadvertently attached improperly the fuse wire will burn off to protect the regulator. New fuse wire is available at the parts department. The remaining pieces of fuse wire can be removed and a new piece soldered in place with rosin core solder.

Equipment manufacturers have developed testers that can measure solid-state regulator settings when they are not connected in a charging circuit. These testers provide a quick, accurate, and easy way to check solid state regulators.

8-3 ALTERNATOR SERVICE

Low alternator output indicates a malfunction in the alternator electrical circuit. Alternator noise, when the alternator is running but not charging, indicates a malfunction in the alternator mechanical parts. An open stator winding will produce a rumble that sounds very much like a rough bearing while the alternator is charging, but unlike a bearing it will stop rumbling when the field wire is disconnected by removing the connector from the regulator.

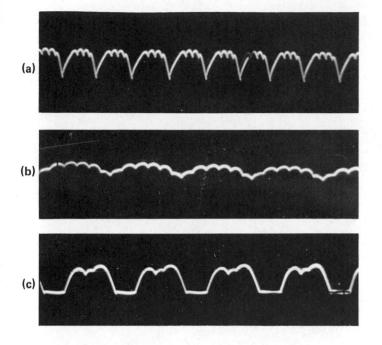

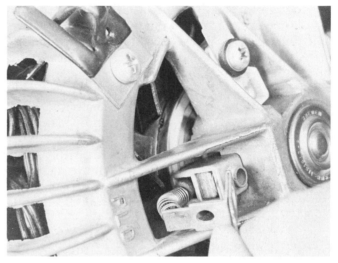

The alternator can then be removed from the engine after the technician disconnects lead wires from the F, R, S, A, and BAT terminals, whichever are used on the specific alternator type. The wire connecting to the alternator BAT terminal is connected directly to the battery so when it is re-

Fig. 8-20 Oscilloscope traces of malfunctioning alternator. (a) Open diode, (b) partly shorted diode, (c) shorted diode or shorted stator.

Ideally, alternator service should be preceded by a scope check to identify the alternator part causing low output. It is a good safety practice to remove the battery ground cable before working on the alternator to prevent accidental grounding.

Fig. 8-21 Removing an externally accessible field brush.

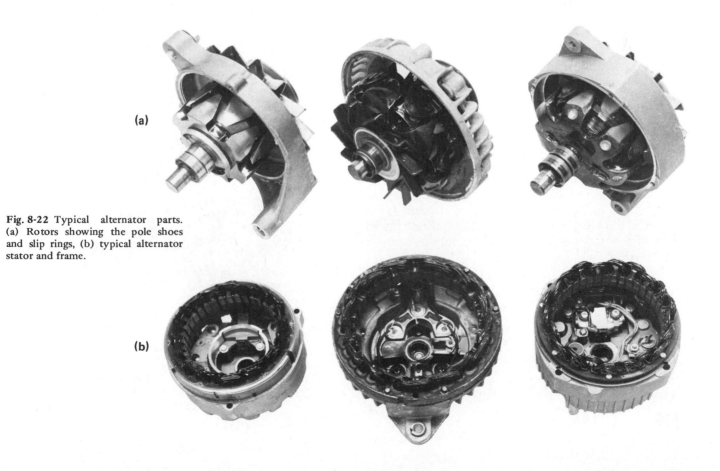

Fig. 8-22 Typical alternator parts. (a) Rotors showing the pole shoes and slip rings, (b) typical alternator stator and frame.

moved from the alternator it must be insulated, preferably by temporarily covering it with electrical tape, to prevent an electrical spark that could occur if the battery ground cable were inadvertently re-attached. The alternator mounting bolts are loosened to allow the alternator to tip, freeing the drive belt. The mounting bolts can then be removed to allow the alternator to be lifted from the engine.

Some alternator makes have externally accessible field brushes. These should be removed before the alternator case is opened. In other makes of alternators, the brushes are not accessible until the two halves of the alternator case are separated. Removing the assembly *through-bolts* that hold the case together will allow case separation. Carefully separate the front case with the rotor as an assembly from the rear case and stator assembly. The stator is connected to the diodes that are mounted in the rear case. With the alternator disassembled to this point all electrical checks can be readily made.

Diode Checks. Diodes are most easily checked with a special diode tester that can be used with the diodes connected in their normal operating manner. One test lead clip is attached to the diode heat sink and the other is touched on the stator lead junction of each insulated diode. Equal readings should be observed. The tester leads are then moved, one lead attached to the alternator case and the other touched on the stator lead of each grounded diode. Again equal readings should be observed. When unequal readings are observed the diode with the low reading must be disconnected from the stator lead and retested. No reading indicates that a diode is faulty. The faulty diode can be replaced separately in some older type alternators. Most modern alternators use a diode bridge. A fault in any one of these diodes will require the replacement of the complete diode bridge. Both diode bridges should have equal but opposite readings.

The use of an ohmmeter operating on a 1.5-volt battery is recommended for use in checking diodes when a special diode test unit is not available. The ohmmeter is connected in the same manner as the special diode tester just described with the diode disconnected. The ohmmeter leads must be reversed at each diode check point. The

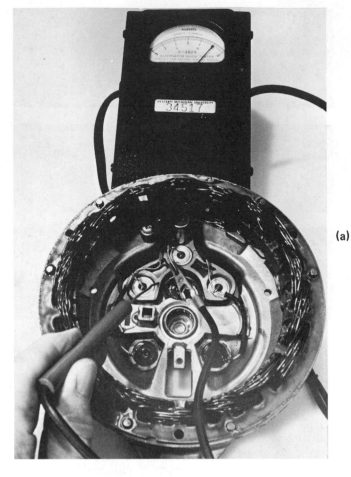

(a)

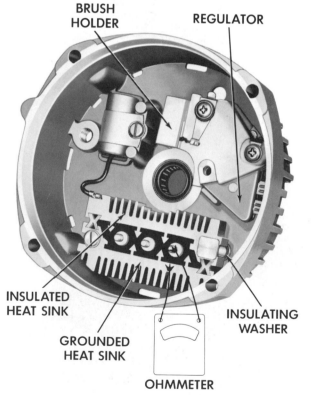

(b)

BRUSH HOLDER

REGULATOR

INSULATED HEAT SINK

GROUNDED HEAT SINK

OHMMETER

INSULATING WASHER

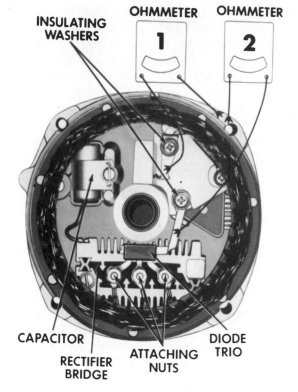

INSULATING WASHERS

OHMMETER 1

OHMMETER 2

(c)

CAPACITOR

RECTIFIER BRIDGE

ATTACHING NUTS

DIODE TRIO

Fig. 8-23 Testing the diode. (a) With a special diode checker, (b) with an ohmmeter (Delco-Remy Division, General Motors Corporation), (c) with an ohmmeter (Oldsmobile Division, General Motors Corporation), (d) with a test light (The Prestolite Company).

ohmmeter should show continuity in one direction and insulation in the other direction. If the reading is the same in both directions, being either high or low in both directions, the diode is faulty. Some variation in the readings between normal diodes should be expected.

A third method can be used to check diodes when neither of the preceding units is available. A test light, consisting of a number 57 lamp bulb connected to a 12-volt battery, can be used to test diodes. It is connected in the same manner as the ohmmeter. The bulb should light when it is connected in one direction and should not light when it is connected in the other direction. If the bulb lights in both directions or does not light in either direction the diode is faulty and must be disconnected and checked separately. Individual replaceable diodes must be checked separately when they are disconnected from the stator. It is, however, a good practice to replace all of the diodes when one is faulty (just as the technician replaces all of the spark plugs when one fails) because the other diodes are likely to be near failure, too. This eliminates come-backs. The entire rectifier bridge must be replaced when any one of its diodes fails.

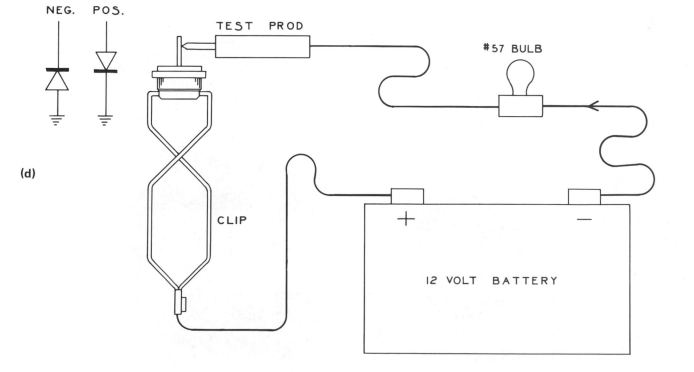

NEG. POS.

TEST PROD

#57 BULB

(d)

CLIP

+ 12 VOLT BATTERY −

Stator Checks. The stator can be checked with a 110-volt test light. The stator leads must be disconnected from the rectifier bridge or diodes. With the test light making a good contact on one stator lead, the second test light lead is connected to each of the other stator leads, one at a time. The test light bulb should light. If it does not the stator is open and will have to be replaced. The second test light lead is then moved to the stator core. With this connection the test light bulb should not light. If it does the stator windings are grounded and the stator will have to be replaced.

Some test procedures specify the use of an ohmmeter rather than 110-volt test light. The ohmmeter is connected in the same manner as the test light and should show continuity between each winding and infinite resistance between the windings and the stator core.

Rotor Field Check. The rotor field can best be checked by measuring the amperage flow when the rotor field is connected in series with a 12-volt battery and ammeter when the leads are placed on the slip rings. The rotor field amperage, called *field current draw,* is not the same on all model alternators. Field current draw must be compared

Fig. 8-24 Rectifier bridge soldered to the stator.

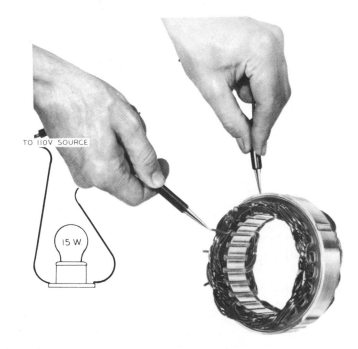

TO 110V SOURCE

15 W.

Fig. 8-25 Testing a stator for grounding (The Prestolite Company).

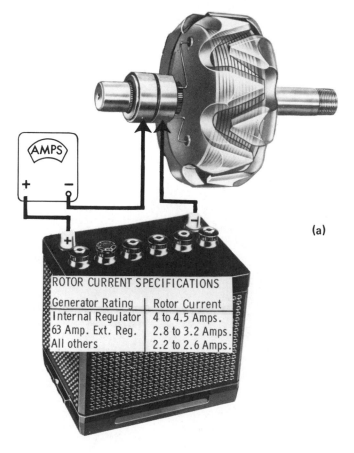

AMPS

(a)

ROTOR CURRENT SPECIFICATIONS	
Generator Rating	Rotor Current
Internal Regulator	4 to 4.5 Amps.
63 Amp. Ext. Reg.	2.8 to 3.2 Amps.
All others	2.2 to 2.6 Amps.

to the alternator specifications to determine if it is normal. Normal alternator field current will range between 1.5 and 4 amperes.

An alternate test method is to check the field with an ohmmeter connected across the slip rings. No continuity indicates an open field. One ohmmeter lead is then touched to the rotor metal. No continuity should be shown if the field is properly insulated from the core.

An alternator rotor can have its field coils replaced. This is done by unsoldering the coil from the slip rings. In some cases the slip rings have to be broken from the rotor. The technician can use special holding fixtures and an arbor press to push the rotor shaft from the rotor core and pole pieces. A new field coil is installed and the rotor reassembled by pressing the shaft into the pole pieces. A new slip ring assembly can be soldered and cemented in place. In practice, the rotor is rarely rebuilt in the service shop but rather it is exchanged for a rotor that has been rebuilt by a company specializing in rebuilding electrical equipment. The repair parts for rotors are seldom stocked by parts houses so exchanging the rotor is the most satisfactory method to correct a faulty rotor problem.

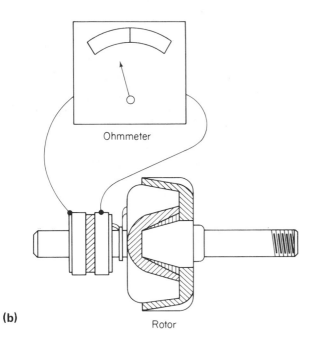

(b)

Rotor

Fig. 8-26 Testing the rotor field. (a) Field current draw (Oldsmobile Division, General Motors Corporation). (b) with an ohmmeter (The Prestolite Company), (c) for grounding with a 110 volt test light (The Prestolite Company).

(c)

Fig. 8-27 Soldering a diode.

Mechanical Service. Alternator mechanical service will usually involve the replacement of diodes, the diode bridge, field brushes, and bearings. Special diode presses are available from tool dealers. They are designed to press the diode from the case or heat sink without damaging either part. The diode should be disconnected from the connector. The connector may be fastened with an electrical terminal or it may be soldered. Electrical terminals can be unbolted. If the joint needs to be unsoldered, a plier should be clamped between the joint and diode. The plier absorbs heat as the joint

Fig. 8-28 Removing a diode with a diode press.

If an integrated internal voltage regulator is faulty it can be replaced with a new one while the alternator is disassembled. When a diode bridge or regulator is installed, the screws, nuts, washers, and insulators must be attached in the correct order to provide insulation or good grounds as required.

Fig. 8-30 A damaged alternator pulley that was removed with the wrong type of puller.

is unsoldered to keep heat from damaging the diode. Then the disconnected diode can be pressed from the case or heat sink.

The press can also be used to install the new diode. Soldered connections again require the use of the plier as a heat sink in the same manner as it was used during disassembly. Diodes using electrical connectors can be attached to their proper terminals. Faulty diode bridges can be unbolted and a new bridge bolted in the case.

The rear needle bearing can be pressed from the frame. Care must be exercised to prevent breaking the aluminum case or frame while pressing. The frame is supported by a tubular member slightly larger than the bearing. The bearing is pressed with a tube or pin slightly smaller than the bearing but large enough to press near the bearing edge. A new needle bearing can be pressed in with the same tools used to remove the old bearing. A soft plug and seal are installed where they are used in specific type alternators.

If the front ball bearing requires replacement the pulley must be removed. Some pulleys are held

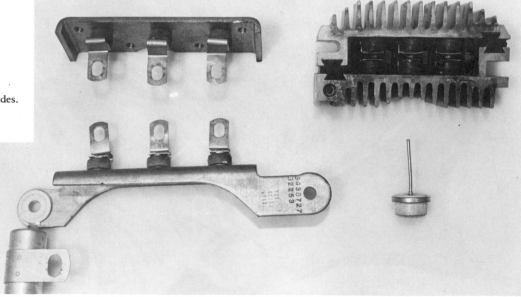

Fig. 8-29 Typical alternator diodes.

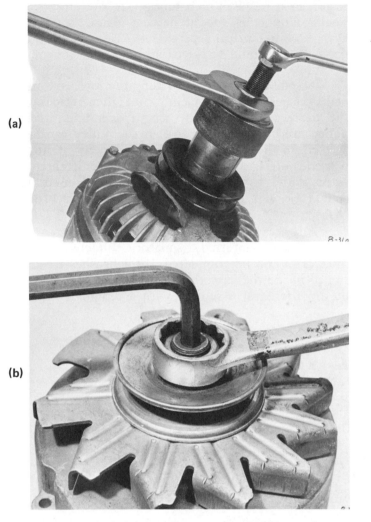

(a)

(b)

Fig. 8-31 Alternator pulley removal. (a) With a puller, (b) by removing a retaining nut.

(a)

(b)

(c)

Fig. 8-32 Removing the front alternator bearing. (a) With a clip retainer, (b) with a bolted retainer, (c) pulling the bearing from the rotor shaft.

on the shaft with a nut and drive the pulley through a key. The nut can be removed, then the pulley can be tapped to free it. Other alternators have the pulley held on the shaft by a press fit. The press-type requires the use of a puller on a pulling ring that is a part of the pulley. The pulley must not be removed by pulling on the edge of the pulley because the edge type puller will bend the pulley so it will have to be replaced with a new one. This is an unnecessary cost to the customer. With the pulley off and a ring spacer removed, the bearing can be freed from the end frame. It may be held in place with a clip retainer or bolted retainer. The retainer is loosened from the frame, then the rotor with the bearing can be pulled from the frame. The parts can then be cleaned and thoroughly inspected for physical damage.

In some models the ball bearing is pressed on the rotor shaft. It must be pulled or pressed off with special tools. The bearing will be discarded, so it can be pulled using its outer race. The retainer must be placed on the rotor shaft before the new bearing is installed. When the new bearing is pressed in during installation the force must be placed only against the inner race. This is best done with a sleeve that nearly matches the size of the inner race. The outer race is a push fit (not a press fit) in the drive end case. Other bearings are a push fit in the housing and on the shaft. These are installed in the case, then the rotor shaft is slipped through the bearing. The front ball bearing is prelubricated and sealed so it requires no attention. In some cases a small amount of special bearing grease, such as Delco-Remy lubricant part 1948791 available at parts stores, should be placed in the bearing retainer cavity.

Assembly starts by installing the rotor and its ball bearings in the drive end frame, then attaching the bearing retainer. The ring spacer and drive pulley are installed next so that the pulley can be pressed on the shaft when this attachment method is used, putting all pressing force on the alternator rotor shaft. If a pulley-retaining nut is used it should be tightened to 70-80 lb-ft (1022-1168 N/m).

Any reassembly of the stator, rear frame, diode bridge, internal regulator, condenser and brushes should be completed. If the brushes are installed inside the case they should be held in place during alternator assembly with a temporary pin.

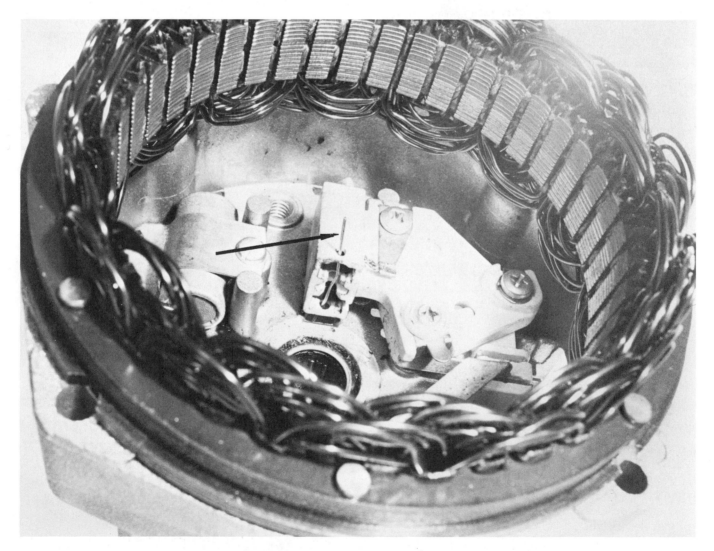

Fig. 8-33 Wire used to retain brushes during assembly.

CHARGING SYSTEM DIAGNOSIS - TRANSISTORIZED REGULATOR

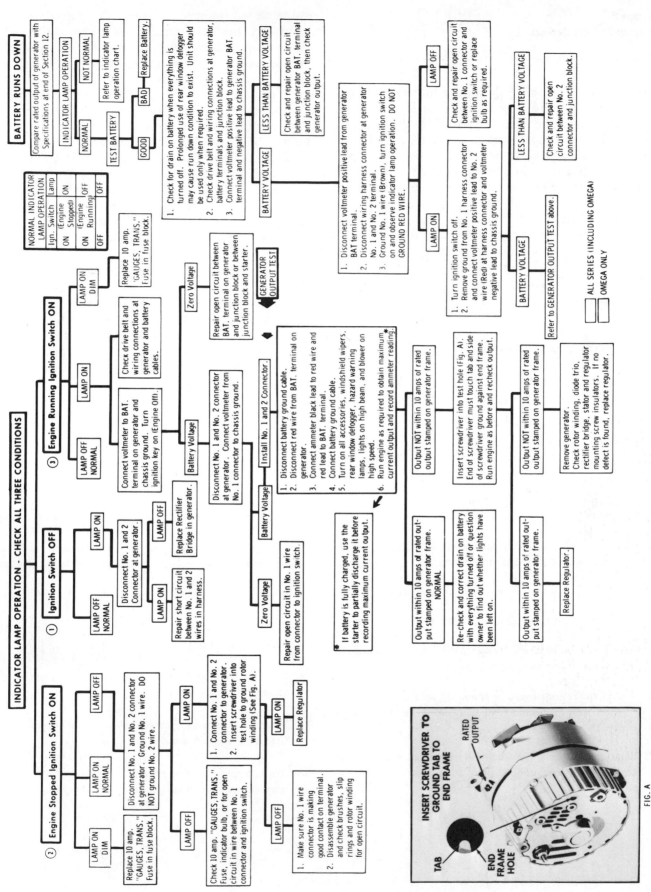

Fig. 8-34 Typical diagnosis procedure for alternators with integrated transistor regulation (Oldsmobile Division, General Motors Corporation).

117

The rear needle bearing should be lubricated with special bearing grease and the rotor shaft should be wiped clean and slid into the needle bearing. With the case halves properly aligned the through-bolts can be installed and tightened to hold the case together. When the pin that temporarily holds the brushes is removed or the externally installed brushes are put in place, the alternator is ready to be tested and then to be put into service.

It is wise to retest the alternator output and voltage regulation on a generator test bench or immediately after it has been reinstalled on the engine. This will assure that the alternator is now working properly.

8-4 TROUBLESHOOTING

Charging system troubleshooting is required when the system fails to charge, as indicated by the ammeter or indicator lamp. The first things to check are the belt tension, wire terminals on the battery, junctions, and alternator for cleanliness and security. If the charging system still does not function an output test should be run. If there is no output during this test the alternator is faulty and should be removed for service. If the alternator has output, the regulator or its lead wires are faulty. The wire can be checked for opens and grounds as described in Chapter 2. If these wires are normal the regulator is faulty. The regulator voltage setting should be checked and corrected if possible. If the regulator does not function it is general practice to replace it, but mechanical regulators can be adjusted as described in the preceding section.

Charging system problems baffle the typical service technician. With practice, following the procedures described in this chapter, the technician can develop a skill that will enable him to rapidly diagnose charging system problems and to make required repairs quickly and correctly so that there will be maximum customer satisfaction at minimum cost while the technician still makes a reasonable wage.

REVIEW QUESTIONS

1. What effect does the voltage regulator have on alternator output?

2. What controls the electrical system voltage when it is less than the voltage regulator setting?

3. When does a voltage regulator begin to operate?

4. What is the most desirable voltage regulator setting?

5. What must be done to the alternator wiring to produce maximum alternator output?

6. What connections must be made on an alternator with an internally grounded field to produce maximum amperage?

7. What connections must be made on an alternator with an externally grounded field to produce maximum amperage?

8. When is a 1/4 ohm fixed resistance inserted in the charging system to test the voltage regulator setting?

9. What charging circuit problems will cause the regulator to limit voltage before the battery is fully charged?

10. What is indicated by excessive use of battery water?

11. Why is it necessary to have a small current flow when checking the voltage regulator setting?

12. When is a battery-starter tester useful in checking the voltage regulator setting?

13. When an alternator requires service, what should be the first item disconnected?

14. What items should be checked when a battery does not stay charged on an automobile used every day?

9

Engine Operating Principles

The automotive electrical system provides the electrical power necessary for cranking the engine and for ignition. An operating engine provides the mechanical power necessary to operate the charging system which handles the electrical running load and moves the vehicle.

An air/fuel mixture is drawn into the engine as the starter motor cranks. This charge is ignited at the correct instant by the ignition system and the engine begins to run. The engine runs by converting part of the energy of the fuel into useful work. Fuel is mixed with the air in the proper proportions by the carburetor or fuel-injection system to form the intake charge. The intake charge is drawn through the intake manifold and an intake valve to fill the combustion chamber; then the valve closes. The charge is compressed and ignited at the precise instant required for proper engine operation. After ignition, the charge will burn very rapidly. Combustion of the charge in the engine is so fast it is usually called an explosion, but if the engine is to function properly the rate of burning of the charge must be controlled. Controlled burning releases the fuel energy in the form of heat. The resulting heat increases the pressure of the gases within the cylinder combustion chamber. In a typical reciprocating engine, the high pressure gases force a piston to move down in its cylinder. Piston movement is transferred to a rotating crankshaft through a connecting rod. When the piston approaches the

bottom of its downward stroke, an exhaust valve opens, releasing the expanded combustion gases into an exhaust manifold and muffler system. The sequence then repeats itself.

It is necessary to look at the operating cycle and major functions of the carburetor to understand how the ignition system timing affects the power, economy, and emissions produced by the engine.

9-1 OPERATING CYCLE

Engine operating cycles are identified by the number of piston *strokes* required to complete the cycle. A piston stroke is a one-way piston movement between top and bottom of the cylinder. Most automobile engines use a *four-stroke cycle.*

The four-stroke cycle starts with the piston at the top of the stroke with the piston close to the head. An intake valve opens as the piston moves down on the first, or *intake stroke,* allowing the combustible charge to enter the cylinder. The intake valve closes after the bottom of the stroke, and, as the crankshaft continues to rotate, the piston moves up on the second stroke, or *compression stroke,* to squeeze the charge into a small space called the *combustion chamber.* Near the top of the compression stroke, the ignition system produces an arc or spark across the spark plug

119

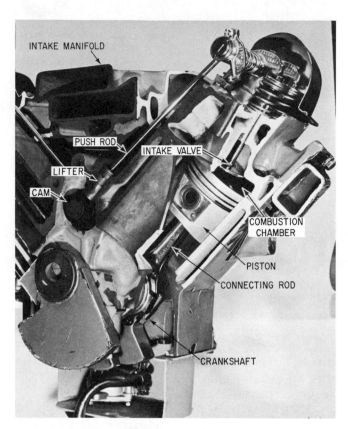

Fig. 9-1 Major engine parts.

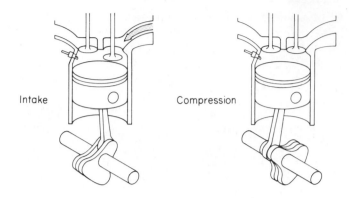

Fig. 9-2 Typical four-stroke engine cycle.

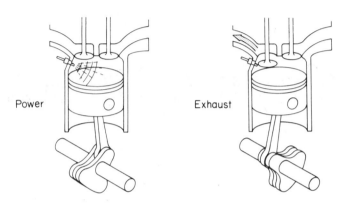

electrodes to ignite the compressed charge so the fuel will burn. The heat released raises the charge pressure and the pressure pushes the piston down on the third, or *power stroke.* Near the bottom of the stroke, the exhaust valve opens to release the spent gases as the piston moves up on the fourth, or *exhaust stroke,* to complete a 720-degree four-stroke cycle. The piston is then in a position to start the next cycle with another intake stroke. The four-stroke cycle is repeated every other crankshaft revolution.

9-2 CARBURETION

The air/fuel charge is mixed in the proper proportions by a carburetor in a modern automobile engine. When the engine operating requirements change, the proportions are changed by a number of specialized carburetor circuits. An idling engine uses a low air flow and requires a rich air/fuel mixture (a high proportion of fuel in the mixture).

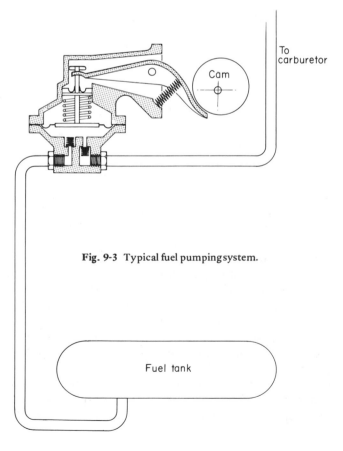

Fig. 9-3 Typical fuel pumping system.

When operating at sustained legal highway speeds, the engine uses a moderate air flow and lean air/fuel mixtures (a low proportion of fuel in the mixture). As engine power requirements approach full throttle, the engine again calls for a large flow of rich air/fuel mixture. The carburetor supplies these needs and, in addition, supplies a rich mixture for starting and for acceleration.

Gasoline is transferred from the fuel tank to the carburetor by a fuel pump. Most of the fuel pumps are mechanically driven by the engine, but some model automobiles use electrically driven fuel pumps. The gasoline is filtered between the fuel pump and carburetor.

Gasoline enters the carburetor float bowl through an inlet needle valve. When the gasoline reaches the required level in the float bowl, a float system closes the needle valve to stop fuel flow. The float system allows gasoline to flow into the bowl at the same rate it is used so the fuel level remains nearly constant.

Air flow through the carburetor is controlled by a throttle plate located at the outlet side of the carburetor passage. As the engine runs, the intake strokes of the cylinders pull air from the manifold. If the throttle plate is closed for engine idling speeds, the intake strokes pull a partial vacuum in the manifold. When the throttle is slightly opened for driving speeds, the amount of air flowing through the carburetor into the manifold will increase. This decreases the manifold vacuum. At full throttle (wide open), the air flows through the carburetor so rapidly that there is hardly any vacuum remaining in the manifold. Manifold vacuum is high when the throttle is closed and low when the throttle is open.

The systems within the carburetor mix the correct amount of fuel with the air flowing through the carburetor to produce an induction charge having the proper air/fuel mixture. A restriction in the air passage, called a venturi, reduces the pressure of the air as it passes through the narrowest part. The low pressure produced at this point is called *venturi vacuum*. The main fuel discharge nozzle is located here. Fuel leaves the float bowl through a main metering jet and enters the main well. Air from a main air bleed also enters the main well to break up the solid stream of fuel. This mixture flows through a passage to the main discharge nozzle where it enters and mixes with the large air flow at the venturi. The air/fuel mixture of this system is controlled by the size of the main metering jet and the air bleed. It is enriched either as the main metering jet is enlarged or as the air bleed is restricted.

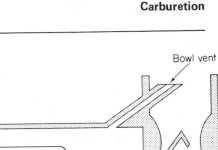

Fig. 9-4 The main fuel system of a simple carburetor.

The main fuel system of the carburetor is used during steady highway speeds. A separate system, called the idle and transfer system, is required for low speed operation. Fuel for this system is taken from the main well in most carburetors. In the rest of the carburetors, fuel for the idle system is taken directly from the float bowl. After fuel enters this system, it is taken above the fuel level where it meets an idle air bleed; then it goes to an idle discharge port on the manifold side of the throttle plate. A fixed restriction within the passage and a variable restriction at the idle passage outlet controls the idle air/fuel mixture ratio. An opening into this idle passage above the throttle plate, called a transfer port, allows extra air to bleed into the idle fuel for better air/fuel mixing. When the throttle is gradually opened past the transfer ports, they are exposed to manifold vacuum that is below the throttle plate. This causes fuel to be delivered through the transfer ports as well as the idle port. Both ports supply enough fuel to the added air flow to maintain a combustible air/fuel mixture ratio. As the throttle is opened still further, the main fuel system begins to deliver fuel. The combination of these systems delivers the correct air/fuel ratio until the throttle is nearly wide open.

A power system comes into operation as the throttle approaches wide open. Either or both manifold vacuum and throttle position are used to open an auxiliary carburetor system, called a power system, that supplies the extra fuel needed for full power. In this system a measured quantity of extra

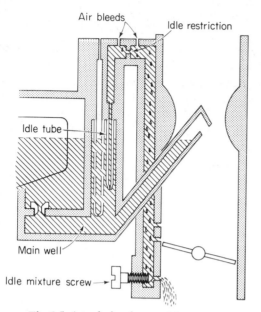

Fig. 9-5 A typical carburetor idle system.

fuel is allowed to flow from the float bowl to the main well to be delivered to the air flow through the main discharge nozzle.

At the moment of rapid throttle opening as the vehicle speed is to be increased, air flow through the carburetor will start to move quicker than the fuel. This will lean the air/fuel mixture delivered to the manifold at a time when a rich mixture is needed. An acceleration pump system is provided to correct this problem. The acceleration pump pulls fuel from the float bowl through an inlet check valve. It is pushed out of the pump through

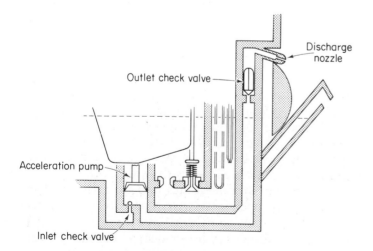

Fig. 9-6 A typical acceleration pump system.

an outlet check valve to a special discharge nozzle located on the atmospheric side of the venturi. A spring system in the operating mechanism provides a fuel delivery for a few seconds duration until fuel begins to flow in the main and power systems. No fuel flows through the acceleration system at any other time.

Carburetors have a choke to aid in starting a cold engine. The choke is a plate in the air horn on the atmospheric side of the venturi. When the engine is cold, the choke plate closes to restrict the incoming air. This applies manifold vacuum on the main discharge nozzle as well as the idle and transfer ports. Fuel delivered from these systems provides a very rich mixture needed to start the engine. After the engine starts, the choke opens slightly. As the engine becomes warm, the choke mechanism gradually opens the choke. It is fully open when the engine is at its normal operating temperature.

The carburetor just described applies to the primary barrel of a single barrel (one bore and one throttle plate) carburetor. A carburetor with two primary barrels (two bores with a throttle plate in each) duplicates all of the parts of the single barrel carburetor, except that each carburetor uses only one float bowl, choke, accelerating system, and in some cases the power system.

The greatest amount of air flow is needed for high speed engine operation. In addition to the two primary barrels, large capacity carburetors have two secondary barrels to provide a sufficient quantity of air. Some small engines use a carburetor with one primary barrel and one secondary barrel. The secondary system may use the same float bowl as the primary system, or it may have a separate float bowl. Secondary systems have a main fuel system designed to operate at the air/fuel ratio needed for full power. Some also contain an idle and transfer system for smooth transition as the secondary throttle plates begin to open. Secondary systems do not use a choke, acceleration system, or a power system.

Carburetors are provided with a number of additional devices to improve drivability, economy, and low emission levels. Among these devices are the fast idle cam, unloader, return check, secondary lock out, idle stop solenoid, and vacuum kick. In addition, the carburetors include vacuum ports for the air silencer, heat damper, EGR valve, carbon canister, and the ignition vacuum advance.

For the study of the ignition system, it is important to understand how the distributor vacuum advance port is connected into the carburetor.

Fig. 9-7 Large secondary throttle plates begin to open as the small primary throttle plates are nearly open.

The port uses the carburetor body but it does not interconnect into any of the carburetor operating systems. There is a direct passage from the external port nipple to an opening in the carburetor bore located just above the high portion of the throttle plate when it is in the closed position. In this location it senses atmospheric pressure when the throttle is closed. As the throttle opens slightly, the edge of the throttle plate moves above the distributor vacuum advance port, exposing it to manifold vacuum. When the throttle plate becomes nearly wide open, the manifold vacuum in the carburetor bore is reduced to nearly atmospheric pressure again so there is no vacuum on the distributor vacuum advance port of the carburetor. To summarize, there is no effective vacuum on the port when the throttle is fully closed against the idle stop or when it is fully open. At part throttle, there is vacuum on the ignition advance port.

Fig. 9-8 Distributor vacuum advance port located just above the closed throttle plate.

9-3 EMISSION REDUCTION

Modern automobile engines have been designed to minimize the harmful emission they produce. Ignition timing has a great deal to do with the way the fuel burns in the combustion chamber and therefore with the emission produced. This makes it very important for the technician to have a basic understanding of what the emissions are, how they are produced, and what has been done to reduce them to the regulated emission standards.

California leads the nation in passing laws requiring new automobiles to produce less emissions of the type that lead to the development of smog. Federal emission control regulations for new automobiles are now in effect for the whole country. Automobile manufacturers met the requirements of the first emission laws by providing the engine with positive crankcase ventilation. Additional regulations followed, and the automobile manufacturers met them. Carburetors and intake systems have been modified to provide each combustion chamber with a mixture that more nearly meets ideal combustion requirements. The ignition system is designed to provide ignition at a time in the combustion cycle that results in lower smog producing emissions. Combustion chamber designs and coolant temperatures have been changed to reduce harmful emissions. The exhaust system has been modified to aid in the final combustion of products not fully burned in the combustion chamber through the use of air pumps and catalytic converters. Vapors from the fuel tank and carburetor are vented to an activated carbon charcoal canister, where, when the engine is not running, they are trapped and stored to keep them from drifting into the atmosphere.

Vehicle emissions come from the engine crankcase, gasoline tank, carburetor, and exhaust. The crankcase vapors from the engines have been completely controlled since 1968. Evaporative vapors from the gasoline tank and carburetor are controlled under almost every condition in automobiles built since 1971. In order to run, the engine will use large amounts of air and expel a large quantity of exhaust, so the engine exhaust cannot be eliminated. Federal standards require the exhaust gases to be modified so that they contain only a very small percentage of harmful exhaust components thus minimizing pollution.

Exhaust Emission Control. Exhaust emission control is accomplished by carefully controlling the air/fuel mixture being sent to the combustion chamber, by controlling the combustion process, and by eliminating any harmful emission products still remaining in the exhaust gases.

Unburned hydrocarbons and carbon monoxide emissions are most critical at idle and during acceleration and deceleration when the engine must run with a rich mixture. Oxides of nitrogen are produced at cruising speeds when the engine runs with high thermal efficiencies, accompanied by high peak combustion temperatures.

Exhaust emission control starts with the carburetor. Emission control carburetors are very carefully calibrated and adjusted to operate as lean as possible while still providing each cylinder with a combustible mixture. With mixtures on the lean side of their design combustible range, the engine may tend to idle rough and it may surge during cruising operation. Careful carburetor adjustment will minimize this tendency.

When the engine is cold, it must be partially choked to operate. Choking provides the engine with a rich air/fuel mixture that produces a large amount of hydrocarbons and carbon monoxide. Emission control engines have their chokes calibrated to open as rapidly as possible and still maintain drivability. This is done by heating the thermostatic choke-spring rapidly or by using a more sensitive thermostatic choke-spring. Some engine models use an electric heater to open the choke more rapidly than is possible using engine heat alone. Hydrocarbon and carbon monoxide emission products that are produced by the engine will reduce as the choke opens.

Many factors affect combustion of the charge once it gets into the combustion chamber. The combustion chamber shape greatly affects the amount of unburned hydrocarbons remaining in the exhaust. The part of the charge that is close to the combustion chamber surface is kept so cool that it does not burn, and these unburned gases form much of the unburned hydrocarbons in the exhaust. The areas within the combustion chamber that quench the charge have been kept at a minimum in emission controlled engines.

The combustion chamber temperature must be high to help burn lean mixtures. Increasing the operating temperatures of the cooling system thermostat helps to provide the high combustion temperatures. Temperatures are also kept high by restricting distributor vacuum advance that normally occurs on non-emission control engines. High engine temperatures cause more rapid hydrocarbon oxidation to lower the amount of hydrocarbons remaining in the exhaust. While idling in traffic, coolant flow through the engine is low because the coolant pump is turned slowly and the fan is driven slowly. This condition may lead to excessive engine temperatures. The distributor vacuum advance system is provided with a temperature-operated by-pass valve to prevent excessive engine temperatures. At an engine temperature of approximately 220°F (104°C), the by-pass opens to apply manifold vacuum to the distributor vacuum advance unit. This allows the engine to run more efficiently, and this in turn increases the engine speed. The resulting higher engine speed increases the cooling pump fan speed to cool the coolant faster and to pass more air through the radiator which results in a lower engine operating temperature.

Engine emission control systems using the features just described to clean up the exhaust are given a number of different names by the automo-

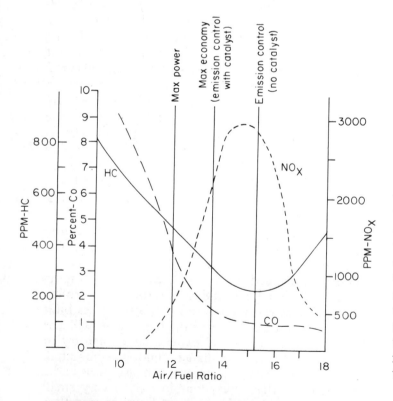

Fig. 9-9 Exhaust gas contaminant changes as the air/fuel ratio changes on a non-emission-controlled engine.

bile manufacturers. They all have essentially the same operating units and go by names such as IMCO (Improved Combustion), CAP (Clean Air Package), CAS (Clean Air System), CCS (Controlled Combustion System), and Engine Modification.

Ignition Timing. Timing on emission control engines is retarded from the best timing, so it is necessary to have the throttle open further to provide the same engine idle speed. This added air allows the engine to be run with a leaner mixture. Lean mixtures, along with the higher temperatures that result from retarded timing, help to reduce hydrocarbon and carbon monoxide emissions in the exhaust. The amount of undesirable exhaust emissions produced by an engine is the result of carburetion and the ignition timing effect on combustion. To operate properly, basic engine timing must be correct. Procedures used for ignition timing are described in Chapter 11.

Ignition systems have two advance systems, mechanical centrifugal and vacuum. The mechanical centrifugal advance is designed to provide the required advance for full throttle maximum power engine operation. Vacuum advance provides the added advance needed for part throttle to give the engine maximum economy. At full throttle, there is no vacuum on the distributor port in the carburetor so the only ignition advance being used is the mechanical centrifugal advance. The vacuum advance unit has no effect on the engine's, full throttle power. The vacuum advance control is modified on emission control engines at part throttle to minimize exhaust emissions.

Distributor vacuum advance in most vehicles is connected to the distributor vacuum port in the carburetor through a temperature operated by-pass valve that may also be called a thermostatic vacuum switch (TVS), ported vacuum switch (PVS),

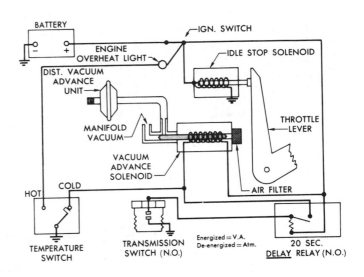

Fig. 9-10 Schematic drawing of a transmission controlled distributor vacuum advance modifying system used to minimize harmful exhaust emissions. (Chevrolet Motor Division, General Motors Corporation).

or distributor vacuum control valve. It provides the distributor with normal distributor vacuum from the carburetor port located just above the closed throttle plate. The connecting hose may also include an advance delay valve that slows the reaction as ported vacuum increases.

There are a number of controls between the carburetor and the distributor vacuum unit. Some of these are electrically operated. They will be discussed, as needed, in the following chapters. The rest of the emission control system is beyond the scope of this book.

REVIEW QUESTIONS

1. What are the strokes of a four-stroke cycle?

2. What does a carburetor do?

3. What operating conditions use a rich air/fuel mixture?

4. What controls the air flow through a carburetor?

5. When does the engine have a high vacuum?

6. When is engine vacuum low?

7. Where does the distributor vacuum port open into the carburetor bore?

8. What type of engine operation produces the most unburned hydrocarbons and carbon monoxide?

9. What distributor advance system has the most direct effect on the products of exhaust emissions?

10

The Ignition System

An air/fuel charge, compression, and ignition are required to make an engine start and run. Of the three, ignition is most critical. The correct amount of fuel mixed with the air is required for proper engine operation; however, the engine will start, even with no carburetor, if a small amount of gasoline is poured into the intake manifold. High compression is required for maximum power and economy, but the engine will start and run with low compression. In all cases the ignition system must be able to produce a spark at the correct instant that is strong enough to ignite the air/fuel mixture after it has been compressed in the cylinder.

Ignition requirements change as engine operating conditions change. Higher compression pressures require a higher ignition voltage. Cold combustion chambers require higher ignition voltages while starting than do warm chambers. Both rich and lean air/fuel mixtures require a higher ignition voltage than the chemically correct mixtures. For proper combustion that leads to engine efficiency, the ignition timing must advance as engine speed increases. Part throttle operation requires more ignition advance than does either full throttle operation or idle. Exhaust emission is affected by ignition timing and so the function of some emission controls is to change ignition timing to minimize polluting exhaust emissions. These changes usually reduce the thermal efficiency of the engine and this will reduce the gasoline mileage.

At the correct instant in the engine cycle the ignition system must provide a voltage that is high enough to form an arc between the spark plug electrodes that will allow the engine to produce the required power, economy, and emission level demanded of modern automobile engines.

The ignition system consists of two parts: a low-voltage *primary* circuit and a high-voltage *secondary* circuit. The primary circuit includes the battery, ignition switch, ballast resistor, cam-operated breaker points, condenser, and the heavy primary windings in the coil with their connecting wiring. The secondary circuit includes the large number of fine coil secondary windings, the distributor rotor, distributor cap, ignition cables, and spark plugs.

When the ignition switch and breaker points are closed in a typical inductive ignition system the primary circuit is completed, through ground, to allow electrical current to flow in the primary circuit. This current flow builds a magnetic field in the coil. As the engine rotates it turns the breaker-point cam within the distributor housing. The cam pushes against the breaker-point rubbing block, forcing the points apart. Breaker-point separation interrupts and stops the primary current flow. When the current flow stops, the magnetic field in the coil collapses through the secondary windings. The condenser within the distributor minimizes contact point arcing as it helps to control the rapid collapse of the magnetic field. Field collapse induces a mo-

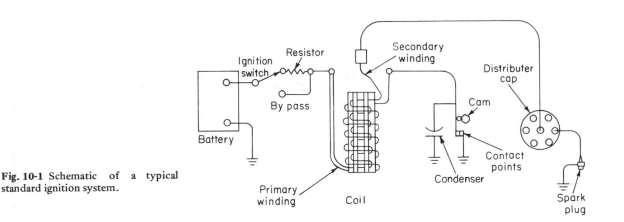

Fig. 10-1 Schematic of a typical standard ignition system.

mentary high voltage surge in the coil secondary windings. At this instant the rotor tip is lined up with the proper distributor cap electrode. This high voltage surge is impressed through the secondary cables on the spark plug in the cylinder to be fired, causing an arc to form across the spark plug gap. This arc ignites the compressed air/fuel

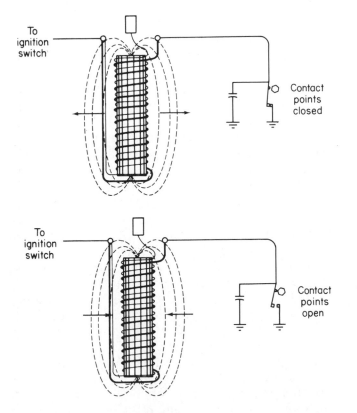

Fig. 10-2 Voltage induced in the coil secondary by the changing primary magnetic field as the ignition points open and close.

charge in the combustion chamber at the correct instant. The resulting combustion increases pressure above the piston to push it down in the cylinder.

The primary current in the ignition system must be great enough to store adequate energy in the coil. This energy will produce a secondary voltage that is required to form the spark plug arc with some additional voltage reserve. When there is no reserve voltage the engine will misfire. To be able to provide high *available voltage* the primary wiring must be in good condition; all junctions in the system must have good electrical contacts; the breaker points must have minimum resistance, normal point dwell and normal point gap; and the coil and condenser must function properly.

The secondary circuit is responsbile for *required voltage.* For minimum required voltage the spark plugs must have clean electrodes with sharp edges; the gap must not be excessive; the spacing between the rotor and cap electrodes must be within limits; and the secondary cables must have good junctions and normal resistance.

As the engine runs, the primary breaker-point contact surface and rubbing block will change and junctions will loosen. These conditions tend to reduce available voltage. Required voltage increases when the secondary circuit condition deteriorates as the spark plug gap grows by about 0.001 in. (0.025 mm) per 1000 miles (1600 km) of operation; as the distributor rotor-to-electrode space increases; and as secondary-cable junctions corrode. When the available voltage decreases and required voltage increases they will eventually become equal, and at that point the engine will misfire from a lack of ignition.

127

10-1 IGNITION TIMING

No matter what type of ignition system is used—it may be a conventional design, it may use transistor switching, or it may use a capacitive discharge system—the spark must be delivered to the spark plug with enough energy to ignite the charge.

It is not only important for the charge to ignite, but it should ignite at the correct instant so that the burning charge will produce maximum useful energy as the hot gases expand within the combustion chamber. The spark arc is timed so that maximum combustion chamber pressure occurs when the crank pin is 5° to 10° after top center. The ignition firing or timing point needs to be adjusted during engine operation for changes in induced air/fuel charge that affect burning rates so that maximum pressure will always occur at 5° to 10° after top center under all operating conditions requiring engine power.

Ignition Timing and Engine Speed. The first 10 percent of the combustion charge burns at a constant rate; that is, it takes a specific length of time to burn, no matter what the engine speed happens to be. To compensate for this, a mechanical timing mechanism is used to advance the ignition firing point as engine speed increases.

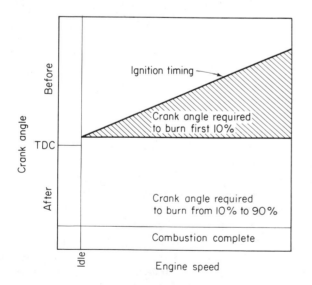

Fig. 10-3 Combustion burning rate in terms of engine speed and degrees of crankshaft rotation.

After the first 10 percent of the charge has burned the combustion rate increase is proportional to engine speed. This is primarily the result of increased turbulence in the combustion chamber created by a high velocity intake charge, combustion chamber squash area (the narrow space between the piston and the head at top center), and flame turbulence. Without this characteristic, engines could not run at high speeds as required in racing. At some high rpm, depending on the engine design, the first 10 percent becomes insignificant so that no further ignition advance is required.

Ignition Timing and Engine Load. The mass or weight of the induction charge that is taken into the combustion chamber, as the result of throttle position and engine load, also affects timing requirements. Under light throttle operation, high manifold vacuum occurs and a *small quantity* of charge is drawn into the combustion chamber. Pressure resulting from compression of this small charge is low and its burning rate is slow. This low pressure type of charge requires high ignition advance to complete combustion at 5° to 10° after top center. At these low compression pressures, the spark plug arc will form at a low required voltage.

During low-speed, full-throttle engine operation, a *large quantity* of charge enters the combustion chamber because the open throttle provides minimum intake restriction. When compressed, this charge is dense and has high pressure. More gas molecules are present between the spark plug electrodes increasing the electrical resistance, and this increases the required voltage. Once kindled, combustion occurs quite rapidly through the dense mixture so timing requires less advance to have combustion complete at 5° to 10° after top center.

Ignition timing could be compared to going to a drag race. If the race began at six o'clock, one would plan to start early enough to arrive on time. His starting time would depend on the road type, the traffic anticipated, and the weather. The ignition system is designed to anticipate the expected length of time to complete combustion; then it must start early enough in the cycle that combustion is completed at the correct time in the cycle.

A vacuum timing-advance mechanism is used to change ignition timing to compensate for throttle position and engine load. Timing is *advanced* under high intake manifold vacuum, light load operation when the burning rate of the combustion charge is slow. It is *retarded* under low intake manifold vacuum, heavy load operation when fast burning rates occur. Vacuum advance is fully retarded at full throttle because it is not required for maximum engine power. The primary function of vacuum advance is to provide fuel economy during part throttle operation by igniting the charge at an advance that will give maximum effective combustion pressure at the engine operating conditions. Restricting vacuum advance is one of the major methods used to control exhaust hydrocarbon emissions.

Ignition Timing and Emissions. The emission quality is greatly affected by the timing-instant that the charge is ignited in the engine cycle. The maximum amount of fuel energy is transformed into useful work when combustion is most efficient. This leaves less heat to be exhausted and so the exhaust gases are at a lower temperature. Exhaust gases from an efficiently operating engine, however, contain excessive hydrocarbons and carbon monoxide in an uncontrolled engine when the engine runs rich with the throttle closed; at idle and especially during deceleration. By retarding the timing, engine efficiency is reduced so the throttle must be opened further to maintain the same speed. The mixture can be leaned when using this larger throttle opening. These conditions result in higher engine exhaust operating temperatures. Increased exhaust heat helps to complete the combustion of hydrocarbons and carbon monoxide as the spent gases flow through the exhaust system. Rapid distributor advance as the engine comes up to power gives the engine normal ignition advance for economy cruise and for high speed operation.

To make sure that the vacuum does not cause the ignition to advance during acceleration some manufacturers have a transmission spark control (TSC) system connected to the transmission to allow vacuum advance only in direct drive.

During deceleration the engine has a high intake manifold vacuum. If the throttle were only partly closed during deceleration the distributor vacuum port would be exposed to manifold vacuum. This would cause the vacuum to advance the distributor timing and produce more hydrocarbons and carbon monoxide. Some automatic transmission equipped engines are fitted with a modified distributor advance unit connected to special carburetor ports to insure full ignition retard during deceleration. They may also have an electric solenoid attached to the vacuum-advance control

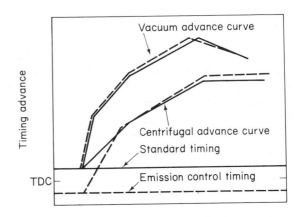

Fig. 10-4 Typical change in the distributor advance curve to reduce hydrocarbon and carbon monoxide at low speeds.

unit. The purpose of the solenoid is to advance the ignition timing during engine cranking to assure quick and easy starting. The timing advance solenoid is only activated during cranking.

In some standard transmission vehicles lower hydrocarbon exhaust emissions will be produced if the ignition timing is advanced during deceleration. This is accomplished by using a vacuum controlled valve in the distributor vacuum hose. With the throttle closed the normal distributor vacuum port in the carburetor is open above the throttle plate where it is exposed to the atmosphere and so it provides no vacuum advance. Under these conditions the vacuum-controlled emission valve connects the distributor diaphragm to the engine manifold to give maximum vacuum advance. This provides a longer period of time for combustion to take place within the combustion chamber before the exhaust valve opens.

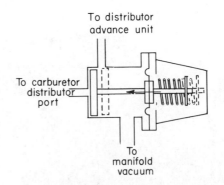

Fig. 10-5 Section drawing of a vacuum control valve used with some standard transmission engines.

10-2 REQUIRED VOLTAGE

Required voltage is the actual voltage produced in the secondary ignition circuit to produce an arc across the spark plug electrode gap. If required voltage exceeds the maximum voltage available, misfiring will occur. Voltage required to arc across the spark plug gap is based upon a number of operating variables and physical conditions existing in the ignition system.

Operating variables that affect required voltage are based on the compression pressure and the air/fuel ratio of the charge in the cylinder. Compression pressure changes as the throttle is opened and closed, being highest when the throttle is wide open and lowest when the throttle is closed at any given engine speed. When engine speed increases, compression pressure lowers as a result of lower volumetric efficiency. The valves open and close so fast that there is little time for air to get into the cylinders. Required voltage is low when the compression pressure is low and high when the compression pressure is high.

The required voltage is lowest when the air/fuel ratio is adjusted to produce best power, approximately 12:1. Any change from this air/fuel ratio, either rich or lean, will increase required voltage. Because emission-control engines operate very lean, increased required voltage is considered to be the result of lean mixtures and reduced re-

quired voltage a result of richer mixtures. For ignition to occur, some of the charge mixture must find its way between the spark plug electrodes, and the spark arc must have enough thermal energy to start a self-propagating, continuous-burning flame in the mixture. In stratified charge engines, as in other engines, there must be a combustible air/fuel charge between the spark plug electrodes.

The spark plug gap is the ignition voltage regulator that controls required voltage. Required voltage is sensitive to the gap spacing between the spark plug electrodes, which in turn is sensitive to compression pressure, the air/fuel mixture and turbulence. A larger gap requires increased voltage. Too small a gap reduces the required voltage but also reduces the opportunity for a combustible mixture to get between the spark plug electrodes. Small spark plug gaps also reduce the air/fuel mixture igniting range. The largest spark plug gap is required at idle speeds when the least amount of turbulence exists in the combustion chamber.

At idle speeds, the combustion chamber turbulence is low and, therefore, the chance of having the correct mixture move into the spark plug electrode gap is also low. The *minimum* spark plug gap that will produce satisfactory engine idle is 0.025 in. (0.625 mm). Most ignition systems use gap specification over 0.030 in. (0.75 mm). As engine speed increases, combustion chamber turbulence will also increase and this reduces the gap requirement. In engines operating above half-load, a gap of 0.005 in. (0.125 mm) will actually provide satisfactory operation. Combustion chamber turbulence must not, however, be so great as to blow the initial flame from between the spark plug electrodes until it becomes hot enough to maintain combustion. If it does the duration of the arc must be long enough to reignite the charge.

The shape of spark plug electrodes, as well as the gap, affects required voltage. New spark plug electrodes have the lowest required voltage. The electrodes become eroded after a number of arcs, rounding off the original sharp edges. This erosion increases the voltage requirement.

Any increase in secondary circuit resistance greater than the resistance of the spark plug gap increases the voltage requirement. Resistance is increased by secondary wiring with loose connections, by a wide gap between rotor and cap electrodes, and by damaged secondary wires. The difference between the voltage available from the ignition system and the required voltage is called *ignition reserve*. Misfiring occurs when no ignition reserve remains.

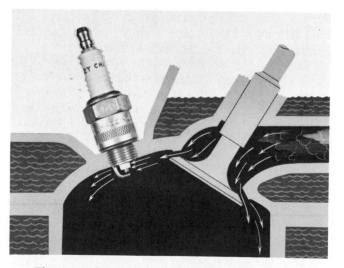

Fig. 10-6 Inducted charge gases reaching the spark plug electrodes (Champion Spark Plug Company).

(a)

Fig. 10-7 Spark plug electrode shape (AC Spark Plug Division, General Motors Corporation). (a) Normal, (b) badly worn.

(b)

10-3 IGNITION MEASUREMENT

In operation, when the points close, battery voltage pushes current through the coil primary windings. This current flow builds up a magnetic field around the primary winding and within the soft iron core of the coil. When the contact breaker points open, the current flow of the primary circuit stops, causing the magnetic field to collapse. During collapse, the magnetic lines of force rapidly cut through the coil secondary windings as they collapse. This rapid relative motion between the magnetic lines of force and conductor induces a high voltage in the secondary windings with sufficient energy to force an arc to flash across the spark plug electrodes. This entire sequence of events must occur each time a spark plug fires. In an eight-cylinder engine running at 4000 rpm, there are 266 spark plug firings each second. It is impossible to follow this action with a meter because the meter cannot move fast enough, so a cathode ray oscilloscope is used to show this constantly changing voltage.

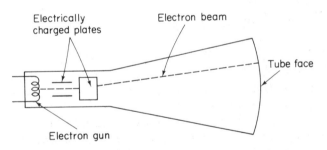

Fig. 10-9 Simplified cross-section of an oscilloscope display tube.

A cathode ray oscilloscope display appears on the face of an electron tube that is similar to a television picture tube. The oscilloscope is powered by electrical and electronic circuits sensitive to voltage and time. The gun in the base of the picture tube emits a stream of electrons, called a beam, that is directed toward the face of the tube between electrically charged plates. The electric charge on these plates deflects or sweeps the beam up and down or sideways. The sideways or horizontal sweep of an oscilloscope is based on time. Sweep speeds are based on centimeters per decimal part of a second, such as: 0.1, 0.01, 0.001, etc. of a second.

The electron beam is focused to hit the tube screen. The screen has a coating so that it momen-

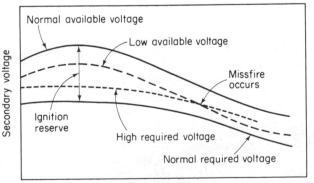

Fig. 10-8 Available and required voltage compared to engine speed.

tarily holds the light, allowing slow decay. As the beam sweeps, it leaves a light beam line on the scope face. The start of the beam movement must be initiated or triggered. When an electrical signal triggers the start of the horizontal beam sweep (x-axis), it will sweep the entire screen, then stop until it is triggered again. Each trigger impulse restarts the beam on the left side of the scope pattern, even if the beam has not completed its sweep across the screen.

Scope controls are provided to adjust voltage sensing (y-axis) and sweep rate (x-axis) as well as vertical and horizontal positioning of the sweep pattern. Using these controls, the operator can measure or look at the characteristics of any portion of the oscilloscope pattern displayed.

The ignition system has its own characteristic oscilloscope pattern. It will be used to describe the details of the ignition system operation. When the details of this pattern are known, they can be applied to ignition scopes as an aid to engine analysis and diagnosis.

10-4 COIL OPERATION

The typical standard automotive ignition coil has from 100 to 180 primary windings of #20 copper wire. The primary winding carries a large current so it becomes warm. It is, therefore, wrapped on the outside of the coil secondary winding to aid in its cooling. The secondary coil has 18,000 winding turns of #38 wire. Both wires are coated with in-

sulating varnish and the winding layers are separated with oiled paper. A laminated soft iron core is placed in the center of the coils and a laminated soft iron shield is wrapped around the outside. The laminations of the core and shield limit magnetic eddy currents that would reduce coil efficiency. This assembly is placed in a can with a ceramic insulator; and the can is filled with insulating transformer oil and sealed. Coils are not repairable. If tests show them to be faulty, or if they leak oil, they must be replaced.

Battery voltage forces a current to flow through the primary coil when the ignition switch and breaker points are closed. The maximum amount of current that flows through the primary circuit is limited by the resistance of the long copper primary wire coil winding and by other resistances in the circuit. When the points close current flow begins. The magnetic field around the primary coil wire expands across adjacent wires and this induces a counter voltage that opposes the input current flow. The counter voltage slows full current buildup causing it to occur over a period of time and crankshaft degrees. This characteristic is called *inductance,* as previously described in Chapter 1. The primary magnetic field buildup induces a voltage in the secondary coil, but it is not strong enough to form an arc across the spark plug electrodes. The voltage change can be seen as the point-closing signal on both primary and secondary scope patterns.

Capacitance is another electrical property that affects the ignition system. When two conductors are close together but insulated from each other, the negative charges in one conductor will attract the positive charges in the adjacent conductor, somewhat like electron attraction in diodes. These

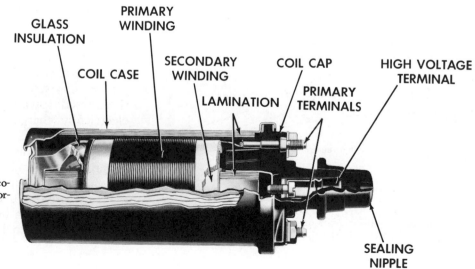

Fig. 10-10 Coil nomenclature (Delco-Remy Division, General Motors Corporation).

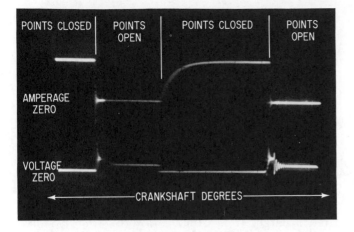

Fig. 10-11 Primary oscilloscope pattern showing what is occurring as the contact points open and close. The upper trace shows the *current* flow in the coil and the lower trace is the standard primary *voltage* trace seen on ignition scopes.

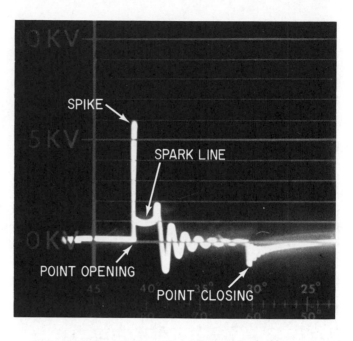

Fig. 10-12 Secondary oscilloscope pattern showing secondary voltage as the contact points open and close and as an arc forms across the spark plug electrodes.

charges will remain as long as the conductors remain insulated from each other. In this way, they are able to store electrical energy. The capacitance of the secondary ignition circuit is based on the design of the secondary coil and on the length, routing, and proximity of the secondary ignition cables to engine metal.

As current flows through the primary coil, its magnetic field continues to build up until full current flows in the primary, at which time the coil has reached magnetic saturation. This stores electrical energy in the coil by induction.

When the breaker points open, primary current flow stops, with the aid of the primary condenser. As the primary current stops, the magnetic field quickly collapses, cutting the coil windings.

Rapid collapse of the coil magnetic field produces voltage in the primary and secondary windings, charging their capacitances. The capacitive portion of the electrical energy builds up in the secondary until it has sufficient voltage to ionize gases between the spark plug electrodes. This voltage produces the familiar spike on ignition scope patterns. The time that it takes to reach required voltage is called *rise time.* Ionization breaks down spark plug gap resistance and the required voltage falls to about one-fourth of the spike-peak voltage as the arc is established. Duration of the arc is fed by inductance as the magnetic lines of force continue to collapse through the secondary windings. This portion of the ignition scope pattern is called the *spark line.* Ignition takes place during capacitive discharge and during the first part of inductive discharge.

The total energy that can be stored in the coil is based on the amperes flowing in the primary circuit and on the length of time the current can flow before the breaker points reopen. Primary current is limited by the current-carrying ability of the breaker points. Normally, the primary current is limited to a 4.2 A flow, which allows the breaker points to last thousands of miles. If primary current flow were increased to 5.4 A, the breaker points would burn in a very few miles. The ability to operate with high primary currents is one of the main advantages of transistor and capacitive-discharge ignition systems. A power transistor can carry twice as much current as breaker points without being damaged. The length of time the primary current can flow to build up the magnetic field is limited by the number of degrees the crankshaft turns while the breaker points are closed and by the engine speed. The longer the current can flow, the more energy will be stored in the coil until the coil is saturated. At low engine speeds, more energy can be stored in the coil than at high engine speeds, as a result of greater coil saturation time by the primary current. The primary circuit is responsible for producing available voltage in the secondary circuit.

The total stored coil energy is dissipated as voltage and current within the arc that forms across the spark plug electrodes. This energy can be released in a very short period of time with high voltage and high current flow or it can be released slowly at a low voltage and low current flow. Energy release from the coil can be compared to electrical energy release through light bulbs. A given amount of electrical energy from a battery can be released through an instantaneous brilliant flash of a flash bulb or through a sustained dim light of a flashlight. For ignition systems, a fast energy release across the spark plug electrodes provides the best ignition of the charge. It is called a *fast rise time* because the capacitive portion of the energy releases rapidly, producing the ignition scope pattern spike. Fast rise time will force the arc to jump across the electrode gap on a partly fouled spark plug; however, this type of operation is demanding on secondary insulation because this same high voltage will try to flash over the secondary insulation, too.

Fast rise time reduces the problem of slight electrical drains. Energy discharge occurs so rapidly

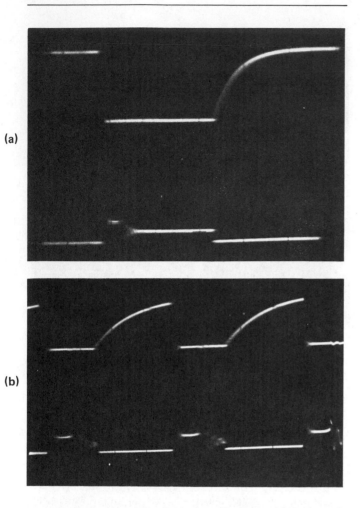

(a)

(b)

Fig. 10-13 Current flowing in the coil primary. (a) Engine running at low speed, (b) engine running at high speed.

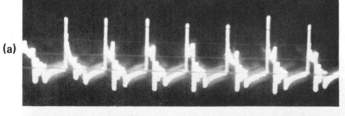

(a)

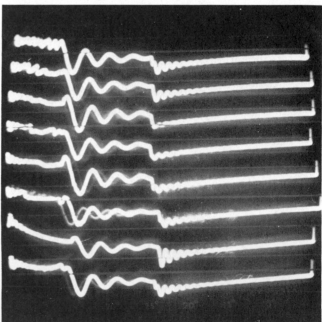

(b)

Fig. 10-14 Typical ignition scope patterns with some malfunctions. (a) Secondary parade display, (b) secondary raster, (c) primary parade display.

(c)

that it does not allow time for slight drains, such as fouled spark plugs, to divert any significant amount of energy. One of the main advantages of C-D (capacitive-discharge) ignition is its very fast rise time.

10-5 PRIMARY CONDENSER

A condenser is installed electrically across the breaker points in the ignition system. It is made from two long strips of electrical conductor foil plates separated by insulating paper. The number of electrons that can accumulate on one side of a plate is limited by the plate size and the distance between plates. The larger and closer together the plates are, the more electrons they can store. This electron storage ability is called *capacitance*. The measurement of capacitance is a *farad*. It is a very large unit, so the smaller unit, *microfarad* (mfd = 10^{-6} farad), is used to describe the capacitance of automotive ignition system condensers.

Fig. 10-15 Parts of an ignition condenser.

The condenser foil strip plates and insulation are rolled together, then placed in a container and sealed. A lead wire contacts one foil strip and the container case contacts the other. The strips of foil are close together so there is electrical attraction between electrons and electrical holes across the insulation paper. The insulation paper keeps the circuit open so the electrons cannot cross to the other plate.

When the breaker points are closed, the primary circuit is complete and a current flows through the primary coil windings. When the breaker points open, the primary current is interrupted, causing the coil magnetic field to start to collapse. This collapse produces an induced voltage that tends to keep the primary current flowing. This induced voltage (shown on the primary scope pattern) may reach 250 V which is high enough to force the electrons across the breaker gap as the points are beginning to open. An arc across the breaker point gap would absorb electrical energy

and reduce available voltage. The condenser provides a place for the electrons in the primary current to go during initial breaker-point opening. The attraction of the positive condenser plate is so great that the electrons move freely into the negative plate, producing a high voltage charge on the negative plate. As the electrons pack into the condenser, they bring the primary current to a quick controlled stop which, in turn, causes a rapid collapse of the primary magnetic field. During this time, the breaker points have opened far enough so that the voltage will not cause flashover across the breaker point gap. The slow buildup and sudden stop of the primary current can be seen in Figure 10-13.

The high electron charge on the negative plate attempts to fill the holes in the positive plate. With the breaker points open, the only way for the electrons to get to the positive plate is back through the battery and primary circuit. As they flow back, they cause a reverse current flow through the coil primary that forces a complete magnetic field collapse from its original direction and produces a magnetic field buildup in the opposite direction. Electrons flow in this direction until they pack into the other side of the condenser plate, leaving holes behind them. This high charge in the reverse direction causes a second reversal and a current again flows forward through the primary circuit producing an oscillation of the primary current. Each cycle has less intensity, until the electrical energy is expended. This can be seen on the primary scope pattern. The entire cycle is repeated when the breaker points close to again store energy in

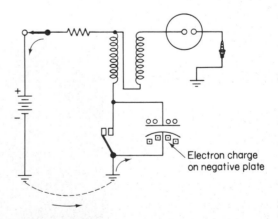

Fig. 10-16 Positive and negative charges on the condenser plates when the contact points open.

135

the coil by allowing a primary current to flow from the battery.

This rapid collapse of the primary magnetic field produces the high secondary voltage (up to 25,000 V) required to ionize the spark plug electrode gap and force the arc across. The primary current flow; the rate of collapse of the coil primary magnetic field; and the coil winding ratio between the primary and secondary windings is responsible for the maximum available voltage in the ignition system. The system seldom operates at this maximum voltage. It will only produce the amount of voltage that is required to fire the spark plug at the operating conditions.

10-6 LEAKAGE

Available voltage is produced from the total energy stored in the coil by the primary current. This energy can be reduced by secondary leakage. Leakage erodes useful available voltage by shunting some of the energy around the spark plug electrodes. One of the main causes of ignition leakage is spark plug fouling. Spark plug fouling occurs when conducting deposits build up on the nose of the spark plug insulator within the combustion chamber. If this leakage is small, the spark plug will fire. As the leakage increases, it drains away electrical energy, so that there is not enough energy remaining to produce the required arc across the spark plug gap. Leakage from spark plug fouling is indicated on the oscilloscope by a low spike with the spark line slanting steeply downward to the right.

The ignition system is designed for a very rapid energy release, or fast rise time, so that the energy will be released faster than it can leak away and, therefore, will be able to flash across the spark plug electrode gap swiftly before appreciable leakage occurs.

Secondary leakage also occurs through weak or cracked secondary insulation, especially at wire-supporting brackets; across dirty coil tops; across dirty spark plug insulators and across dirty distributor caps. Moisture and carbon tracks inside the distributor are other paths of electrical leakage. This type of leakage is indicated by a higher spike with the spark line slanting steeply downward to the right.

Corona accompanies high secondary voltages. It is an external leakage along ignition wires that is sometimes visible in the dark. Corona increases as the conductor becomes wet and dirty. Eventually, corona will lead to insulation failure and secondary leakage.

From the foregoing discussion, it would seem desirable to increase ignition system energy to overcome all required voltage and leakage. An over-capacity ignition system, however, rapidly erodes the spark plug electrodes and insulators to give short spark plug life. It also overloads the secondary insulation so that it will fail permaturely.

In summary, ignition systems are designed to supply enough energy to the spark plug electrode arc to raise the temperature of the charge located between the electrodes to kindling temperature and vaporize any remaining liquid fuel. This must be hot enough that the small flame is not quenched by the cool spark plug parts and the cool cylinder head. The ignition system energy must be large enough to meet ignition requirements and still be able to give maximum service life without overloading the ignition system.

Fig. 10-17 Secondary scope pattern showing a fouled spark plug in the center pattern.

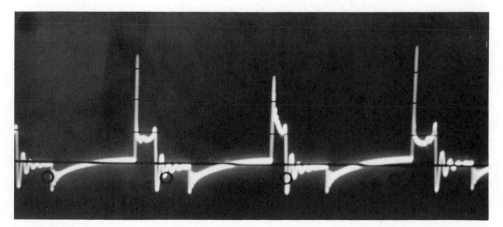

Twelve-volt automotive ignition systems use a resistor or ballast in the primary circuit to control available voltage and total energy stored in the coil. This may be a separate resistor or a resistor wire between the ignition switch and coil. With current flow the resistance increases as its temperature increases. During low speed operation, the ignition breaker points are closed for a longer period of time than at high speeds, so more current will flow. The current reduction resulting from increased resistor temperature reduces breaker-point burning during low speed operation. At high engine speeds the points are closed for shorter periods of time and so the resistor cools and its resistance drops. This allows higher voltage to reach the coil for more rapid coil saturation. This change can be observed on a voltmeter with the positive lead on

the resistor side of the coil and negative lead on ground. When the ignition is first turned on with closed points, voltage will be high. As the resistor heats the voltage drops.

The ballast type of resistor is designed to maintain constant resistance regardless of its temperature. It limits primary current at low temperature while still providing an adequate current at high temperatures.

The ignition resistor provides about one-half of the total resistance in the primary circuit and is the only part of the ignition system that is temperature-compensated.

During cranking, the ignition resistor is bypassed so that the entire electrical-system voltage is placed across the coil, as shown in the accompanying illustration. This provides a momentary overload for a few cycles until the engine starts. The voltage in the electrical system during cranking is lowered to about 10 V by the heavy starter current draw and therefore the voltage is not excessive for the coil. When the engine starts, the electrical system voltage increases to the regulator voltage setting, about 14 V. The resistor then becomes effective to limit the running voltage of the coil to approximately 7 to 8 V when the breaker contact points are momentarily closed as the engine operates.

(a)

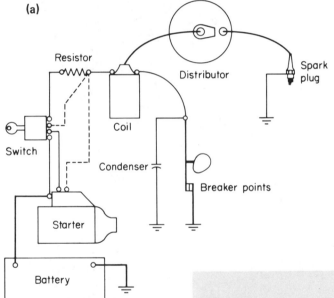

(b)

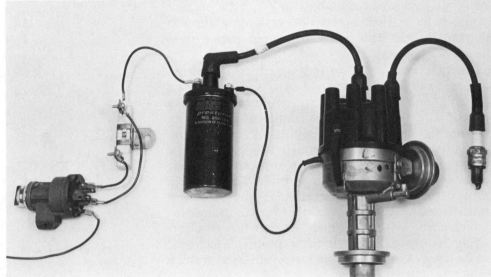

Fig. 10-18 Typical ignition system.
(a) Schematic, (b) parts connected together.

10-8 SEMICONDUCTOR IGNITION

The conventional inductive ignition system just described, invented by Charles Kittering, is the most economical type of ignition system to produce. It has some shortcomings that can be overcome by using one of the ignition systems incorporating semiconductor electronics that were first introduced commercially in 1962.

Secondary available voltage is limited by a 5-ampere maximum current flow which the breaker points can handle. Electronic ignition systems remove the breaker points from the coil primary circuit. A primary current as high as 10 amperes is carried by a power transistor to increase coil saturation and this, in turn, increases available voltage. One type of system uses breaker points, without a condenser, to send an electrical pulse which will trigger a transistor. The transistor will transmit electrical energy from the battery to the coil in a more efficient manner than the breaker points alone can do. When used as a pulse trigger, the breaker points are required to carry only 1.0 ampere so they will not burn as rapidly as conventional points. This gives the breaker-point contact surfaces an extended service life.

Breaker points have further limitations even when they are used with transistors. The low current flow across the contact surfaces allows the points to become dirty and so they will not conduct electricity. Breaker points still have rubbing block wear and therefore require periodic replacement, even when the contact surface is excellent. At high engine speeds, above 6000 rpm, breaker points tend to float or bounce, causing ignition to become erratic. This limits high-speed engine operation.

A second type of semiconductor ignition system replaces the breaker points and cam with a rotating *pole piece, armature,* or *reluctor* and a pickup coil to form a *breakerless* ignition system. In normal operation the transistor circuit conducts primary current through the coil. As the pole piece, armature or reluctor turns, the magnetic field across the pickup coil reverses. This momentarily stops current flow through the switching transistor. This turns off the power transistor, which abruptly stops primary current flow as effectively as opening the breaker points. Electronic circuitry delays the power transistor from turning

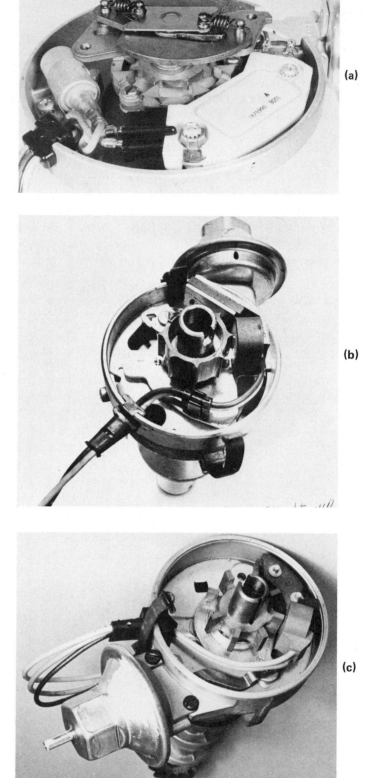

(a)

(b)

(c)

Fig. 10-19 Breakerless distributors. (a) Armature, (b) reluctor, (c) pole piece.

back on until the spark plugs have fired; then it immediately turns back on. This effectively provides a dwell over 40 degrees on eight-cylinder engines.

The conventional inductive Kittering ignition system can be replaced by a capacitive-discharge (C-D) system. A third type of ignition system uses breaker points to trigger a C-D system, while a fourth type is a breakerless C-D ignition system triggered by a rotating pole piece similar to the second type of ignition system previously described.

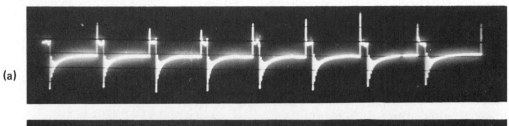

(a)

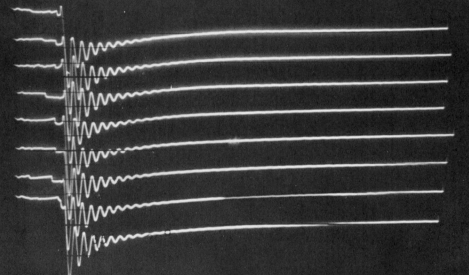

Fig. 10-20 Ignition scope pattern of an electronic ignition system. (a) Secondary display, (b) secondary raster, (c) primary raster.

(b)

(c)

Modern semiconductor technology and devices make it possible for automotive electronic engineers to produce any desired type of ignition pulse that is needed. They can change the ignition system electrical energy content, available voltage, rise time, and spark duration. The ignition engineer has to balance the required ignition pulse against the complexity and cost of the system.

Ignition electrical energy must be able to produce enough heat in the arc to ignite the combustion gases surrounding the spark plug electrodes. Some of the discharge energy of the arc may be required to vaporize a small part of the fuel mixture that remains as a liquid before combustion can take place. If this is not done by the capacitive portion of the arc discharge, the additional heat energy for this vaporization must be provided by the inductive portion of the arc discharge. To get more electrical energy from the coil it must be saturated with more electrical energy (electrical energy = watts = amperes × volts). The ignition primary system voltage is limited by the battery and the charging

system regulator which means that any increased electrical energy in the Kittering ignition system must be the result of increased current flow. The use of a power transistor allows the primary current to be raised while at the same time it lowers the current flow through the breaker points to eliminate breaker-point burning. The power transistor also allows the use of breakerless transistor switching.

Increasing the electrical energy content of the ignition system provides the system with more available voltage. Secondary available voltage much above 30 KV is of questionable value to engine operation and it is above any required voltage used by spark-ignited internal combustion engines. Late-model engines with lower compression ratios for emission reduction have a lower required voltage than the high-compression-ratio engines built a few years ago. This is offset by the high voltage required to fire lean mixtures. Secondary voltage above 30 KV (1 KV or kilovolt = 1,000 V) will tend to break down secondary insulation and produce cross-firing inside the distributor cap, across the rotor, or through the secondary ignition cables. Secondary components with very high insulation are used with high energy ignition systems.

(a)

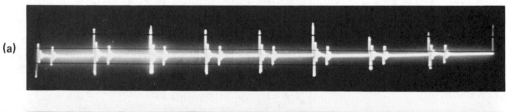

Fig. 10-21 CD ignition system scope patterns. (a) Secondary display, (b) primary raster.

(b)

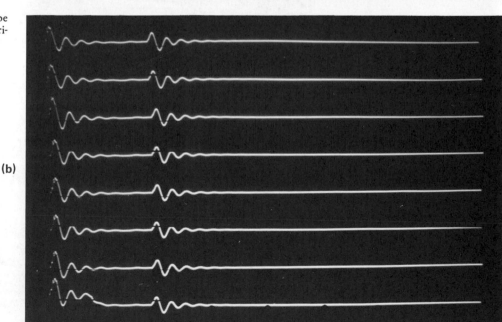

Rise time is the time it takes the secondary voltage to reach the required voltage level. On an ignition scope this appears to be instantaneous and forms the spike on a typical secondary firing pattern. If the sweep speed of the scope is increased it can be seen that the spike actually does take a very short time to rise to the required voltage level.

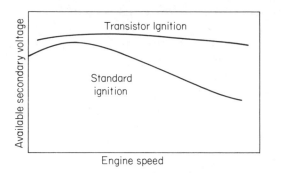

Fig. 10-22 Available voltage compared between standard ignition and transistor ignition.

This time is measured in microseconds (one microsecond = 0.000001 sec). As soon as the voltage starts to rise some electrical leakage occurs. This is most evident as spark plugs foul with electrically conducting deposits. With a slow rise time electrical energy bleeds off nearly as fast as the coil secondary produces it and so no spark can occur across the spark plug gap. A fast rise time will build up required voltage and form an arc before the energy can leak away.

Spark duration must be long enough to form a good self-propagating flame in the combustion chamber. Turbulence in the combustion chamber that is produced as the charge is compressed may blow the initial flame from the spark plug before a good flame-front is established. If the spark duration is too short the charge will not reignite and the cylinder will misfire. Lean mixtures, especially at part-throttle cruising speeds, require more heat to ignite them than rich mixtures do, and so increased spark duration is helpful. More of the ignition electrical energy will be available for spark duration if the rise time is kept short.

The conventional Kittering ignition system has an average available voltage of 24 KV, a rise time of approximately 120 microseconds, and a spark duration near 1200 microseconds. Breakerless transistor ignition systems have an average available voltage of 30 KV, a rise time of 180 microseconds and a spark duration of 1800 microseconds. Capacitive-discharge ignition systems have an average available voltage of 32 KV, a rise time

of 3 to 35 microseconds, depending on the design, and a spark duration of 200 microseconds, which releases the coil energy in a shorter time and thus produces a more intense spark because there is a higher momentary current flow in the arc. Spark duration is shown as the length of the spark line on the secondary scope pattern.

None of the systems is best for all conditions. Under part throttle engine load using high distributor-vacuum advance, a condition which occurs at freeway cruising speeds, a long spark duration is required. This is beneficial to smooth operation because combustion may not take place until more than 200 microseconds have elapsed after the spark plug gap is ionized during the voltage rise. This condition would cause misfire on a C-D system because the C-D system has a very short spark duration. Fast rise time of the C-D system will, however, reduce electrical leakage loss so it is possible to operate spark plugs in a fouled condition where the standard and transistor electronic ignition systems would not operate. This ability of the C-D ignition system will also aid in easy engine starting. It also works well on engines with rich air/fuel mixtures. With any type of ignition system, engine performance will be lost when the secondary available voltage is no longer high enough to form an arc across the spark plug gap, causing a misfire that will reduce high-speed performance and fuel economy and will produce large amounts of unburned hydrocarbon emissions.

Semiconductor ignition has been an available option on some automobiles since 1962. A number of after-market kits and system diagrams are available. Generally speaking, the semiconductor ignition systems are sophisticated and complex. This increases their cost. They have no advantage for emission control, performance, or economy as long as the engine can continue to fire each cylinder and each power stroke at the correct instant. They require special radio-frequency suppression when the automobile is using UHF radio equipment. In operation the conventional ignition system deteriorates and no longer correctly fires the charge, or the timing changes as a result of point and distributor wear. The breakerless semiconductor ignition system, on the other hand, may continue to function properly. The main advantage to a breakerless semiconductor ignition system in a passenger car is that it minimizes the need for ignition system maintenance, except for spark plugs, spark plug cables, rotors, and distributor caps. This has become sufficiently important on emission-controlled engines that Chrysler Corporation made breakerless transistor ignition standard on certain engines in 1972 and on all engines in 1973. Other manufacturers soon followed, and in 1975 all engines were equiped with these systems. Many owners neglect and fail to properly maintain the standard ignition system and so their engines operate poorly and produce an abnormal quantity of hydrocarbon emissions. The breakerless transistor ignition system will remain at peak efficiency. If it fails, the engine stops and the faulty component will have to be replaced. The electronic components cannot be repaired. If the system is going to fail about one-third of the failures will occur in the first 100 miles (160 Km) and two-thirds will occur in the first 2000 miles (3200 Km), well within the warranty period. After 2000 miles (3200 Km), the chances of system failure are extremely low.

The first semiconductor ignition systems made use of low-cost germanium transistors. These frequently failed if they were warmed above 160°F (15.5°C). Under-hood temperatures of emission-controlled automobiles go above this temperature. Silicon semiconductors have replace germanium transistors to provide ignition system reliability throughout a temperature range from –40°F (-40°C) to 225°F (108°C). The electronic components of the semiconductor ignition system are fastened to printed circuit boards. These circuit boards are secured in a metal case and the case is then filled with epoxy resin to prevent vibration failures, to seal the components from moisture, and to act as a heat sink which will transfer heat from the electronic components to the surrounding air.

Ignition coils used with conventional Kittering ignition systems have a winding ratio of 100 secondary turns to one primary turn. Some transistor systems operate with the same coil while others have fewer primary windings to make a ratio as high as 250 to 1. This reduces primary resistance, allowing more current to flow. Some C-D systems use a close-coupled coil with a winding ratio as low as 10 secondary windings to one primary winding because they have a very high primary current resulting from a primary voltage as high as 400 volts which occurs for a very short period of time. The secondary winding may be connected directly to

ground rather than grounded through the primary as is done in the conventional ignition system. For satisfactory operation it is important that the correct coil be used with each system.

Breaker points degrade because of pitting and oxidation buildup on the contacts. This is a result of heat produced during point opening as a small arc is formed. They may also degrade by becoming dirty from lack of sufficient current flow. In addition, the rubbing block will wear, changing dwell and basic timing. The mechanically operating points can float or bounce at high speed, causing misfiring. Using a breakerless pulse generator in the distributor eliminates all of these problems.

The pulse is created as a rotating pole piece, armature, or reluctor is turned past a magnet. The magnet in the distributor is made from powdered metallic barium-ferrite bonded with phenolic resin. When protrusions or projections line up, the magnetic lines of force are free to concentrate through the pole pieces, armature, or reluctor. This reduces the system *reluctance,* which is the resistance to magnetic lines of force. An instant after this alignment occurs the magnetic lines of force reverse through the pickup coil to produce a voltage pulse signal which is sensed by the ignition amplifier. The amplifier produces the current required to trigger the ignition coil.

Fig. 10-23 Electronic ignition system amplifiers.

The distributor used in the semiconductor ignition system is similar to the distributor used with the conventional ignition system. It uses the same mechanical advance and vacuum curves because these are made to match the ignition timing requirements of the engine. The mechanical characteristics of the distributor are more critical if the system is to be service-free while it maintains ac-

(a)

(b)

Fig. 10-24 Breakerless ignition systems. (a) CD system components, (b) parts of a unitized high energy ignition system with the coil located in the distributor cap.

curate timing. Distributor bearings must be accurately aligned and sized, permanently lubricated, and rigidly supported to provide required rotor shaft alignment for a long service life.

A trend toward maintenance-free electronic controls in automobile components has been firmly established. This trend has been rapidly increasing as technology, manufacturing capacity, and reliability increase and as cost is reduced. The trend is also apparent in the use of electronic components to control no-skid braking and no-spin acceleration systems. Electronic fuel injection is within the capability of manufacturing but the need for it at this time is not as great as its higher cost. It is becoming more and more important for the automotive technician to have a good understanding of operating procedures and testing principles used in semiconductor controlled systems.

10-9 DISTRIBUTOR OPERATION

The ignition distributor is driven from the engine camshaft at one-half crankshaft speed. The breaker points, condenser, rotor, cap, and timing-advance mechanisms are located in the distributor. This arrangement puts all of the moving parts of the ignition system into a single unit.

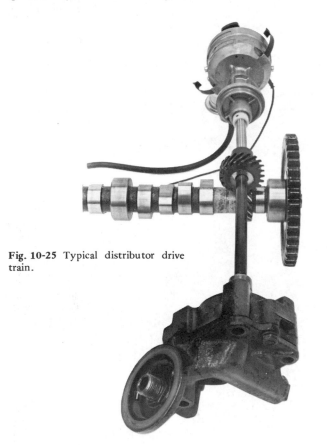

Fig. 10-25 Typical distributor drive train.

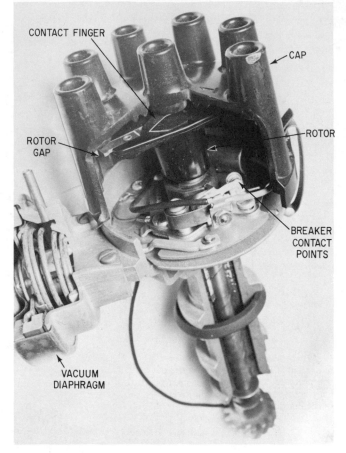

Fig. 10-26 Typical parts in a distributor.

The distributor gets its name from the portion that directs the secondary output to the spark plugs in the correct order to match the engine firing order. Coil secondary output is fed to the center distributor cap tower. It flows through the tower to a button inside the cap. A spring clip contact finger on the rotor contacts the center button. The rotor has a conductor plate from the spring clip to an extended tip that comes close to the distributor cap electrodes as the rotor turns. It lines up with each distributor cap electrode in sequence as the breaker points open. This allows the secondary impulse to be directed through each spark plug lead to the spark plug in the correct firing order.

It is convenient to locate the breaker-point cam on the same shaft as the rotor because these two parts must always maintain their relative position for rotor and electrode alignment. A breaker-point contact set is attached to the breaker plate within the distributor. Adjustments are provided to allow the points to be positioned closer to the cam for a larger point gap or away from the cam for a smaller point gap.

One cam lobe is provided for each cylinder. Four-cylinder cam lobes are spaced at 90°; six-cylinder cam lobes are spaced at 60°; and eight-cylinder cam lobes are spaced at 45°. Within each of these cam angles, the points must be closed long enough to store electrical energy in the coil and must open far enough to minimize point arcing. The points are normally closed from 65 to 70% of the cam angle to provide coil saturation. This is known as the *dwell angle.* Any change in the breaker point gap will change the dwell approximately one degree for each 0.001 in. (0.025 mm) change in point gap.

The distributor cam opens the breaker points and a breaker point spring closes the points. A weak

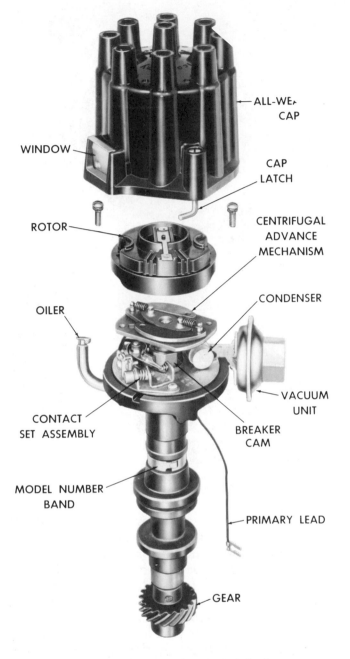

ALL-WEA
CAP

WINDOW

CAP
LATCH

ROTOR

CENTRIFUGAL
ADVANCE
MECHANISM

OILER

CONDENSER

CONTACT
SET ASSEMBLY

VACUUM
UNIT

BREAKER
CAM

MODEL NUMBER
BAND

PRIMARY LEAD

GEAR

Fig. 10-27 Exploded view of a typical distributor
(Delco-Remy Division, General Motors Corporation).

breaker point spring will allow the points to be
thrown clear of the cam and so they will float and
bounce when they close. When this happens, the
points will not be able to close fast enough, the
dwell period with the points closed will be short-
ened, and consequently the available voltage will be
reduced. Excessively high breaker point spring
tension will cause rapid rubbing-block wear and the
point gap will reduce. This will also reduce available voltage.

Fig. 10-28 Breaker contact points in distributors.

145

Fig. 10-29 Typical mechanical advance mechanisms.

Original-equipment distributor points are designed to maintain constant breaker point gap and dwell. Normal breaker points gradually burn, which tends to enlarge the gap. This is countered as the breaker-point rubbing block wears on the cam, which tends to close the gap. These two service wear conditions counteract each other to keep the breaker-point gap nearly constant. If wear caused the breaker-point gap to decrease, the engine's basic timing angle would be retarded. If wear caused the gap to increase, the timing would advance.

The breaker-point cam is driven by the distributor shaft through a mechanical advance mechanism. The advance mechanism consists of centrifugal flyweights that are retained by springs. As the distributor shaft rotates faster, the flyweights swing outward against spring pressure. Cam surfaces on the flyweights will advance or move the breaker-point cam position forward in the direction of cam rotation in relation to the distributor shaft position. The distributor shaft drive is timed to a specific crankshaft angle with the distributor advance mechanisms in full retard. The distributor shaft always maintains this position in relation to the crankshaft while the distributor advance mechanism moves from this timing base that is called *basic timing*. The mechanical centrifugal advance is sensitive to engine speed, advancing the ignition timing as engine speed increases to compensate for the constant

combustion rate that occurs while the first 10% of the combustion chamber charge burns. Flyweights and springs control the amount of timing change at any specific engine speed by turning the cam in the direction of shaft rotation so that the contact points open sooner. In service, the amount of advance is checked on a distributor machine or advance controls on a timing light. The actual advance is compared against advance specifications. Corrections in advance rate are usually made by changing the counterweight springs or by adjusting the spring hanger position.

The breaker plate, upon which the breaker points mount, is movable within the distributor housing and is held in position by a link from a vacuum diaphragm. To sense vacuum at a port within the carburetor, the outside portion of the vacuum diaphragm is connected by tubing. High, ported-vacuum pulls the diaphragm which, in turn, pulls the breaker plate in an advance direction against the direction of rotation; this opens the contact points sooner. During high ported-vacuum operation, the engine runs with a less dense lean

Fig. 10-30 Typical vacuum advance diaphragm assemblies.

charge mixture is more dense and usually richer as the manifold vacuum drops. This requires less advance to complete combustion at $5° - 10°$ after top center. The vacuum advance mechanism is sensitive to manifold vacuum which, in turn, is sensitive to engine load and throttle position.

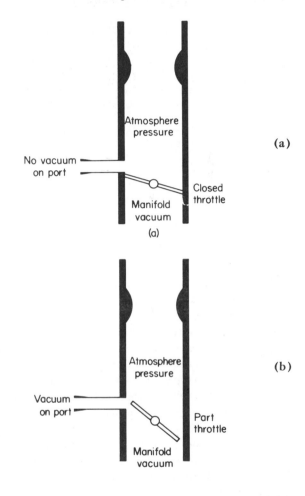

Fig. 10-31 Vacuum port in a carburetor. (a) Opening above the closed throttle, (b) opening below the partly open throttle.

mixture that burns slowly and, therefore, requires a high advance to complete combustion at the correct $5° - 10°$ after top center. As the throttle is opened, manifold vacuum is reduced. This lowers ported vacuum causing the vacuum advance mechanism to retard the breaker points. The combustion

In most carburetors, the vacuum-sensing port is located just above the high portion of a closed throttle plate. At full idle, with the throttle closed, no vacuum is applied to the distributor vacuum diaphragm, because the port opens into atmospheric pressure above the throttle plate. As the throttle is opened, the port is exposed to manifold vacuum so it will sense engine vacuum to advance the distributor.

147

The breakerless pulse generator located in the distributor uses the same mechanical centrifugal advance mechanism to provide the engine with the advance required by engine speed. The pickup coil is mounted on a movable plate just as breaker points are so it will be moved to provide advance that is sensitive to engine load and throttle position.

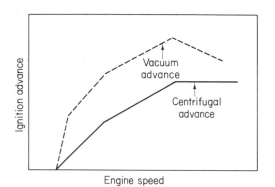

Fig. 10-32 Curve showing centrifugal and vacuum advance in relation to engine speed.

Mechanical and vacuum advance mechanisms work together to provide the engine with the advance required to give the most efficient combustion and lowest practical emission level at each operating condition. A change in the basic timing or advance mechanisms will cause normal performance to deteriorate. If, on the other hand, the engine is modified from the original manufacturer's configuration, timing and advance curves would also have to be modified to produce the most efficient performance. References on emission controls should be consulted for control devices used to modify the vacuum advance for minimum exhaust emissions.

10-10 SPARK PLUGS

The entire ignition system culminates in an arc between the spark plug electrodes. If the correct spark plug is not used, ignition will malfunction, resulting in a misfire. The spark plug must concentrate the conversion of the electrical energy to heat energy at a location in the combustion chamber which will ignite enough of the charge so that combustion of the remaining charge will proceed in a normal manner.

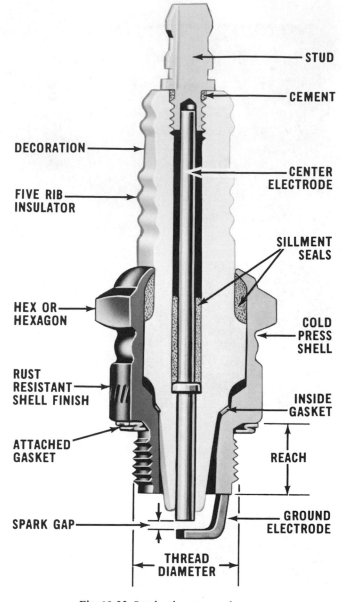

Fig. 10-33 Spark plug nomenclature (Champion Spark Plug Company).

The spark plug consists of three major parts: the shell, the insulator, and the electrodes. The shell supports the insulator and has threads that screw into the head. The thread portion must be long enough to allow the electrodes to enter the combustion chamber. This length is called the spark plug *reach*. If the reach were too long, it could damage the valves or piston. Threads on the spark plug are universal throughout the world; metric 14 mm and 18 mm threads are used. The shell seals the combustion-chamber spark plug hole. Some shells seal with a tapered spark plug seat. Others seal with a metal spark plug gasket.

The ceramic spark plug insulator is sealed inside the shell, so that it makes a pressure and

Fig. 10-34 Typical spark plugs used in modern automotive engines. The four on the left use gaskets. The two on the right have conical seats.

RESISTOR

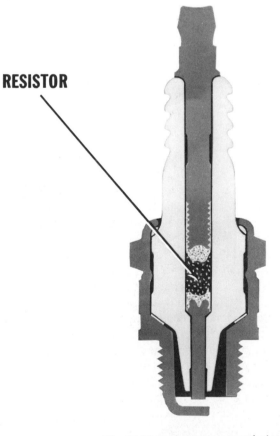

Fig. 10-35 Resistance-type spark plug (AC Spark Plug Division, General Motors Corporation).

thermal seal. Much of the spark plug development work has been concentrated on the insulator. It must withstand high thermal and mechanical stress as well as insulate high secondary voltage. During manufacture, the insulator ingredients are made into a putty-like consistency. The putty is formed in the insulator shape, then fired in a furnace. The finished insulator has close-to-diamond hardness. It is placed in the shell with sealing material, then the shell is crimped around the insulator to produce a gas-tight seal.

The center electrode is placed in a hole through the center of the insulator. Modern center electrodes are made from two pieces, one on which to attach the conductor and the other to extend into the hot combustion chamber. Using two pieces allows the spark plug manufacturer to select the type of metal that will best meet the requirements under which it must operate and to keep cost at a minimum. The electrode is sealed with a gas-tight electrically conducting seal material.

Some spark plug types have a resistor installed between the two sections of the electrode. Its 10,000-ohm resistance changes the ignition secondary oscillating frequency at the instant the arc is established across the electrodes. This change in frequency moves the electrical radiation out of the television and radio frequencies to suppress radiation noise interference. The resistor also provides long spark plug electrode life by cutting down peak current that flows in the arc across the electrode gap.

149

Spark plugs must operate within a specified temperature range. If the spark plug is too cold, it will foul with deposits. These deposits will bleed off coil electrical energy, so the spark plug will not fire. If the spark plug is too hot, it will erode rapidly and will cause preignition. Preignition will lead to physical engine damage. The minimum spark plug temperature for nonfouling operation is 650°F (350°C). Above 1500°F (825°C), preignition will occur. Spark plugs must operate within these temperatures under all normal operating conditions.

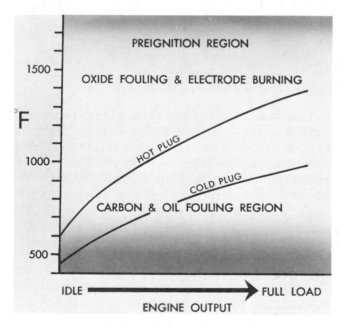

Fig. 10-36 Spark plug operating temperature heat limits controlled by the spark plug's heat range (Champion Spark Plug Company).

When an engine is running under heavy loads, such as in sustained high speed driving, the combustion chambers become hot. During these operating conditions, a cold spark plug is required to prevent spark plug overheating that would cause preignition. Engines that have a tendency to foul from oil or from light-duty operation may require hot spark plugs to keep their temperature high enough to eliminate fouling. Drag racing operation is such a short-time operation on each run that cold spark plugs may not be necessary. Spark plug temperature is controlled by designing different distances through which heat must pass to cool the spark plug nose. Hot spark plugs have long cooling

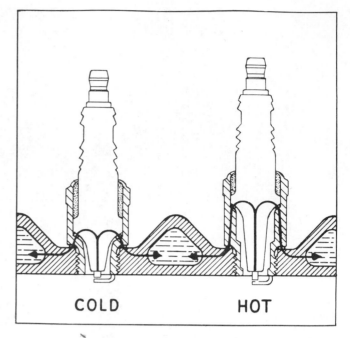

Fig. 10-37 The spark plug's cooling path controls its heat range (Champion Spark Plug Company).

paths while cold spark plugs have short cooling paths.

A cold spark plug transfers heat from the spark plug nose through the shell faster than a hot spark plug. The spark plug heat range selected for replacement spark plugs should match the manufacturer's specifications. Modified engines may require a different spark plug heat range than that specified for the original engine. Spark plugs for modified engines should be selected by working up from cold spark plugs. If fouling occurs, the next higher heat range that does not foul should be used. In this way, it is possible to avoid preignition.

The center electrode of the automotive spark plug normally has negative polarity. Hot bodies have increased electron activity. The center electrode is the hottest part of the spark plug and, therefore, requires the lowest voltage to free the electrons which form the arc. The hot negative center electrode helps to keep required voltage low. If the polarity is reversed, required voltage will increase. Secondary polarity can be changed by reversing the primary coil leads, and so care is required to see that coil connections are made correctly.

The appearance of the combustion-chamber end of a spark plug can indicate a number of things about the engine. If the spark plug is brown or gray and relatively clean, it is a normally operating spark plug. Dry fluffy carbon deposits indicate incomplete combustion. Oil pumping past the rings will produce oil-wet heavy deposits. Badly burned elec-

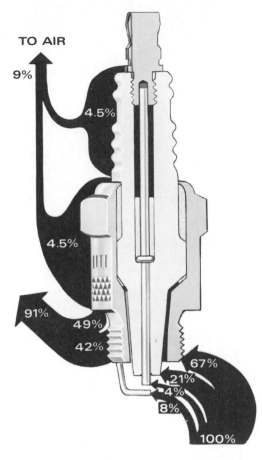

Fig. 10-38 Heat flow through a spark plug (Champion Spark Plug Company).

10-11 SPARK PLUG CABLES

Modern engines use nonmetallic resistance-type conductor secondary cables. As with spark plug resistors, these cables provide ignition radiation suppression (IRS cable) or television and radio noise suppression (TVRS cable) of radio-frequency emissions from the ignition system. Aluminum distributor cap electrode inserts are used with suppression-type ignition cables. Old model engines used metal conductor secondary cables with copper distributor cap inserts. Mixing distributor caps and cable types will produce corrosion which will add resistance to the secondary circuit.

Suppression-type ignition cable should not be replaced with metal conductor cable. Ignition systems are designed to satisfactorily handle the resistance built into the cable. The use of metal conductor cables on these systems will lead to rapid spark plug electrode erosion and to radio-frequency emission that causes interference in nearby radios and television sets. Federal Communication Commission laws prohibit the use of metal conductor secondary cables.

Emission-controlled engines run much hotter than nonemission control engines. Old style ignition cables will not last in these high under-hood temperatures. Care must be exercised to make sure that the proper high-temperature secondary cables are used for replacement in emission-controlled engines. High temperature cable insulation is made from either hyplon or silicone materials.

trodes are the result of overheating. Thermal shock from excessive timing advance or from detonation will break pieces out of the insulator nose. The practice of examining the spark plugs to determine engine conditions is often called *reading the plugs.*

Fig. 10-39 Typical spark plug conditions (The Prestolite Company).

151

REVIEW QUESTIONS

1. What distributor advance mechanism is sensitive to the load on an engine?

2. What distributor advance mechanism provides fuel economy?

3. How does volumetric efficiency affect the required voltage?

4. How does the air/fuel ratio of the charge affect required voltage?

5. What happens when required voltage is above available voltage?

6. When should maximum pressure occur in the combustion cycle?

7. What part of the combustion requires a specific time to complete?

8. What part of the combustion is proportional to engine speed?

9. When are compression pressures highest in the combustion chamber?

10. What induces a high voltage in the coil secondary windings?

11. How do the coil primary and secondary windings differ?

12. Why are the coil primary windings wrapped on the outside of the secondary windings?

13. What limits the maximum current flow through the primary windings?

14. What slows the rate of full primary current buildup?

15. What minimizes arcing across the breaker points as they open?

16. What causes the primary voltage to rise as high as 250 volts?

17. What part of the ignition scope pattern results from the capacitive discharge?

18. What part of the ignition pattern results from the inductive discharge?

19. In an ignition system, what is responsible for producing available voltage?

20. What causes spark plug fouling?

21. What reduces the problems that are caused by secondary leakage?

22. Why do contact breaker points last longer in transistor ignition systems than in conventional ignition systems?

23. How much change would be expected in dwell when the point gap changes 0.003 inch?

24. What change will occur in engine timing as the contact breaker point gap decreases?

25. What problem may be encountered when the spark plug heat range is above the normal range?

26. How can the correct spark plug heat range be safely found for a modified engine?

27. Why is the spark plug center electrode negative?

11

Ignition System Service

Ignition system service is necessary (1) to recondition the ignition system so that it will be able to produce its original high available voltage at the correct instant in the cycle and (2) to reduce required voltage to its normal low value.

All types of ignition systems use spark plugs. These operate in a combustion chamber with the hot combustion gases along with some oil that leaks past the piston rings and valve stems. Combustion deposits that are formed while the engine runs will coat the entire combustion chamber including the exposed portions of the spark plug. In some cases these deposits are electrically conducting. These tend to bleed electrical energy from the ignition system and so either a weak spark or no spark will form between the spark-plug electrodes. This condition is called *spark plug fouling*. In other cases insulating deposits build up on the spark plug between the electrodes. These deposits prevent the charge gases from getting between the electrodes where they must be to ignite. In either case the ignition system required voltage is affected and so the spark plugs must be serviced.

Ignition systems can deteriorate as the primary wires and secondary cables develop resistance or become shorted. Ignition system service includes checking the condition of all wires and cables, including their terminals and junctions. Distributor caps can crack or form an electrical path called a *carbon track* which will allow the secondary electrical energy to leak to ground or cross-fire to another cylinder. A faulty rotor will allow leakage to ground or will increase secondary resistance as the rotor tip erodes away.

Distributor timing-advance mechanisms operate mechanically. They are subject to wear and sticking which affects ignition timing for efficient engine operation, required engine power, and minimum engine exhaust emissions.

Ignition systems controlled by the typical breaker points require additional service. As the rubbing block wears the breaker point gap will reduce. This causes retarded ignition timing. Burning of the contact surface of the breaker points will change the point gap. This too will cause a change in timing. The breaker-point contact surface deterioration will also increase the resistance of the primary circuit. This resistance reduces primary current flow, which results in less coil saturation and less available voltage.

Using correct testing and servicing procedures, the technician can recondition the ignition system so that it will deliver the same performance as it did when it was new.

153

11-1 IGNITION TESTERS

The ignition system and the spark plug operation can be tested with meters and with an oscilloscope. Meter equipment is usually less costly than an ignition scope. Some meters require the use of spark plug adapters to pick up the secondary voltage signal while others pick up the desired signal electronically by using a selector switch. Instructions are furnished with the specific test equipment. Because there are rapid changes in test equipment design and in the number of makes on the market, it serves no purpose to give, in this text, a detailed procedure for any one specific test unit. In general, two types of tests are run with meter test equipment. One test measures the voltage being delivered to each spark plug. This is *required voltage*. The other test measures ignition output or *available voltage*. Output or available voltage is produced by removing one spark plug cable from the spark plug, thereby increasing the secondary ignition voltage requirement to the maximum voltage that the ignition system can produce. This should be done as quickly as possible on converter equipped engines to avoid converter damage.

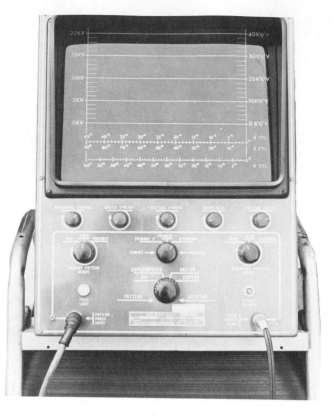

Fig. 11-2 Typical ignition oscilloscope.

An oscilloscope is similar to a television picture tube. An electron beam in the back of the tube is sent toward the front screen. If it is not disturbed it will make a light spot. Electronics cause the electron beam to sweep from the left side of the screen to the right at a specific speed when it is triggered. This forms a line on the scope screen. If it is not re-triggered, the beam stays on the right. If the beam is triggered half way through the sweep it starts over at the left of the screen.

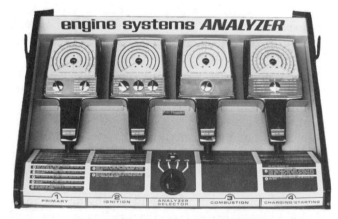

Fig. 11-1 Meter-type test equipment.

Ignition scopes are advanced test instruments to be used only after one understands all other tests. This discussion will present the ignition scope pattern that appears as normal on an operating engine to help the reader understand the operation of the ignition system. When an abnormal scope pattern exists other tests will usually have to be made to locate and verify the specific cause of the abnormality.

Fig. 11-3 Chassis of an ignition scope.

In ignition oscilloscopes a second signal, voltage, is sent into the scope. The greater the voltage the higher the sweep line will be. With less voltage the sweep line will be lower. When the electron beam sweep is occurring and the voltage is changing at the same time the line on the scope forms a number of characteristic patterns that indicate different types of ignition-system operation. Some ignition testers, both scope and meter types, have switches to short-out selected cylinders for more rapid diagnosis.

11-2 IGNITION SYSTEM TESTING

A short review of the ignition system will be helpful in understanding ignition system testing. The job of the ignition system is to supply high voltage to the spark plug at the correct instant to ignite the combustion charge so that it will burn efficiently to produce the required engine power.

Two circuits make up the typical induction ignition system that has been used in automobiles since the early days of the magneto. A primary system is connected into the automobile electrical system through the ignition switch to carry low-voltage primary current. The ignition primary system consists of a resistor, breaker points, a condenser, and the primary side of the coil. In electronic circuits a power transistor is used in place of the points. High voltage is developed in the secondary coil windings by magnetic interaction of the primary and secondary coil windings. This high voltage is carried in the ignition secondary circuit by highly insulated secondary ignition cables to the distributor cap, distributor rotor, and spark plugs. Both primary and secondary circuits are completed through the electrical conduction of the engine metal.

An instantaneous voltage high enough to force a small current through an arc formed between the spark plug electrodes is built up in the coil secondary windings at the moment the primary circuit breaker points open to stop primary current flow. The breaker points then close allowing primary current to flow again. This will magnetically resaturate the coil. When the points reopen there will be sufficient electrical energy stored in the coil to again produce an electrical surge having sufficient voltage to produce an arc across the spark plug gap. Even though the coil has capacity to develop a much higher voltage, the voltage produced will only be as high as necessary to form the arc. The excess electrical energy is dissipated through a longer arc duration.

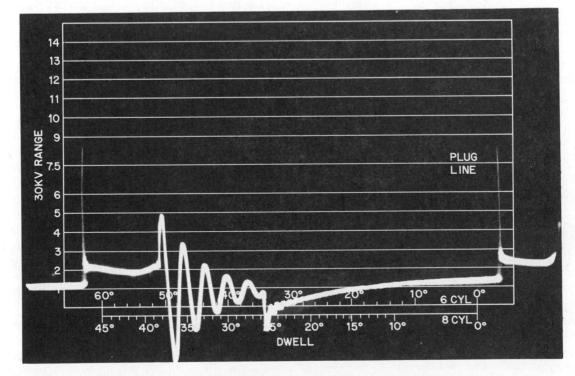

Fig. 11-4 A normal secondary ignition pattern of one cylinder.

Scope Patterns. The oscilloscope used in ignition-system testing is useful to give an overall view of the engine condition as it operates. The ignition scope has a voltage pickup on the coil-to-distributor secondary cable to measure secondary voltage. A second scope lead is connected to the number one spark plug cable as a trigger. Each time the number one spark plug fires, the scope is triggered and the pattern starts on the left side of the scope screen.

The ignition system must build up a sufficient voltage to force its way across the largest gap in the secondary circuit. This gap normally is the spark plug electrode gap. It requires about 7 to 8 KV as indicated by the top of the pattern spike. As soon as the electricity arcs across the gap it ionizes the charge gases between the gap to allow a small milli-amp current to flow; this reduces the voltage needed to maintain the arc. The lower arc voltage is indicated by the spark line that results from the immediate fall of secondary voltage to about 25% of the original required voltage, or to about 2 KV, as the coil dissipates its energy while it is providing current for the spark plug arc. After the arc is formed a small milliamp current flows in the secondary circuit. Because current is flowing, any resistances that are in the secondary system will affect the voltage level of the spark line portion of the scope pattern. Factors that produce secondary circuit resistance normally cause the spark line to slope downward toward the right. Factors that increase secondary circuit resistance in a spark plug cable or spark plug will cause the spark line voltage to be higher and shorter than normal, while factors that lower the resistance produce a spark line that is lower and longer than normal.

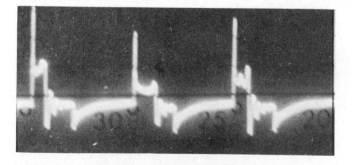

Fig. 11-5 Three variations of an ignition pattern. The left cylinder pattern shows a cylinder having high secondary resistance, the second shows low resistance, and the right pattern is normal.

When the coil energy is no longer sufficient to maintain an arc across the spark plug the spark line stops. This is followed by a series of five or more oscillations as the ignition system energy dissipates. Abnormal operation of the coil or condenser will reduce the number of these oscillations.

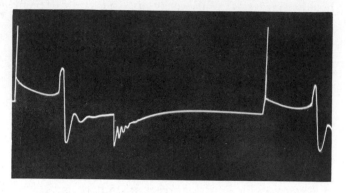

Fig. 11-6 An ignition pattern with a faulty coil-condenser oscillation immediately to the right of the spark line.

Breaker-point closing causes a momentary reverse voltage signal that produces a sharp dip in the pattern line. The pattern line comes up to normal as the coil saturates before the points open to produce a spike for the next cylinder firing. The horizontal line from the point closing signal to the next firing is the total time the points are closed and it is called *dwell*. Dwell is from 65 percent to 70 percent of the total distance between firing spikes. Most scopes are designed to allow a single pattern to be positioned over a scale that can be used to read dwell directly without the aid of a separate dwell meter.

The preceding discussion of the scope deals with the voltage that is actually being required to operate the engine. Required voltage is considered to be the voltage reached by the top of the spike on a scope pattern. The engine will run as long as the ignition system has more voltage available than that required by the engine. The available ignition system voltage can be measured on the scope by setting the scope pattern dwell line on the zero volt line and then removing one spark plug cable to force a voltage increase on that cable, causing the ignition system to develop full voltage. For normal operation the ignition system should be able to produce more than 20,000 volts to fire the spark plug.

Ignition scope checks are first used to check the coil output voltage while the engine is cranking. Then the engine is started. If the scope pattern is upside down the coil polarity is reversed. Reversed polarity can be corrected by reversing the primary

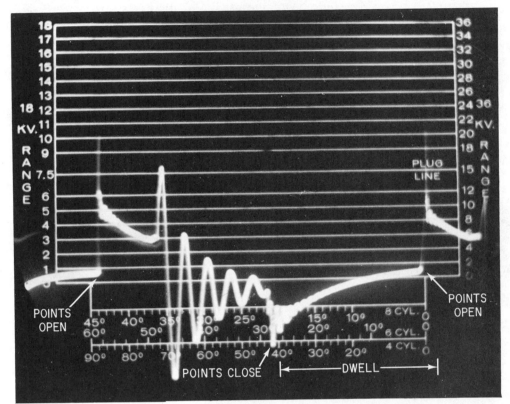

Fig. 11-7 A cylinder pattern with the spark line sloping to the right as a result of standard resistor ignition cables and a dwell of 28° for a 6-cylinder engine is shown.

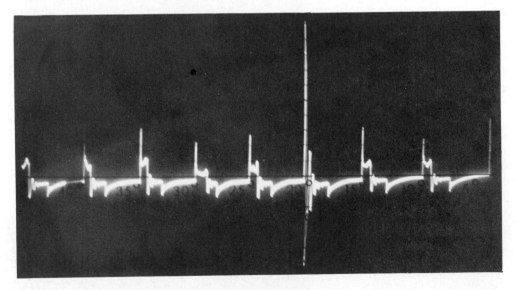

Fig. 11-8 A parade display pattern of eight cylinders with one spark plug wire removed to indicate available voltage. Notice the tail of the high available voltage spike is about one-half its height. Moving from left to right, the first cylinder pattern has a rising firing line indicating turbulence in the cylinder. The second pattern shows a fouled spark plug. The third indicates high resistance, the fourth low resistance, and the fifth is normal. Available voltage is shown on plug six, and the last two are normal.

wires attached to the coil. Coil polarity is important because required voltage is lower when the spark plug center electrode is negative than it is when the ground electrode is negative. Coil polarity can also be checked using a voltmeter. The meter should swing up-scale when the positive voltmeter lead is attached to the engine metal and the negative lead is touched to one of the spark plug cable terminals while the engine is running. Engines that have normal scope patterns need only routine maintenance on the ignition systems.

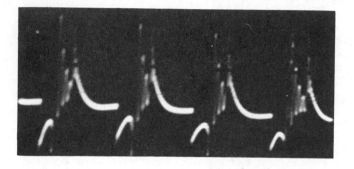

Fig. 11-9 An inverted scope pattern indicating reverse polarity.

Engine required voltage can be read directly on the scope as the height of the pattern spikes. It can also be read as a number or in a green band on some test instruments when one lead of the instrument is touched to the spark plug cable terminal of a running engine, and the other lead is connected to the engine metal.

The secondary circuit consists of the coil secondary windings, secondary ignition cables, distributor cap, rotor, and spark plugs. Voltage requirements increase as the spark plug gap increases or as other resistances develop in the system that are greater than the spark plug gap. Normal spark plug gap will increase about 0.001 in. (0.025 mm) each 1000 miles (1600 km) of operation so the required voltage gradually increases after a tune-up. If a secondary ignition cable is damaged its resistance can increase above the spark plug resistance to increase the required voltage. Normal ignition cable resistance should be below 20,000 ohms when measured with an ohmmeter. It is normal for long cables to have more total resistance than short cables. New cables have less than 9,000 ohms per foot (300 mm).

Breaker-point action cannot be seen on an instrument dial but it is clearly visible on the ignition scope. Faulty breaker point action is indicated by abnormal pattern characteristics at both the opening signal and the closing signal. If the points do not break cleanly the pattern will be hooked or curved at the base of the spike; there may also be a bright spot in the spike. Breaker-point arcing does not allow the secondary to provide maximum available voltage. This reduces the energy available for ignition which may result in misfiring. Point closing problems show up as multiple closing signals or as a momentary reverse voltage at the point-closing signal. A rough dwell line indicates a loose connection in the primary. These malfunctions reduce available voltage.

Electricity will not arc across the spark plug electrode gap when the voltage required is greater than the available voltage. This condition is most likely to occur at full throttle and at high speeds. Secondary circuit problems that causes unusually high required voltage are the spark plug gap and secondary resistance. Secondary resistance does not affect available voltage, which is developed by the primary.

Resistance and insulation breakdown are encountered in the secondary circuit. Secondary voltage builds up to 7 to 8 KV to strike an arc across

Fig. 11-10 A pattern showing arcing points. In this case, it was done with high condenser series resistance on an ignition simulator.

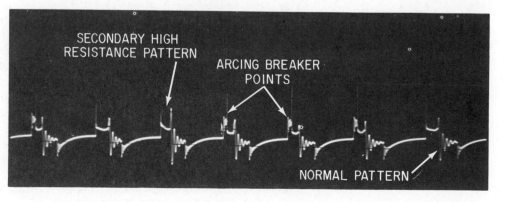

(a)

CARBON TRACK

(b)

FLASH-OVER
CRACK

Fig. 11-11 Flash-over that resulted from open secondary cables. (a) Cap, (b) rotor.

energy will go directly to ground. The secondary cables can crack and short at their supporting brackets. Flashover can occur on a rotor or within the distributor cap. It can even occur at the coil secondary tower. In each case less electrical energy remains to form the spark plug arc.

Ignition system leakage can be determined by using the ignition scope at the same time that available voltage is being measured. Available voltage is measured by pulling one of the spark plug cables from the spark plug to force the voltage as high as possible. The spike peak should go over 20 KV. The pattern also has a tail that should be approximately half the length of the upper spike. If leakage occurs the tail will be short, intermittently missing, or gone altogether. This test is done by *momentarily* removing each spark plug cable, in turn, to fully check the secondary insulation. Cross-firing between spark plug cables or within the distributor cap will show up as secondary leakage.

Available voltage depends upon the maximum electrical energy that can be stored in a coil between spark plug firings. The maximum electrical energy that can be stored in the coil depends upon the amount of current flowing in the primary circuit and the length of time it is allowed to flow. The amount of current that can flow depends upon good, resistance-free conductors. The length of time it flows depends upon how long the breaker points are together between each ignition firing. This is based on the engine speed and the number of degrees the breaker-point cam allows the points to remain closed during dwell. Dwell is mechanically set to specifications. As engine speed increases the energy stored in the coil becomes less, thus reducing coil magnetic saturation and available secondary voltage.

the spark plug electrode gap. This may go higher on lean-operating emission engines. If the secondary insulation is weak it will breakdown at these voltages, allowing some of the electricity to leak to ground. This is especially noticeable at full throttle when voltage requirements may go as high as 15 KV. When this happens the engine will misfire.

The secondary circuit can short or flash over the external spark plug insulator so that electrical

Fig. 11-12 Secondary leakage indicated by the short tail on available voltage spike when one spark plug was removed.

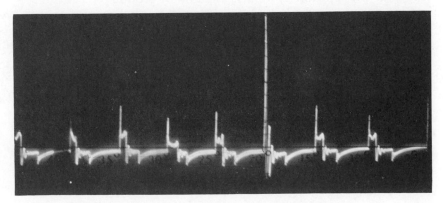

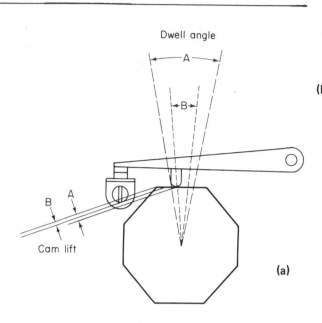

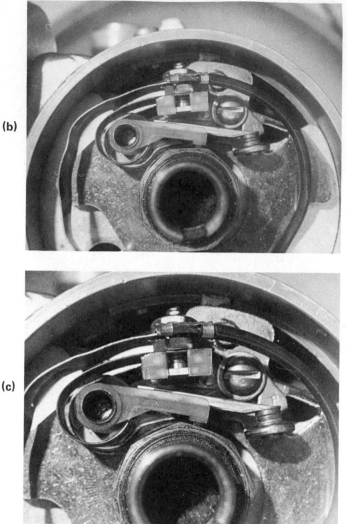

(b)

(c)

Fig. 11-13 Dwell. (a) A drawing showing how gap affects dwell, (b) the breaker points just closing as dwell begins with the cam turning clockwise. (c) the points just ready to open at the end of the dwell period. The degrees the cam rotates with the points closed is called dwell.

Semiconductor ignition systems can be checked using standard ignition test equipment found in service shops. Specialized testers are manufactured for specific ignition systems for rapid tests of the components. These units use switches and lights to indicate the component condition. When a fault occurs in the ignition circuit it can be traced in the same manner as in the standard Kittering ignition system.

Ignition Circuit. The mechanic can do two things, in addition to replacing faulty parts, to be sure that the ignition system is capable of producing maximum available voltage. First, he can be sure that there is no abnormal resistance in the primary circuit. Second, he can adjust the distributor point dwell if it is incorrect.

Electrical resistance in most automobile circuits is checked by the voltage drop method. With the normal current flowing in the circuit (ignition switch on and points closed), the leads of a sensitive voltmeter are placed at each end of the circuit being tested. About half of the normal circuit resistance is in the ignition resistor and the rest is in the primary windings of the coil.

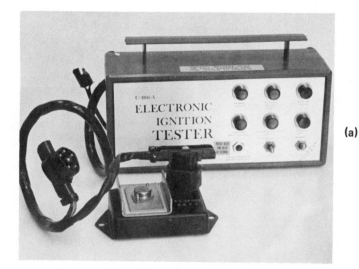

(a)

160

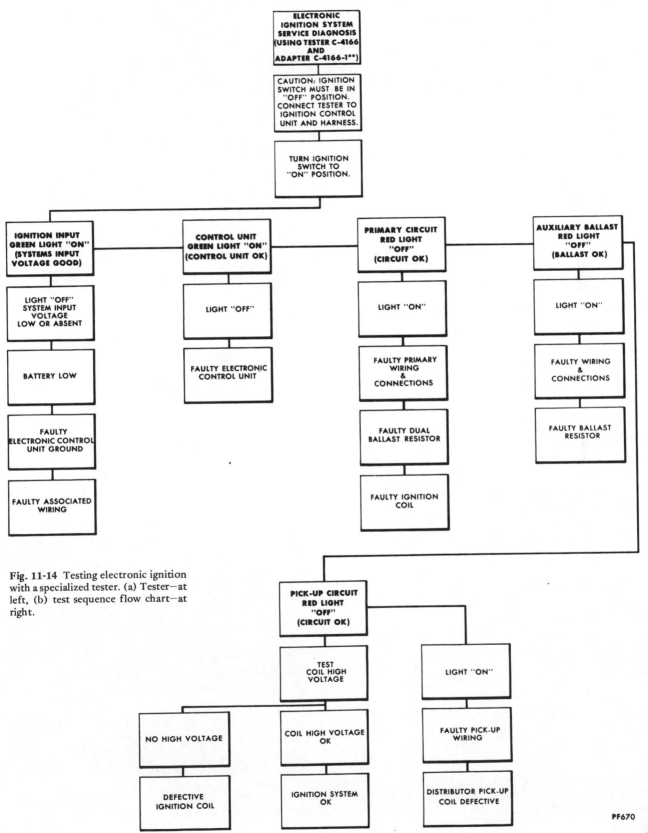

Fig. 11-14 Testing electronic ignition with a specialized tester. (a) Tester—at left, (b) test sequence flow chart—at right.

(b)

PF670

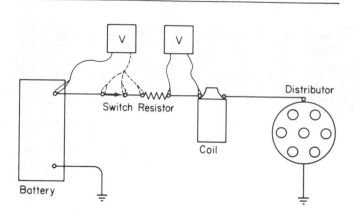

Fig. 11-15 Method used to measure the ignition circuit resistance with the points closed and the switch "on."

With the primary current flowing a large part of the circuit can be checked by placing the positive voltmeter lead on the positive battery post and the negative voltmeter lead on the switch side of the ignition resistor. A normal ignition system will have a maximum voltage drop of 0.5 volts. A voltage reading of less than 0.5 volts indicates a satisfactory primary ignition system while readings above 0.5 volts indicate abnormal resistance somewhere in the primary system. This resistance can be located by leaving one voltmeter lead attached to the battery and moving the other lead junction-to-junction along the primary ignition circuit, taking voltage drop readings at each junction. These junctions include the bulkhead connector, both ignition switch terminals, and the power pickup junction. The excessive resistance will be located at the last junction having an abnormally high voltage drop.

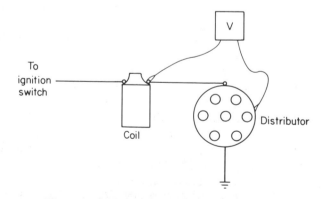

Fig. 11-16 Measuring the resistance of the breaker contact points with the ignition switch "on" and the points closed.

A second part of the primary circuit can be checked by placing the positive voltmeter lead on the coil side of the resistor and the negative lead on the resistor side terminal of the coil primary. With the ignition on and the points together there should be less than 0.1 volts reading on the voltmeter.

The last circuit test places the positive voltmeter lead on the distributor side of the coil primary and the negative lead on the distributor housing. With the ignition switch on and the points closed the voltmeter should read less than 0.1 volts. Voltages higher than this indicate distributor resistance, usually in the breaker-point contacts. It is helpful in understanding ignition if the engine is rotated to open the breaker points with this same voltmeter hook-up. When the breaker points open they have a resistance so high that no primary current can flow. The voltmeter will then read battery voltage.

The only other primary circuit tests are measures of the total resistance of the ignition resistor with an ohmmeter. An ohmmeter may be used to check the coil primary winding resistance but the coil is usually checked on a *coil tester.* Both resistors and coils are either good or bad. If they are not good they are not repairable and must be replaced, no matter whether the malfunction is a broken resistor or is in the primary or secondary coil windings.

An open secondary cable can cause an unusually high scope spike. Spikes over 10 KV at idle usually indicate an open cable. Excessive secondary cable resistance does not affect the spike height but it will affect the spark plug firing line. Excessive resistance causes the line to slope down steeply to

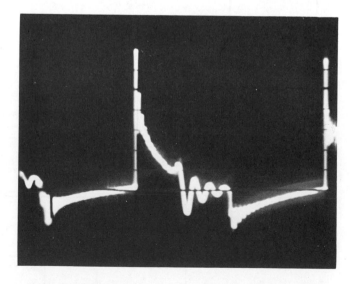

Fig. 11-17 Excessive resistance in ignition cables shown by the sloping spark line.

the right. A slight slope is normal with suppression ignition cables. Secondary resistance is affected by the distributor cap and rotor as well as by secondary ignition cables.

With the ignition scope in operation the engine should be given several momentary snap accelerations. These place a higher load on the ignition system. The scope spike will stretch upward. Carefully watch the spikes to make sure they are all nearly even. They usually will not go over 15 KV. This snap acceleration will also be a check of the carburetor acceleration pump. The engine should not hesitate or stumble during the acceleration.

11-3 POINTS AND CONDENSER

It is the usual practice during each periodic tune-up on engines with standard ignitions to change the breaker points and condenser without testing them. The condenser rarely causes trouble and seldom needs to be replaced, but the customer has had both points and condenser changed on tune-ups over the years so he usually expects to have a new condenser installed as part of the periodic tune-up. Often he feels cheated if a new condenser is not installed. Breaker points do wear. Their contact surfaces become pitted and the rubbing block wears. In breakerless electronic ignition systems this step is not required during a tune-up.

Breaker points are provided as an assembly set. Sometimes a cam lubricant is packaged with them so the cam will receive the correct type of

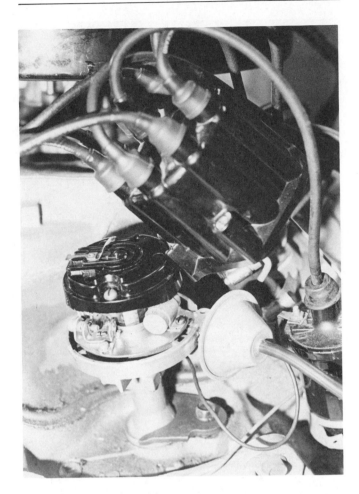

Fig. 11-19 Distributor with the cap removed exposing the rotor and points.

lubricant. Some parts suppliers selling to do-it-yourself consumers put all of the normally replaced ignition components in a single package. These would include points, condenser, spark plugs, rotor, and, sometimes, a distributor cap.

Two methods can be used to replace points and condensers. The amateur mechanic will usually change them while the distributor is installed in the engine, because he does not want to disturb the basic engine timing. The professional technician will usually remove the distributor from the engine because he can do a better and usually a faster job of replacing the breaker points and condenser. It also gives him a chance to examine the rest of the distributor for potential problems.

Breaker point replacement starts with removal of the distributor cap. It is fastened with spring clips, screw driver lock clips, or screws. The cap is

RUBBING BLOCK WORN

BURNED POINT

Fig. 11-18 Normal wear on high mileage ignition breaker contact points.

163

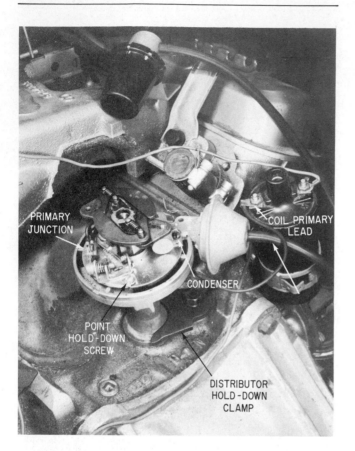

Fig. 11-20 Location of parts that are used when replacing the points and condenser.

PRIMARY JUNCTION

COIL PRIMARY LEAD

CONDENSER

POINT HOLD-DOWN SCREW

DISTRIBUTOR HOLD-DOWN CLAMP

loosened and placed at the side of the distributor with all of the ignition cables remaining in the cap. If the distributor is to be removed from the engine the vacuum advance unit and rotor positions should be noted and marked on the distributor housing so that the distributor can be replaced in the same position after the points and condenser are installed. The primary lead is removed from the coil and the vacuum hose from the vacuum-advance unit nipple; then the distributor hold-down clamp is removed so that the distributor can be pulled straight out of its engine opening. Heavy internal engine deposits will sometimes make distributor removal difficult. Careless prying can break the housing and bend the shaft. As some distributor models are removed the distributor shaft will turn a small amount, as a result of their angled-drive gear teeth. This rotation should be noted to ease reinstalling the distributor. The following breaker

point changing procedure will be the same if the distributor is in the engine or if it is on the bench.

The distributor rotor is removed. On distributors having the centrifugal mechanical advance below the breaker points, the rotor is merely pulled off from the shaft. Two screws will have to be removed from the rotor to free the rotor from distributors having the mechanical advance mechanism above the breaker points. If the rotor tip or distributor cap electrodes show excessive burning, they should be replaced with new parts, especially if the engine has been misfiring prior to the distributor service. Contact breaker points are exposed when the rotor is removed on most distributors. Some distributors require the removal of a metal shield dust cover to expose the points.

The primary wire and condenser are attached to the breaker points at a single junction. The junction may have a screw or a bolt and nut, or it may be held by a spring pressure fit. The junction is separated and the single hold-down screw is removed so the points can be lifted from the distributor. If the condenser is to be replaced it can also be removed by taking out one hold-down screw. After wiping the cam a new condenser and breaker point set can be installed in the reverse order used to remove them. If a screw is dropped into the distributor the screw must be retrieved because it will break the distributor or distributor drive when it jams within the distributor. Cam lubricant should be wiped smoothly over the cam surface and a drop of oil should be put on the felt plug inside the cam. Excessive lubrication will get on the points and cause them to burn. The dis-

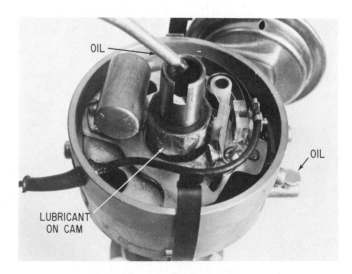

OIL

OIL

LUBRICANT ON CAM

Fig. 11-21 Lubricating points on a distributor.

tributor bearings should be oiled if an oiler is used on the distributor. Most modern distributor bearings have permanent lubrication or are lubricated with motor oil from within the engine.

When a distributor is in good mechanical condition the ignition point dwell will be correct if the breaker point gap is correct. A breaker point gap between 0.016 inch (0.04 mm) and 0.018 in (0.045 mm) will allow the engine to start and will usually place the dwell within the correct range. Some four-cylinder engines require a breaker point gap of 0.025 in (0.055 mm). The gap is adjusted while the breaker-point rubbing block is on the highest part of one of the breaker-cam lobes. Some technicians adjust the points to the correct dwell, rather than putting a thickness gauge between the points, since a gauge may accidently put dirt between the points.

(b)

(a)

Fig. 11-22 Point gap adjustment. (a) Gap is adjusted with the rubbing block on the high point of the cam, (b) point adjustment with an allen wrench, (c) adjustment with a screwdriver in the notches.

(c)

Breaker-point sets are usually adjusted properly for maximum service. They should be checked for contact point alignment and for spring tension. Contacts can be aligned by carefully bending the stationary contact to align it with the movable contact. Point spring tension of 19 to 23 oz is checked with a spring scale. Tension can be increased by pushing the point spring into the holding screw, and it can be reduced by sliding the spring from the holding screw. After any point adjustment the gap or dwell should be rechecked. In a professional shop the centrifugal and vacuum advance mechanisms would be checked at this time. Details of these checks are given in the next section of this chapter.

(a)

(c)

(b)

Fig. 11-23 Point alignment. (a) Bent, (b) twisted, (c) straightening with a bending tool.

The rotor should be installed. If the distributor is out of the engine the rotor should be turned to the same position it had when the distributor was removed. With the vacuum advance unit correctly positioned the distributor can be installed and engaged with the drive mechanism. The distributor will be close to the correct timing with the engine to allow starting if the engine has not been rotated. The primary wire can then be connected to the coil. The engine can be started and the timing set. If the engine has been rotated while the

Fig. 11-24 Measuring breaker point spring tension.

Fig. 11-25 Ignition timing marks on the engine vibration damper.

distributor was out of the engine the procedure to be used to reset the engine basic timing is given in the following section.

11-4 TIMING

Assume that the engine has not been cranked and the distributor is positioned and reinstalled correctly. A quick check of the distributor timing can be made without special timing tools. The engine should be turned with the starter a little at a time until the damper timing marks line up. This procedure is called *bumping* the starter. If the rotor is not pointing toward the number one ignition-cable terminal, turn the engine one additional revolution. By turning the crankshaft either with the starter or with a wrench on the front crankshaft nut, adjust the timing mark at the specified basic engine timing degree. This may be found in the owner's handbook, service manual, or specification sheets. With the distributor hold-down clamp loose, move the distributor housing in the direction opposite to the normal rotation of the rotor until the points just start to open with the rotor pointing to the ignition cable terminal that leads to number one cylinder. The control arm of the vacuum unit points in the direction of distributor rotation. This will be as close to the correct timing as it is possible to get without the use of a timing light. Tighten the hold-down clamp and reinstall the distributor cap, being careful to fit the cap into the aligning notch. Replace any of the spark plug cables have come out of the distributor cap while the cap was off the distributor. With the vacuum hose attached the engine should run.

The amateur mechanic is often completely confused if he has forgotten which way the rotor pointed or if the engine has been inadvertently cranked while the distributor was out of the engine. The key to retiming the ignition is to set the engine crankshaft to the position that number one cylinder *should* fire. The distributor is turned to the position that *will* fire number one cylinder. With both positioned, the distributor can be installed on the engine. The resulting timing will be close enough to start the engine.

Finding the crankshaft angle needed to fire number one cylinder is the most confusing part of basic timing for one who has never done it. Either of two methods will assure satisfactory results. Number one spark plug must fire as the piston moves up on the *compression* stroke with both valves closed. The number one piston top center position is marked as zero on the crankshaft damper timing mark. Automotive engines have a four stroke cycle so the timing mark passes the zero mark at the end of the exhaust stroke as the intake stroke begins as well as the end of the compression stroke. The correct piston position can be found by holding a finger over number one spark plug hole to feel pressure as the piston comes up on the compression stroke while the engine is being cranked. When pressure is felt in number one spark plug hole bump the starter switch enough so that the timing marks align. This is the correct crankshaft position to fire number one spark plug. Correct crankshaft position can also be found by watching the valves of number one cylinder if the rocker cover is off. If the number one exhaust valve is closing and the intake valve is opening as the marks line up, the crankshaft must be turned one complete revolution and the timing marks realigned. This sets the correct crankshaft position for timing.

The first consideration when the distributor is to be timed to the engine is to make sure the housing will be correctly aligned on the engine so that the vacuum advance unit will be positioned properly. The second consideration is the location of the cap tower in which the number one ignition cable is located. The rotor is turned in the normal direction of rotation until the rotor approaches the number one electrode and the breaker points are just ready to open. This is the position the distributor rotor should have when the distributor is installed in an engine that has had its crankshaft positioned correctly. Be sure the distributor vacuum advance unit is aligned properly as the distributor is installed. The distributor with a tang drive will fit directly in the drive slot if the drive has not been rotated. Distributors with a gear drive will turn a few degrees as the gear is engaged with the engine gear and so the shaft must be positioned to compensate for the gear angle. This might require lifting the distributor and engaging the next tooth if it does not line up correctly the first time it is installed. A little practice will enable the technician to quickly estimate the amount of turn.

Sometimes the distributor does not go all the way down into the engine because the oil pump drive does not mesh. A simple method to get the distributor to line up with the oil pump drive is to crank the engine with the distributor installed in the engine as far as possible. As the engine is cranked the oil pump drive will line up and the distributor will fully seat. The engine will have to be cranked through two full revolutions to correctly realign the timing marks on the compression stroke. With the distributor hold-down clamp loose, the distributor housing can be rotated slightly in a direction opposite to rotor rotation to visually set the breaker points in a position so that they are just ready to be opened by the distributor cam. This position is close enough to start the engine. Final timing should be done with a timing light as the engine runs.

If the ignition cables have been removed from the distributor cap they can be easily reinstalled in the correct cap tower. Number one cable goes into the tower toward which the rotor points when the timing marks line up as number one cylinder is on its compression stroke. Following around the cap in the direction the rotor turns, the ignition cables are installed according to the engine firing order. The cylinder firing order is usually shown in raised cast numbers on the manifold. If it is not, it will have to be found in a specification book. Crank the starter slightly to positively identify the direction of the rotor rotation. The vacuum advance unit control arm points in the direction of rotation. Place the spark plug cable leading to the next cylinder in the firing order into the next distributor tower. Follow this by inserting each succeeding cable into the cap towers in the proper firing-order sequence. If the engine is not going to be timed

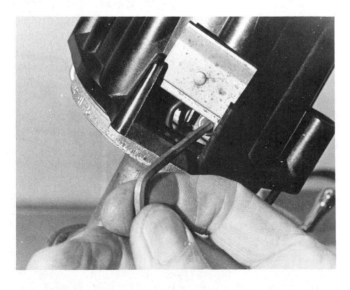

Fig. 11-26 Adjusting dwell with an external adjustment.

with a timing light reinstall the vacuum hose. With the parking brake set and the transmission in neutral, start the engine.

If a dwell meter is available, it should be attached and the ignition point dwell checked. Dwell can be easily adjusted on an external-adjustment distributor with the engine idling. If dwell is incorrect on the other types of distributors the engine will have to be stopped, the distributor cap removed, and the gap changed sufficiently to bring the dwell into specification. Some dwell meters can be used to check dwell while the engine is being cranked. If one of these meters is used the rotor will have to be removed and the dwell adjusted as the engine is cranked. Timing should *always* be reset after adjusting dwell.

If a timing light is available connect the pickup cable to the number one ignition cable and connect the light to its proper power source, either the vehicle battery or the shop 110-volt line. It is critical on most emission control engines to attach this timing light pick-up to number one spark plug cable even if it is not as accessible as one of the other spark plugs. Set the parking brake and place the transmission in neutral; then start the engine. Let it run slowly at curb idle speed with the vacuum line to the distributor removed and plugged so air does not go into the carburetor. With the timing light aimed at the timing marks and the hold-down clamp slightly loose, adjust the distributor until ignition occurs at the specified degree. Tighten the hold-down clamp and recheck the timing. Readjust the timing as necessary; then reconnect the distributor vacuum line.

In addition to basic timing the timing light can be used to determine if the distributor mechanical centrifugal advance and vacuum-advance mechanisms are operating. Remove and plug the distributor vacuum line so air does not enter the carburetor port. With the timing light aimed at the timing marks, gradually increase the engine speed. The timing marks should appear to move in the advance direction when the mechanical centrifugal advance is operating. With the engine running and held at approximately 1200 rpm, watch the timing marks with the timing light as the vacuum line is reconnected. The timing mark will again move in the advance direction if the vacuum-advance mechanism operates. This test will indicate that the distributor advance mechanisms are operating, but it does not indicate that the advance mechanisms are operating correctly.

Some timing lights are made with built-in advance meters. When doing basic timing the technician must be sure to have the meter turned rotor position should be marked on the edge of the distributor housing, then the distributor hold-down clip is removed and the distributor is lifted from the engine.

The distributor should be given a thorough visual examination. This includes looking for abnormal conditions on the shaft drive gear or tang, bearing looseness, breaker-point condition, breaker-plate looseness, electrical conductor and junction security, cam wear, and deposits. This will give the technician an indication of problem areas that require close attention.

The rotor, points, and condenser are removed and replaced as described in the previous section. The distributor is placed on a distributor machine to make final checks and adjustments. The distributor machine is designed to control the distributor rotating speed. It is also equipped with a special light that illuminates a pointer located on a

Fig. 11-27 Checking engine timing with a timing light.

off so that it will operate as a simple timing light. After basic timing is set, the engine is brought up to a specified speed. At this speed the advance meter control is adjusted so that the timing light makes the timing mark appear to be in the same position as it was while the basic timing was set. The meter reading indicates the number of degrees the distributor has advanced. This advance check can be done with the vacuum line off to measure mechanical centrifugal advance and the vacuum line reconnected to measure the additional advance produced by the vacuum-advance mechanism. The distributor vacuum advance line must be connected at the end of this test. If the timing advance is not correct the distributor will have to be tested on a distributor machine.

11-5 DISTRIBUTOR SERVICE

For major service the distributor must be removed from the engine. The distributor cap, vacuum line, and distributor primary wire are removed. The

Fig. 11-28 Timing pointer used when checking a distributor on a distributor machine.

disc rotating within a ring marked with degrees. An ignition system within the distributor machine flashes the light, very much like a timing light, each time the distributor breaker points open. The position of the pointer shows up on the degree wheel at each flash. Observing the angle when each flash occurs allows the technician to check cam lobe wear or shaft bend.

Specifications for distributor advance are given in the service manual and on special specification sheets. The distributor is rotated at very slow speeds and the degree wheel is lined up so that one of the illuminated pointers is at 0°. The distributor speed is slowly increased until the pointer begins to advance. This is the first specification check point for the mechanical centrifugal advance. Two or more additional specification check points are given. They specify a certain degree advance at a given rpm, one at medium speeds and one at high speeds.

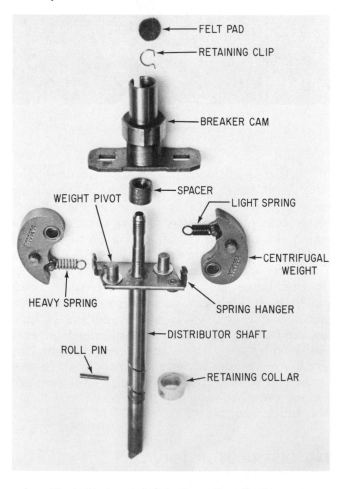

Fig. 11-29 A mechanical centrifugal advance mechanism with a small advance spring on the left and a heavy one on the right.

The centrifugal mechanical advance of the distributor is produced by two weights hinged at one end and balanced with springs. As the rotating speed increases the loose ends of the flyweights move outward against spring pressure to pull the cam forward. Often two different size springs are used, one on each weight. A small lightweight spring fits snugly on the hanger to control advance at low speeds. The second heavier and stronger spring is mounted loosely and does not control until the speed becomes high enough to stretch the small spring far enough so that the control with both springs occurs. The distributor advance test-point speeds are at the start of the small spring movement, at the start of the large spring movement, and at the total control of both springs at high speed.

If the distributor centrifugal mechanical advance is incorrect some distributors are designed so that the spring hangers on the centrifugal weights can be adjusted. Other types will require new springs. Sometimes the weight, cam pivot points, or breaker cam pivot gets sticky and restricts movement. Whenever the centrifugal mechanical advance does not meet specifications it is a good plan to disassemble, clean, and relubricate the weight and cam pivots. This is most easily accomplished on a distributor that has the mechanism directly under the rotor.

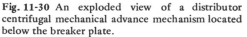

Fig. 11-30 An exploded view of a distributor centrifugal mechanical advance mechanism located below the breaker plate.

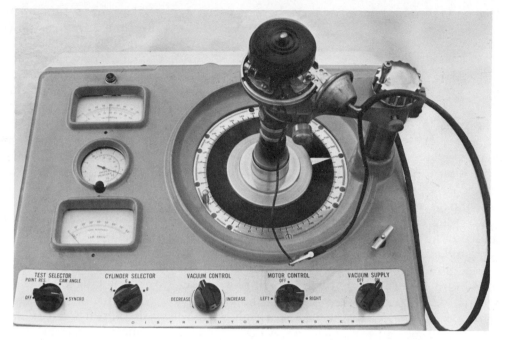

Fig. 11-31 Checking distributor vacuum advance on a distributor machine.

Many centrifugal mechanical advance mechanisms are under the breaker plate. The breaker plate is removed by first removing the primary wire, then removing two screws to free the vacuum-advance mechanism. Some models require that a clip holding the vacuum-advance link to the breaker plate be removed before the advance mechanism can be lifted from the distributor housing. Three additional housing screws are removed to free the breaker plate so it can be lifted from the distributor housing exposing the centrifugal weights. The weights can often be cleaned and lubricated without further disassembly. When required, they can be removed by taking the felt pad from the center of the cam, then removing the retaining clip freeing the cam. The cam and weights can readily slide from the distributor. After cleaning the weights can be lubricated and reassembled in the reverse order with new springs if the old ones are distorted or worn. It is important to have the correct spring set to provide proper centrifugal mechanical advance for the specific engine requirements. Recurving a distributor is usually accomplished with different springs. After reassembly the distributor should be rechecked on the distributor machine.

Vacuum advance is also checked on the distributor machine. The distributor machine has a vacuum pump with a vacuum gauge and control. The distributor is rotated at approximately 1000 rpm and vacuum is gradually applied to the vacuum-control unit. Advance should start at a given vacuum. Several other check points are specified to

determine the correct rate of advance. It is a good practice to remove the vacuum hose and block it with a finger, then adjust the machine to 15 in. (383 mm) Hg of vacuum. Without changing the settings, reconnect the vacuum line to the distributor. If the vacuum diaphragm does not leak the gauge will go right back up to 15 in. (383 mm) Hg. If a leak exists the vacuum will be lower. This condition can only be corrected by replacing the vacuum-control unit.

If the vacuum advance does not function correctly it could be the fault of the vacuum-control unit. Before condemning the vacuum unit, make sure that the breaker plate is clean and operating freely. If the breaker plate moves freely the problem is in the vacuum-advance unit. Most modern vacuum-advance units are not adjustable but must be replaced when they are faulty. A few models of vacuum-advance units can have their return springs adjusted with washers, shims, or an adjusting screw.

When the distributor functions normally on the distributor machine it can be reinstalled on the engine and the timing can be set as previously described. Breakerless distributors used with semiconductor ignition systems require the same distributor mechanical and vacuum advance as the breaker-point type distributors. Their timing advance can be checked on a regular distributor machine if the distributor machine is equipped with a pulse amplifier. The advance mechanisms are serviced in exactly the same manner as the breaker-point type distributors.

171

11-6 SPARK PLUG SERVICE

The spark plug is the end point in the ignition system. It is located in the combustion chamber where it is subjected to combustion deposits, erosion, and corrosion. Spark plugs require periodic service regardless of the type of ignition system used.

Spark plugs are removed by first removing the spark plug cable. This is done by carefully twisting and pulling the boot that fits over the spark plug to remove it without damaging or stretching the cable. Blow air around the spark plug to remove any loose material. Use a good spark plug socket, with an internal cushion, to remove the spark plug without damage. Generally the spark plugs are removed and laid out for inspection. A better practice to follow when a compression test is to be run while the spark plugs are out of the engine is to loosen the spark plugs about one-quarter turn, and reattach the spark plug cables; then start the engine and speed it up two or three times. Any carbon chips that have broken loose from the combustion chamber surface as the spark plugs are turned will be blown from the engine and will not get under a valve and cause erroneous compression test readings.

When the spark plugs are removed they should be examined critically. This examination is often called *reading the plugs.* The condition of the electrodes and the type of carbon on the spark plug nose give a good indication of how that particular cylinder has been operating.

The most obvious spark plug condition is the type of carbon on the spark plug nose. Normal spark plugs will have a light tan to gray deposit, depending on the additives in the gasoline that has been used in the engine. If the deposits are slight and white with badly eroded electrodes the spark plug has been running very hot. Heavy sooty deposits indicate rich air/fuel mixtures and heavy wet deposits indicate high oil consumption. Some engines, especially ones with high mileage, tend to develop heavy white deposits that bridge the gap. This results from oil consumption which forms the deposits. Spark plug manufacturers supply full color pictures of these conditions so that the technician can compare the spark plug appearance and diagnose the problem.

Spark plugs can be cleaned and serviced; however it is the general practice to install new spark plugs on a tune-up that is done on a customer's engine. The customer usually plans to get over 10,000 miles (18,537 Km) before the next tune-up and so new spark plugs are expected. Maintenance on automobiles equipped with a catalytic converter specify new spark plugs at specific service intervals. Spark plug servicing takes the technician's time for which he does not usually get paid, so it is obvious that he can make more money in less time by installing new spark plugs which the customer expects anyway.

Cleaning is the first step when spark plugs are to be serviced. Spark plug cleaners are available to sand blast the electrode end of the spark plug in order to remove carbon deposits. Excessive sand blasting should be avoided because it will erode the spark plug insulator nose and the electrodes. The spark plug threads should be cleaned with a wire brush and the top insulator and terminal should be wiped clean. The spark plug can then be given a good visual inspection to see that the insulator shows no signs of cracking and that the electrodes are not excessively burned. The gap of each serviceable spark plug is somewhat enlarged so a point file can be inserted between the electrodes to file the center electrode flat. This reduces the voltage required to fire the spark plug. The gap is reset to specifications and the spark plugs are now ready for reinstalling. It is considered a good practice to use a wire gauge for measuring spark plug gaps.

Spark plugs are manufactured in a number of heat ranges. The heat range is part of the spark plug numbering code. It is always advisable to reinstall spark plugs with the same heat range when the used spark plug nose appears normal. If the removed spark plug appears burned a colder heat range spark plug can be installed, and if the removed spark plugs have heavy carbon deposits a hotter range spark plug can be used. The engine manufacturer's recommendation should be followed. If excessively high heat range spark plugs are inadvertently installed in an engine they will run so hot that they will cause preignition, which will damage the pistons and may damage the valves. Spark plugs that are too cold will foul and misfire, producing unburned hydrocarbon emissions.

It is a recommended procedure to run a spark plug tap through the spark plug hole to clean the threads before reinstalling the spark plugs, although this is seldom done. The electrode gap of all new spark plugs should be checked and adjusted to specification before they are installed to correct any gap change caused by careless handling. Where spark plug gaskets are used, new gaskets are generally recommended for use on both new and used

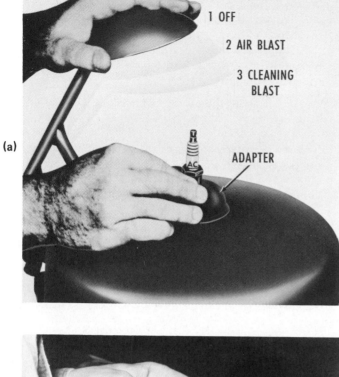

(a)

1 OFF

2 AIR BLAST

3 CLEANING BLAST

ADAPTER

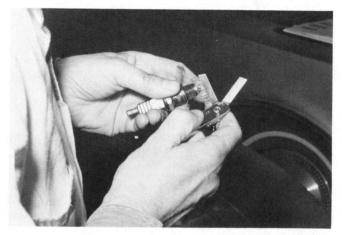

(c)

Fig. 11-32 Servicing spark plugs (AC Spark Plug Division, General Motors Corporation). (a) Cleaning, (b) filing the gap, (c) gap measurement, (d) gap adjustment.

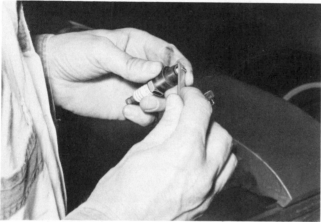

(b)

(d)

spark plugs to give the proper seating contact that helps transfer nearly half of the heat from the spark plug to the engine head. Spark plug manufacturers recommend correct spark plug tightening torque to provide maximum service life. The recommended torque is achieved by turning the spark plug about one-half turn past finger-tight when a *new* gasket is used. Taper-seat spark plugs should be seated firmly enough to assure a gas-tight seal. Spark plug cables should be properly supported in the clips provided on the engine. In some cases the spark plug cables are purposely crossed to eliminate cross-firing caused by induction between the cables.

When new secondary spark plug cables are required it is critical for maximum service to get cables that will withstand the under-hood tempera-

tures of emission controlled engines. Some engines require expensive silicone insulation on the cables to meet high-temperature requirements. It is the responsibility of the technician to install the correct type of secondary cable. All modern engines use resistance-type secondary cables minimizing radio and television interference.

The correct operation of secondary cables is checked using an engine scope or an ohmmeter. All of the secondary ignition system can be checked at one time by observing the secondary scope pattern. Each wire can be checked individually. Normal ignition cable resistance will be between 5,000 and 9,000 ohms per foot. Cables having excessive resistance should be replaced to minimize the possibility of misfiring, especially on engines equipped with converters.

REVIEW QUESTIONS

1. What can be done to insure that the ignition system is capable of producing maximum voltage?

2. What is the minimum normal available voltage?

3. What should be done to correct an inverted ignition scope pattern?

4. What causes the required voltage to increase as the vehicle mileage increases?

5. What is the normal maximum resistance in suppression-type ignition cables?

6. Where can arcing points be observed on an ignition scope pattern?

7. On a scope pattern how does an open ignition secondary cable differ from a cable with a high resistance?

8. In what direction should the distributor housing be turned to advance the basic timing?

9. What service can be done on an inoperative vacuum-advance unit?

10. What is indicated by small amounts of light tan to gray deposits on the spark plug nose?

12

Electrical Accessories

Technicians usually find it difficult to service electrically operated accessories and instruments. Most of the technician's work involves mechanical parts whose movement can be seen or touched while electrical parts seem to operate in a mysterious fashion with no visible moving force. When electrical force or power is understood, often in terms of hydraulics or pneumatic analogies, the technician will have little difficulty in diagnosing electrical system problems and in locating and correcting the malfunctioning unit.

Electricity is the flow of an enormous amount of electrons, which are extremely small negatively charged particles, along a conductor. A *conductor* is any material through which electrons will flow. In automobiles one-half of the electrical system conductors are wires and the other half is the vehicle metal. Materials that do not conduct electricity are called *insulators*. In automobiles the wire conductors are covered by a special plastic insulation to keep the wire from touching other metal, thereby directing the electricity along the wire.

Electricity is allowed to flow through a complete circuit and is stopped from flowing by a *switch*. When the switch contacts are touching, electricity can flow through the switch and when the contacts are separated, electrical flow will be stopped. Any device that reduces or restricts the flow of electricity is called an electrical *resistance,* while any device that increases the flow of electricity is called an electrical *load.*

The battery and the charging system provide the electricity source in automobiles. Electricity is directed to the operating unit through conductors and a conductor is used to provide a return path to the electrical source to complete the electrical circuit. A technician must know that an electrical unit must have this complete circuit to function. To function efficiently the circuit must not have leakage that drains away the needed electrical energy or resistance that will slow the electrical flow.

12-1 ELECTRICAL CIRCUIT REQUIREMENTS

A short review of electrical circuit requirements will reinforce the reader's comprehension of the factors that cause electrical units to malfunction. Conductors of adequate size are required to carry the electrical current needed to operate an electrical unit and to return the current to the electrical source. This is similar to a closed hydraulic system, such as the automobile power-steering system. In the power-steering system the fluid is pumped through a hose to the steering gear and returned to the pump through a second hose. If any part of the hose is too small it will restrict the amount of fluid that can flow in the system. In an electrical system a loose or corroded connection reduces the contact area of the connection, which will reduce the current flow. This type of malfunction is called a *resistance.*

175

The possibility that there is an electrical resistance in an electrical circuit is indicated to the technician by slow or weak operation of the electrical unit because full electrical power is unable to move through the resistance. Electrical resistances can best be located by checking the operating circuit for *voltage drop* with a voltmeter. The part of the circuit having high voltage drop is the part of the circuit having high resistance. The resistance point will be unusually warm.

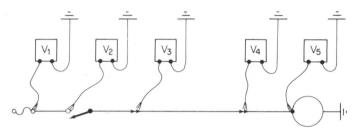

Fig. 12-1 Typical connections used to measure voltage drop along a circuit. The switch must be closed to measure voltage drop.

If a conductor is separated so no current can flow it is called an *open*. With the circuit switch closed and the black voltmeter lead fastened to the body metal, the red voltmeter lead is touched to junction points along the faulty circuit. On one side of the open point the voltmeter will read battery voltage while at the other side it will read zero. Once the open portion of the conductor is located it can be replaced or repaired using procedures described in Chapter 2.

Sometimes the insulation around a conductor fails. This may be the result of cracks from age, from heat, or from wearing or abrasion as the wire

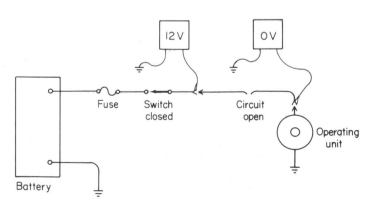

Fig. 12-2 Locating an open in a circuit.

vibrates against the engine or vehicle metal. When the insulation is no longer effective the conductor will touch the vehicle metal. This allows current to go directly to *ground* without going through the operating unit. It may allow so much current to flow that the safety device (fuse, fusible link, or circuit breaker) opens or "blows." If the circuit were not protected against excess current flow the high current flow would burn the insulation and overheat the wire until the wire melted. This would probably ignite flammable materials in the vehicle, destroying the vehicle. Circuits should always be protected by the correct size and type of safety device.

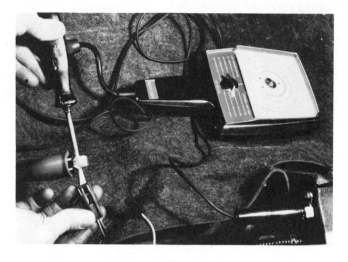

Fig. 12-3 Testing a circuit with a voltmeter at a body junction.

Grounds can be located by separating the circuit at the circuit junction blocks, then installing a new fuse or closing the circuit breaker. Starting at the fuse block, reconnect the circuit, a junction at a time until the fuse or circuit breaker blows again. The ground is in the last section connected. Placing a 12-volt test light or voltmeter across the fuse block terminals allows circuit testing without blowing fuses. This procedure takes a lot of time but it is still more positive than the "guess method" often used. A far better method of locating electrical grounds (which are a form of short circuits) is to use a short finder. A short finder consists of a circuit breaker similar to a directional indicator flasher unit that is connected in place of the blown fuse. It turns the circuit on and off as the system is being checked. A magnetism indicator, for example the type of inexpensive current indicator instrument that is held against a starting or charging system wire to measure current flow, is moved along the circuit wire. As long as electricity is pulsing through the wire the indicator will swing up and back. When the ground is reached the indicator will no longer move. This indicates the exact location of the ground.

A *short* is similar to a ground in its action. It provides an alternate path back to the electrical source by-passing the operating unit. The short can be located by using the short finder just described. It can also be found by looking for a burned spot in the circuit insulation. The short finder method is faster and more positive than the visual method.

With a basic understanding of the methods used to locate opens, shorts, and grounds, the technician can follow malfunctioning electrical circuits and pinpoint the fault. Electrical circuit diagrams are most useful in directing the technician to the circuit, junction, and components in the electrical circuit giving the problem.

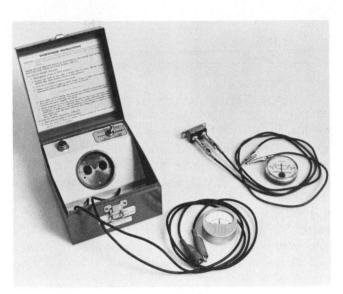

Fig. 12-4 A professional short finder on the left and a homemade short finder on the right.

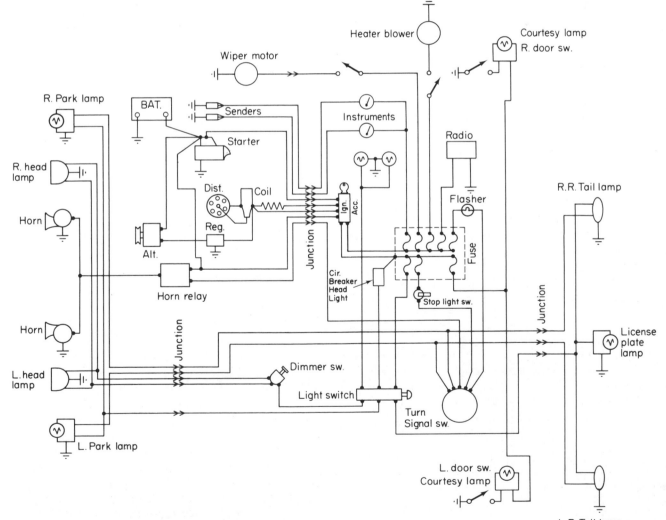

Fig. 12-5 Simplified automotive electrical circuit.

177

12-2 WIRING DIAGRAMS

An electrical circuit must be a complete circuit to operate a unit. One-half of the circuit in automobiles is the automobile metal. A connection anywhere on clean vehicle metal will form the ground half of the circuit. The other half of the circuit, the insulated half, is the wiring with operating units, switches, junction, safety devices, resistors, and connecting wiring. It is the second or insulated half of the circuit that is diagrammed on the electrical circuit drawings.

A wiring diagram is essentially a road map of the electrical system. Like a road map of states with accompanying small maps of cities, the wiring diagram may have an expanded diagram of congested junctions or special electrical equipment. All of the lines and symbols are confusing at the first glance. With a little study the electrical circuit can be understood.

The Fisher Body Service Manual has over 100 full-page schematic wiring diagrams for the GM automobile, omitting the engine compartment wiring. It is obviously impossible to present this type of detail here.

The schematic drawing, Figure 12-5, is a simplified automotive electrical system that combines pictorial units and electrical symbols interconnected with lines representing wires. In the automobile the electrical wires are fastened together in a harness, bundle, or loom to keep the insulation neat and to protect the wires from damage. This makes it difficult to follow a single wire. The lines on the wiring diagram are given letter and number designations. The actual wire in the vehicle has the same color as the color indicated on the wiring diagram. This is helpful in locating the specific wire in the circuit to be checked when the wire is one of a group of wires in a harness or bundle.

When an electrical unit fails to operate it is necessary to pinpoint the malfunctioning unit. For example, the most common cause of single light bulb failure is a burned bulb. Bulbs wear out with use and one usually fails before the others. Light bulbs, sometimes called lamps, are replaced as de-

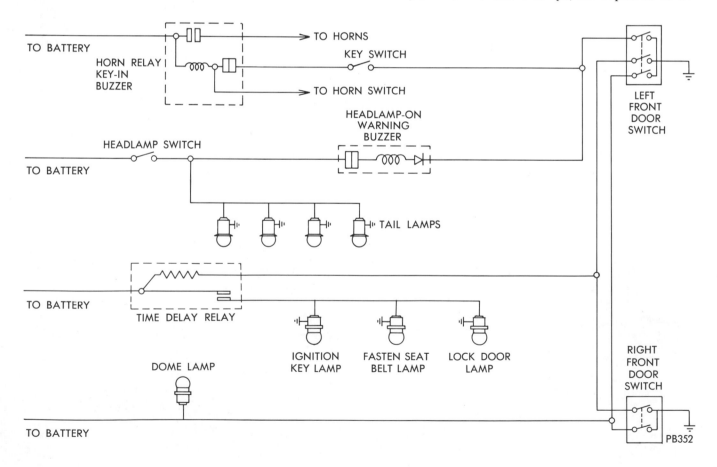

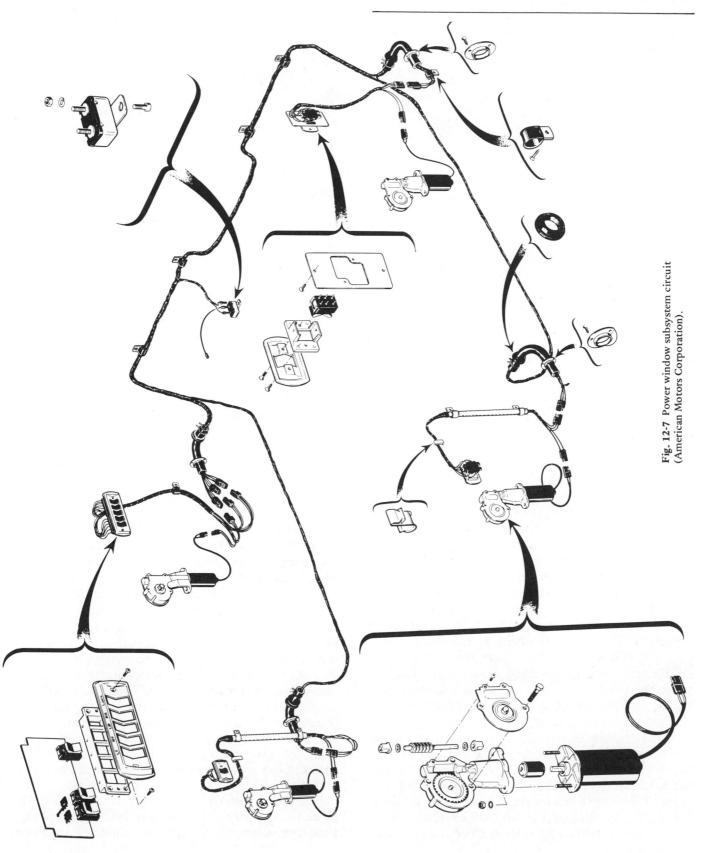

Fig. 12-7 Power window subsystem circuit (American Motors Corporation).

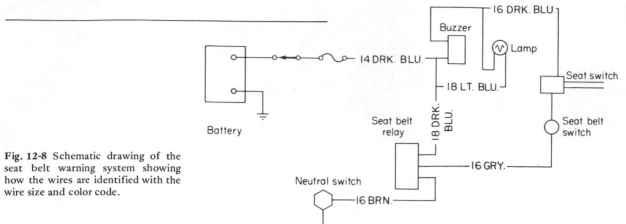

Fig. 12-8 Schematic drawing of the seat belt warning system showing how the wires are identified with the wire size and color code.

scribed in Chapter 2. Sometimes a light bulb socket becomes corroded so that it makes a poor electrical contact to the vehicle metal. The poor connection becomes a resistance that causes a dim light. If the bulb filament isn't burned out, a jumper wire can be connected between the light bulb base and clean vehicle metal. If this causes the bulb to light normally the socket ground should be cleaned to form a good electrical contact.

If a whole set of lights go out at once it is usually the result of a burned-out fuse, fusible link, or circuit breaker. A new fuse may correct the immediate problem; however, assuming the correct size fuse was used, a burned-out fuse is usually the result of excess current flow in the circuit. The only way excess current can flow in a standard electrical system is through a short or ground in the wire or operating unit. Modified systems can be overloaded by the addition of motors, lights, solenoids, etc. to the circuit. Dead shorts or grounds will quickly burn out the fuse. These can be located by procedures described in the preceding section. Intermittent shorts or grounds are difficult to find, especially if they only occur as the vehicle goes over a rough road. In these cases the wiring in the circuit will have to be given a thorough visual inspection. This is one of the times it will be necessary to consult the wiring diagram in order to identify the wires forming the circuit.

One of the easiest ways to follow a circuit on a wiring diagram is to cover the diagram with a sheet of thin paper. The electrical symbol of the malfunctioning unit is located on the wiring diagram. The circuit can be clearly identified by starting at the symbol of the unit to be tested, then following the circuit by tracing the circuit lines on the paper overlay and identifying the wire color code. The line will go to the switch, junctions, fuse and to the battery. If any part of the circuit that is traced also supplies current to normally operating units, that part of the circuit does not contain the malfunction. Terminal connectors in the circuit are convenient places to separate the circuit for testing and for isolating the problem. Using a voltmeter, test light, or short finder the technician can check the circuit at the junctions, while the circuit is both connected and disconnected at the operating unit.

12-3 COMMON ELECTRICAL CONTROL UNITS

A number of electrical control units are common to the different electrical circuits. They are devices that complete or break an electrical circuit. In its basic form the device is called a *switch*.

A switch has contacts made of special metal alloys that resist burning and corrosion by small electrical arcs that always form as a switch is closed and opened. Switches are designed to move with a snap action which will minimize arcing time.

A switch will fail if the contacts eventually become so pitted and burned that they will no longer carry an electrical current; or if the contacts seize together and so they carry electrical current all of the time. A second type of failure is mechanical. The snap action mechanism may fail and so the contacts will not move, staying either open or closed.

A basic test of an automotive switch can be made using either a 12-volt test light or voltmeter. First the voltmeter or light is connected between

Fig. 12-9 Typical automotive switches.

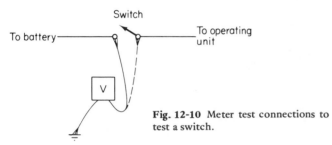

Switch

To battery

To operating unit

V

Fig. 12-10 Meter test connections to test a switch.

ground and the battery side of the switch in the "off" position. Voltage should be shown by the test bulb illumination or by battery voltage indicated on the voltmeter. If no voltage is shown, the fuse and the rest of the circuit should be checked before any further checking of the switch can be done by this test method. Then the lead is moved from the battery side of the switch to the operating unit side of the switch. With the switch off there should be no test light illumination or voltage. With the switch on there should be illumination and voltage shown on the operating unit side. If the switch carries electricity when it is in the off position it is a faulty switch. Faulty switches are not normally repaired but are replaced with new switches.

A *relay* is a remote-controlled switch. It is usually used in circuits carrying high current flow where long heavy wires are expensive and awkward and have high resistance. Examples of relays in automobiles are the horn relay, starter relay, head lamp time delay relay, concealed head lamp relay, air conditioning relay, seat belt relay and power window relay. The relay is usually mounted in a location that forms a short path between the battery and the operating unit. It is operated by a remote switch.

Fig. 12-11 Typical automotive relays.

The relay consists of two heavy contacts, one stationary and one on a movable armature arm. A spring hinge on the armature arm may hold the points closed (normally closed points) or it may hold them open (normally open points), depending on the application. A coil, consisting of many turns of fine wire wound around a laminated soft iron core, forms an electromagnet. When a remote switch connected to the relay coil is closed it will allow current to flow through the coil. This forms a strong electromagnet that attracts the armature arm to separate normally closed contacts or close normally open contacts. In this way a remote switch with a small current, operating through a relay, can control switching of a circuit carrying a heavy current.

Fig. 12-12 A starter switch circuit relay with the cover off showing normally open points.

The contact points of a relay are checked in the same manner as a switch is checked. The control circuit operation can be checked by connecting a test light or voltmeter to the relay switch terminal. Voltage should be indicated when the remote switch is turned on and no power when it is turned off.

A *solenoid* is somewhat similar to a relay and it may incorporate a relay. Essentially, a solenoid has a movable core within the coil of wire. When the coil is energized by closing a remote switch,

Fig. 12-13 Typical automotive solenoids.

the magnetism attracts the movable core toward the center of the coil. This core movement is usually connected to a mechanical device to produce a mechanical movement. One of the most common solenoids on automobiles is the starter solenoid. Solenoids are also used for air-conditioning-clutch engagement, remote door locks and throttle stops. In some cases, such as the starter solenoid, full movement of the movable core pushes relay contacts together to complete an electrical circuit. When coil current is turned off a spring returns the movable core to its original position. This can be seen in the illustrations of starter solenoids in Chapter 5.

If a solenoid does not move it could be because no electrical power is reaching the solenoid, or it could be the result of a mechanically jammed movable core or a faulty solenoid coil. Many times the core can be moved by hand to assure proper mechanical operation. Electrical operation can be checked by connecting the test light or voltmeter at the solenoid electrical lead. When the remote switch is turned on the light or voltmeter should indicate that electrical power is getting to the solenoid. If it does not the problem is in the switch circuit. If power gets to the solenoid but there is no action the solenoid coil is faulty.

Flashers are a special form of switch. A flasher has a stationary contact and a contact on a bimetallic arm held in the normally closed position. As current flows through the bimetallic arm it becomes warm. The increase in temperature causes the bimetallic arm to bend, separating the contacts and stopping current flow. The bimetallic arm cools quickly with no current flowing and the contacts close to reestablish the current flow. The flasher operating cycle repeats to open and close the circuit to produce a flashing turn signal or warning light.

(a)

(b)

Fig. 12-14 Typical automotive circuit breakers and flashers. (a) Exterior, (b) interior.

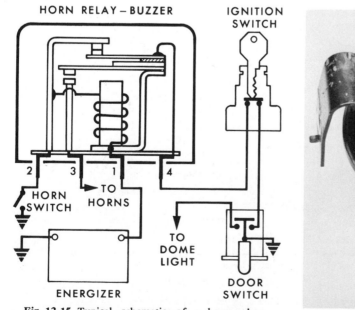

Fig. 12-15 Typical schematic of a horn relay-buzzer (Chevrolet Motor Division, General Motors Corporation).

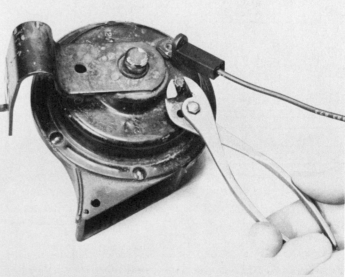

Fig. 12-16 Adjusting the sound of a horn.

183

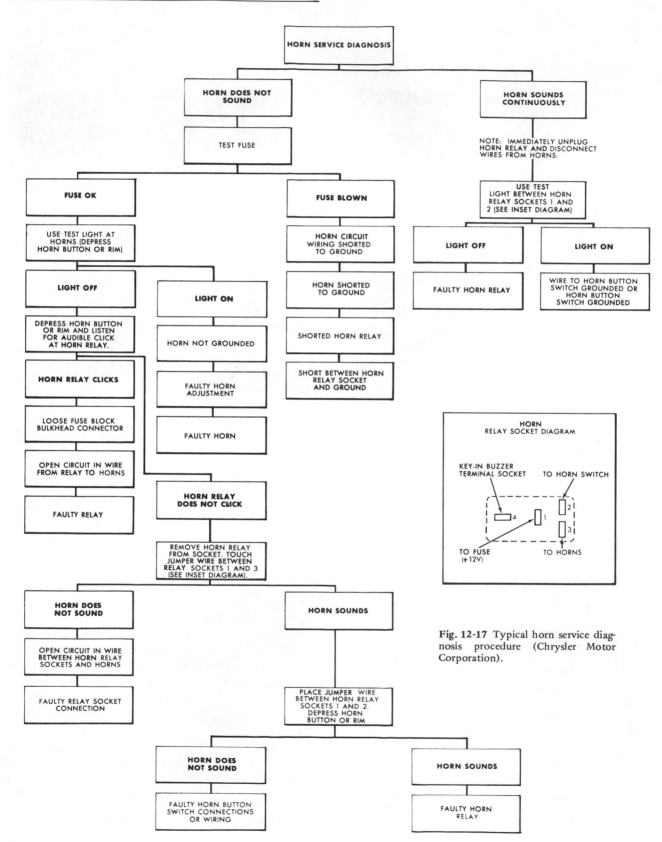

Fig. 12-17 Typical horn service diagnosis procedure (Chrysler Motor Corporation).

A *buzzer* is another type of specialized switch used in automobiles. It works in a fashion very similar to a flasher except that it has a high switching frequency to produce a buzzing sound to alert the driver to some abnormal condition.

When either the buzzer or flasher fails to operate, first determine that there is electrical power at the terminal. If power is at the terminal, the faulty flasher or buzzer will require replacement. Neither is reparable.

The *horn* contacts act like a buzzer, but the armature is connected to a large metal diaphragm; the diaphragm vibrates to produce the horn sound. Fast vibration produces a high-pitched sound; slow vibration produces a low-pitched sound.

If the horn does not sound the switch lead of the horn relay should be momentarily grounded using a jumper wire. If this causes the horn to sound the problem is in the wire or horn contact in the steering column. If this jumper position does not sound the horn the jumper should be momentarily connected between the horn relay BAT and HORN terminals. If this causes the horn to sound the relay is at fault. If the horn still does not sound the wire, horn ground, or horn is at fault. A jumper momentarily connected between the insulated battery post and the terminal on the horn will cause the horn to sound if the horn is normal. If the horn still does not sound the problem is a faulty horn or a poor horn ground. A jumper between the horn and clean body metal will eliminate a ground problem.

Temperature switches have been used in increasing numbers as part of the emission controls on automobiles as well as for coolant temperature lights. Temperature switches consist of a bimetallic arm holding a movable switch contact point against a stationary contact point. When the operating temperature is reached the thermostatic arm bends to open the switch and break the electrical circuit. In some cases the points are normally open and the bending arm closes the contact to operate an electrical circuit. These switches are not reparable and must be replaced if they receive electrical power and fail to function properly. Other temperature switches have both normally open and normally closed contacts.

Some switches are operated by vacuum or pressure. The movable switch contact is mounted on a diaphgram. As vacuum or pressure changes it moves the diaphgram to open or close the points, depending on the purpose and design of the switch. Vacuum and pressure switches are not reparable.

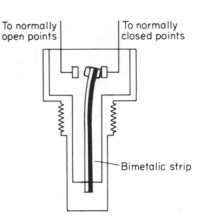

Fig. 12-18 Typical electrical temperature switch with both normally open and normally closed points.

12-4 SERVICING COMMON ELECTRICAL UNITS

The majority of the automotive electrical units are of the throw-away type. They are therefore not reparable at the service garage. Sometimes they can be exchanged and repaired at a rebuilder when no repair parts are available to the service technician.

Generally speaking, light-duty switches, relays, flashers, temperature senders, and pressure senders are replaced when they do not function. They are inexpensively assembled by machine and enclosed in a can with the edges crimped so that they can not be opened without ruining them. They can usually be by-passed with a jumper to check their operation. If the system functions normally when the jumper is used the switch is causing the system malfunction and it will need to be replaced.

Relays generally carry heavier currents than switches. After extended use their contact points become burned. Most relays, like switches, are not reparable; however, parts are available to repair some relays, such as the starter relay portion of a starter solenoid. The relay can be disassembled and new contact parts installed.

Solenoids can generally be disassembled. They should be checked to make sure that the core moves freely; that the coil is not open or grounded and that it has the proper current draw; and that all of

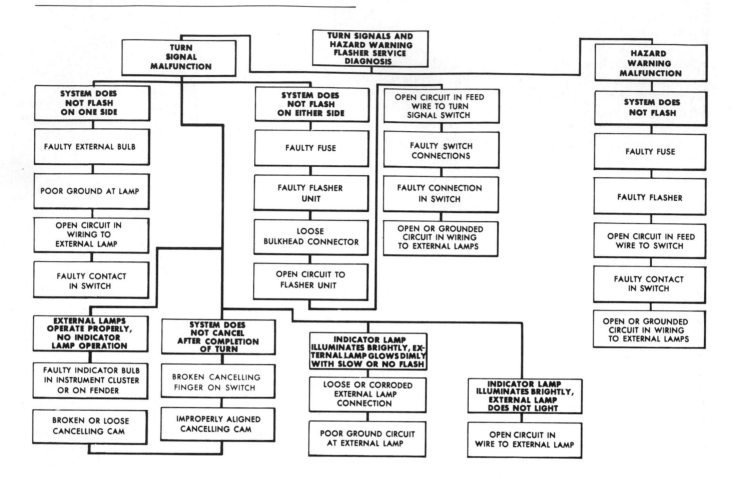

Fig. 12-19 Flasher diagnosis procedure
(Chrysler Motors Corporation).

the insulation is in good condition. New coils are available for some types of solenoids but the entire solenoid is usually replaced with a new solenoid if the coil is faulty. Some solenoids require sealing to keep dirt and moisture out. This is done with gaskets, O rings, and in some cases with RTV (Room Temperature Vulcanizing) rubber type paste.

The horn seldom gives trouble. The horn button or horn ring on the steering wheel grounds a horn relay coil circuit to complete the circuit and energize the relay coil. When a relay is used, the relay coil pulls the contacts together to energize the horn circuit and sound the horn. If the horn switch does not function the steering wheel will have to be removed to repair the leads or clean the contacts. Applicable service manuals should be consulted for steering wheel removal details. Sometimes the horn relay points stick, causing the horn

to sound continuously. The simplest way to stop the horn is to remove the wire from the horn. The relay will then require replacement.

A horn may not operate or it may not sound right. An adjuster is usually provided to clear up the horn sound. The adjuster should not be turned while the horn is operated. It is turned one-quarter of a turn and the horn sounded. If the sound improves the process is continued until the horn produces a clear mellow sound. When operating correctly, each horn will draw from 4 to 6 amperes. A faulty horn that cannot be made to sound properly by turning the adjuster should be replaced.

Most faulty headlight operation results from burned-out or improperly adjusted sealed-beam headlight bulbs. If all of the headlights go out at once the problem is usually caused by the wiring,

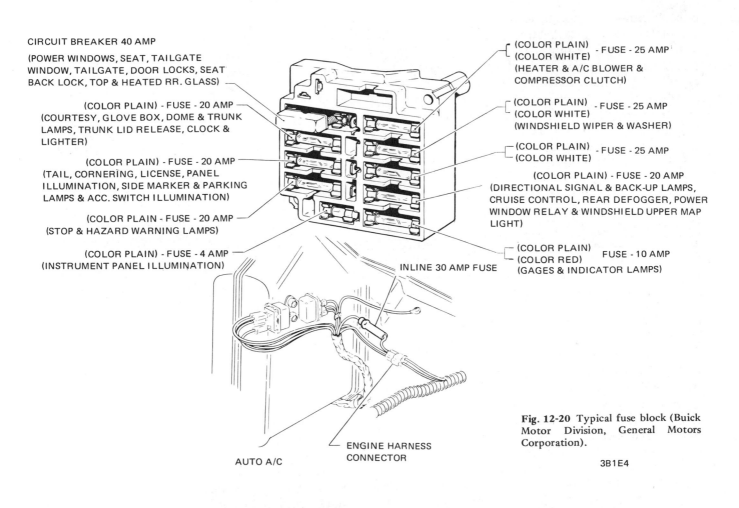

CIRCUIT BREAKER 40 AMP

(POWER WINDOWS, SEAT, TAILGATE WINDOW, TAILGATE, DOOR LOCKS, SEAT BACK LOCK, TOP & HEATED RR. GLASS)

(COLOR PLAIN) - FUSE - 20 AMP
(COURTESY, GLOVE BOX, DOME & TRUNK LAMPS, TRUNK LID RELEASE, CLOCK & LIGHTER)

(COLOR PLAIN) - FUSE - 20 AMP
(TAIL, CORNERING, LICENSE, PANEL ILLUMINATION, SIDE MARKER & PARKING LAMPS & ACC. SWITCH ILLUMINATION)

(COLOR PLAIN - FUSE - 20 AMP
(STOP & HAZARD WARNING LAMPS)

(COLOR PLAIN) - FUSE - 4 AMP
(INSTRUMENT PANEL ILLUMINATION)

(COLOR PLAIN) - FUSE - 25 AMP
(COLOR WHITE)
(HEATER & A/C BLOWER & COMPRESSOR CLUTCH)

(COLOR PLAIN) - FUSE - 25 AMP
(COLOR WHITE)
(WINDSHIELD WIPER & WASHER)

(COLOR PLAIN) - FUSE - 25 AMP
(COLOR WHITE)

(COLOR PLAIN) - FUSE - 20 AMP
(DIRECTIONAL SIGNAL & BACK-UP LAMPS, CRUISE CONTROL, REAR DEFOGGER, POWER WINDOW RELAY & WINDSHIELD UPPER MAP LIGHT)

(COLOR PLAIN) FUSE - 10 AMP
(COLOR RED)
(GAGES & INDICATOR LAMPS)

INLINE 30 AMP FUSE

AUTO A/C

ENGINE HARNESS CONNECTOR

Fig. 12-20 Typical fuse block (Buick Motor Division, General Motors Corporation).

3B1E4

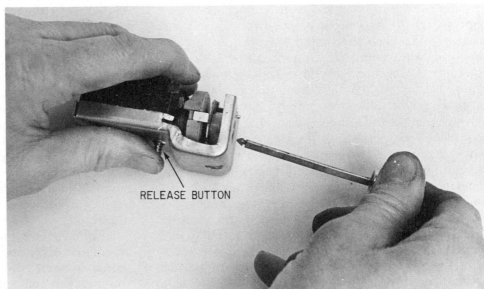

Fig. 12-21 Pressing the release button to remove the pull knob from the headlight switch.

RELEASE BUTTON

circuit breaker, or switch. The wiring can be checked for opens, shorts, or grounds, as described at the beginning of this chapter. The circuit breaker can be checked as an open circuit and the light switch as an open switch. A faulty circuit breaker or light switch will require replacement. If both high-beam or both low-beam lights do not function the problem may be the dimmer switch.

The light switch does more than merely turn the headlights on. It controls the exterior lights, interior courtesy lights, and instrument lights. If all of these fail to operate at the same time it is the result of a blown fuse or a faulty light switch. A fuse will burn out when the system is shorted or grounded and so the short or ground should be corrected before a new fuse is installed. Because the light switch carries so many circuits it is removed more often than many other vehicle switches.

Most pull-type light switches must have their pull knob and pin removed from the switch before the switch can be removed from the dash panel. The switch has a release button that is depressed to allow the control pin to be removed from the switch. With the battery ground cable removed to prevent accidental shorts, the switch retaining nut can be removed, thus freeing the switch. The switch can then be removed below the instrument panel for examination. If the switch is to be replaced the wires can be removed, one at a time, from the old switch and transferred to the new switch to avoid misconnections. Some automobiles use a junction block-type connector on the light switch. It is a good practice to connect the battery and check the switch operation before remounting the switch. If the switch operates satisfactorily the battery ground is again removed and the switch reinstalled. The knob and pin will snap into place when they are pushed into the switch.

The automotive technician will be expected to remove and install the radio, speaker, and antenna when required and to trim the radio antenna. Most automobile radios are located behind the instrument panel and are held to the panel with a brace and with nuts located behind the radio knobs. To work under the dash it may be necessary to remove some defroster and air conditioning ducting to expose the back of the radio. Again, it is a good safety policy to remove the battery ground cable to eliminate any chance of an accidental electrical short. The radio electrical lead, antenna lead, and

Fig. 12-22 Burned instrument light rheostat on the back of a headlight switch.

speaker leads are removed from the radio chassis. If a brace is used on the back of the radio it should be loosened. The knobs are pulled from the front of the radio. In some rare cases they may be held with set screws. This exposes the nuts holding the radio chassis to the dash. The nuts are loosened while the chassis is supported. When free, the radio chassis can be lowered from below the dash. If the front speaker needs to be replaced it is usually exposed and can be removed after the radio chassis is out. The speaker can be removed from its mounting after taking off the four retaining nuts. The radio chassis and speaker are usually sent to a radio repair shop for internal repair when this type of repair is required.

The radio is reinstalled by reversing the procedure used during removal. The speaker is remounted, the chassis installed, and the retaining nuts tightened. This is followed by attaching the speaker wires, antenna, power lead, and knobs. When the radio is installed the battery ground can be connected and the radio turned on. The radio should be tuned to a weak station near 1600 KC and the antenna trimmer screw located near the antenna connection should be turned to obtain the

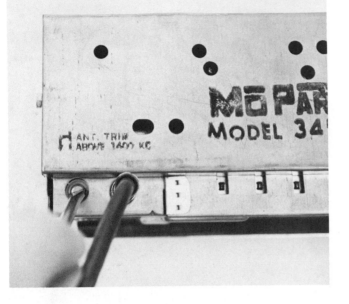

Fig. 12-23 Adjusting the antenna trim screw on a radio.

loudest signal. This trims the antenna to the radio. Heater and air conditioner ducting can then be re-assembled.

Sometimes it is necessary to replace the antenna. Most original-equipment whip antennas are one-piece units from the fender to the radio chassis. Replacement requires removing the antenna lead from the chassis and sliding the lead wire through grommets to remove it with the antenna. The antenna can be removed by unscrewing a trim nut on the fender mounting and pushing the antenna into the fender. It can be threaded out behind the fender from the under-hood area. The new antenna is installed in the reverse order. Windshield antennas are only replaced when a new windshield is installed.

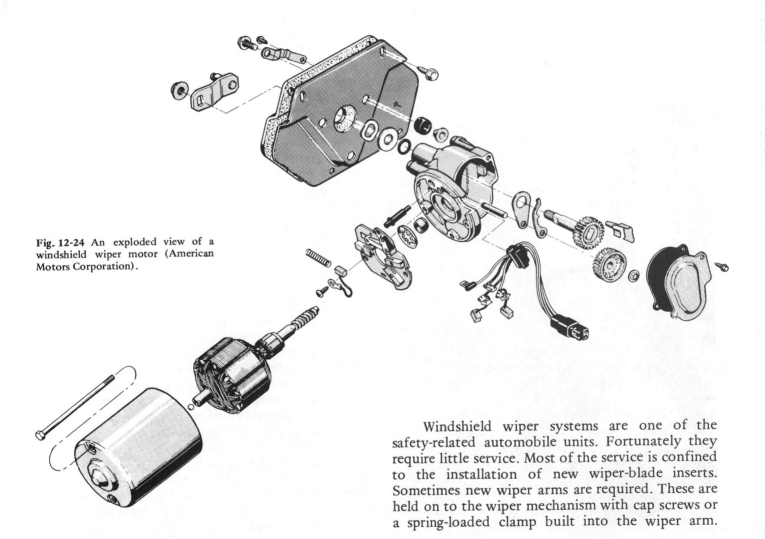

Fig. 12-24 An exploded view of a windshield wiper motor (American Motors Corporation).

Windshield wiper systems are one of the safety-related automobile units. Fortunately they require little service. Most of the service is confined to the installation of new wiper-blade inserts. Sometimes new wiper arms are required. These are held on to the wiper mechanism with cap screws or a spring-loaded clamp built into the wiper arm.

Windshield wipers use an electric motor driving the wiper through a gear train that is connected to a crank. As with any electromechanical device, it can fail. If the wiper motor fails it can be checked using the same procedure used on other automotive-type electric motors. The motor must receive electricity through wires and switches. If it does the fault is in the wiper assembly. If it does not the wiper electrical circuit will have to be checked. The mechanical linkages of the wiper should be carefully inspected for binding before the assembly is removed for service. The complete wiper motor and gear assembly is usually replaced in order to accomplish speedy repairs. Parts are available to recondition the wiper assembly, but if they are not in stock they would have to be special-ordered. Sometimes it is expedient to combine the parts of several used wiper assemblies to make one operational unit.

Fig. 12-26 Components of the windshield washer.

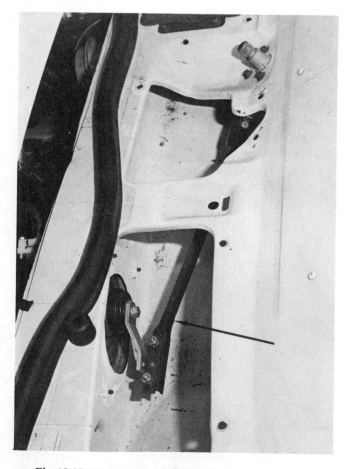

Fig. 12-25 Windshield wiper linkages in the intake plenum for the body interior air.

Windshield washers are another safety-related item used on automobiles. They consist of a fluid reservoir, an electric pump, hoses, and washer nozzles. The electric pump may be a diaphragm type pump that puts pulses of washer fluid on the windshield or it can be a turbine pump that sprays a steady stream of washer fluid. The most common washer failure results from an empty washer-fluid reservoir. A second common cause of failure is plugged or poorly adjusted nozzles. Plugging can be checked by removing the washer pump pressure hose and operating the pump. If the pump supplies fluid the nozzles are plugged. Plugged nozzles can usually be opened with air pressure. Sometimes a small soft wire, such as those used on shipping tags, will have to be used to open the nozzle holes. If this fails, the nozzle will have to be replaced. If the washer pump does not deliver fluid the pump is not functioning properly. Here again the electrical circuit should be checked to make sure electricity is being delivered to the pump. If the circuit is satisfactory the pump will have to be replaced. Washer motors and pumps are not normally reparable.

Instruments are used to indicate many vehicle operating conditions. All vehicles are equipped with a speedometer and an odometer to show vehicle speed and distance traveled. Some means is provided to indicate low engine oil pressure, high engine temperature, and battery discharge. A fuel gauge is provided to show the amount of fuel remaining in the tank. Each vehicle has an indicator to show the operation of high-beam headlights and directional signals.

Many vehicles have additional instruments to give the driver more information about the operation of the vehicle. These would include instruments such as a tachometer, clock, and compass.

Indicator Lights. Many operating conditions are shown by indicator lights. Even though he is concentrating on driving the vehicle, a driver's attention is immediately called to a light signal that indicates a problem. It is interesting to note that the aerospace industry uses lights to indicate abnormal operating conditions to alert the pilot to the problem; the pilot may also have a gauge to check the actual operating value.

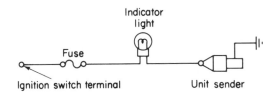

Fig. 12-27 Typical indicator light circuit.

Indicator lights pick up their power at the engine unit. The circuit goes through to the indicator light bulb, then on to the ignition switch where it is attached to a junction block to complete the circuit. It should be noted that these indicator light bulbs are some of the few in the vehicle that are not grounded at the bulb. The engine units are electrical switches that connect the circuit to ground to turn the indicator light on.

A diaphragm in the oil pressure unit opens points when sufficient oil pressure exists. When the pressure drops dangerously low, the points close to turn on the oil pressure indicator light. Points on a bimetal arm are used in the temperature unit. When engine temperature is excessive, the heat bends the bimetal arm in the engine unit so that the points close to complete the circuit and turn on the warning light. In some cases, the temperature unit is equipped with a second set of points to indicate low temperature. These points are normally closed to keep the cold signal light on. As the engine warms the bimetal arm bends enough to separate the points, which turns the cold signal light out.

Charging system discharge lights operate in a different manner. They use a light relay or a field relay, usually located within the regulator, as described in Chapter 7. When the generator is charging, the relay is energized to open the points of the light relay or to close the field relay. The closed field relay puts equal voltage on both sides of the indicator bulb so it does not light. When the system is not charging, the points switch to the opposite position to light the indicator lamp.

A number of other warning lights may be used, such as indicators for the parking brake, low fuel level, seal belt fastening, door ajar, etc. Each helps to improve safety and convenience, but adds to the original cost and to maintenance costs.

A relatively new indicating method makes use of a fiber optic conductor, which consists of a bundle of plastic filaments that transmit light. The optic conductor is used to show the driver if lights are on or off. One end of the bundle is at the light source and the other is visible to the driver.

Gauges. Instrument gauges are used where it is important to know values, such as vehicle speed and remaining fuel. Oil pressure gauges, engine temperature gauges, and charging-ampere gauges also are used to indicate impending failure before it occurs. Gauges are generally more expensive than indicating lights and many drivers would not notice or recognize an incorrect reading, and so lights are usually used. Gauges are standard equipment on certain sport and performance model cars and optional equipment on many other cars.

The speedometer is a mechanical device, making use of induction between a rotating magnet and a cup. The cup position is retained by a hair spring. As the magnet rotates, the magnetic force pulls the cup against the hair spring an amount proportional to the rotating speed of the magnet. The cup is connected to an indicator needle to show speed. The rotating magnet is driven by a flexible shaft which, in turn, is driven by a gear in the transmission output shaft or by a gear on the left front wheel. An odometer is geared to the shaft to indicate distance traveled.

Fig. 12-28 Typical speedometer hair spring.

Most of the other gauges are electrically operated. In one type a coil of resistance wire is wound around a bimetal arm. The more current that flows through the coil, the more it heats and bends the bimetal arm. The movable end of the arm is connected by a linkage to an indicator needle. Different scale panels are placed behind the needle to show the correct value.

Another method used to operate instruments uses a balanced-coil principle. A series coil carries full instrument current. The current then splits, part going to a variable resistance in the sending

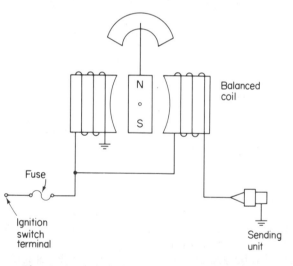

Fig. 12-30 Typical instrument circuit using a balanced coil.

unit and the rest going to the shunt coil. Current flowing through the sending unit changes as its resistance changes and this weakens and strengthens the shunt coil. High resistance in the sending unit increases the shunt coil magnetic strength and a low resistance weakens the shunt coil magnetic strength. The indicator needle is deflected by the difference in the magnetic strength of the sensing and shunt coils.

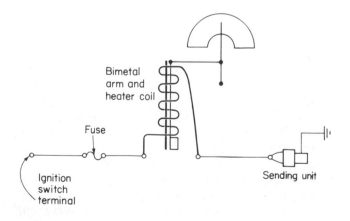

Fig. 12-29 Typical instrument circuit using a heated bimetal spring.

Fig. 12-31 The interior of a vibrating voltage regulator used with electrical instruments.

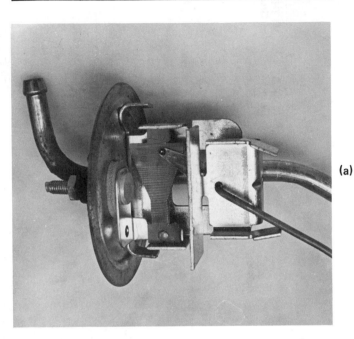

(a)

Because the gauge mechanism is sensitive to current flow, it is important to have a constant voltage source for accuracy. In most cases, electrical instruments are supplied from a vibrating-point voltage regulator that keeps the voltage at a con-

Fig. 12-32 Fuel gauge tank units. (a) Variable resistance, (b) float assemblies.

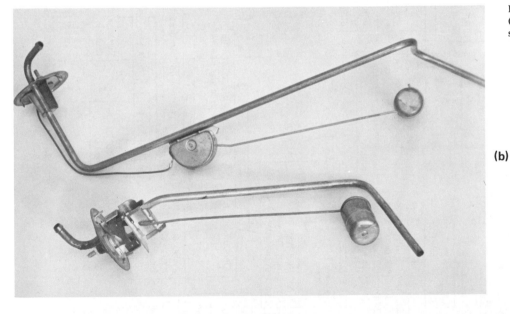

(b)

stant value, usually five volts. The regulator may be a separate unit mounted in the fuse block or it may be part of the fuel level gauge.

The gauge sender, which is a tank unit or engine unit, actually connects the system to ground where it indirectly connects to the negative side of the battery to complete the circuit. A variable resistance rheostat is connected to the hinged tank float in the fuel gauge sender. When the fuel level is high, the gauge circuit connects directly to

ground, allowing full current to flow through the instrument coil. This moves the instrument needle to the top of the scale. As fuel is used, the float drops. This causes the instrument circuit current to flow through part of the variable resistance, adding resistance that reduces current flow. The reduced current flow lowers the instrument coil temperature so the gauge reading decreases. The gauge reading is, therefore, proportional to the tank fuel level.

FUEL GAUGE DIAGNOSIS

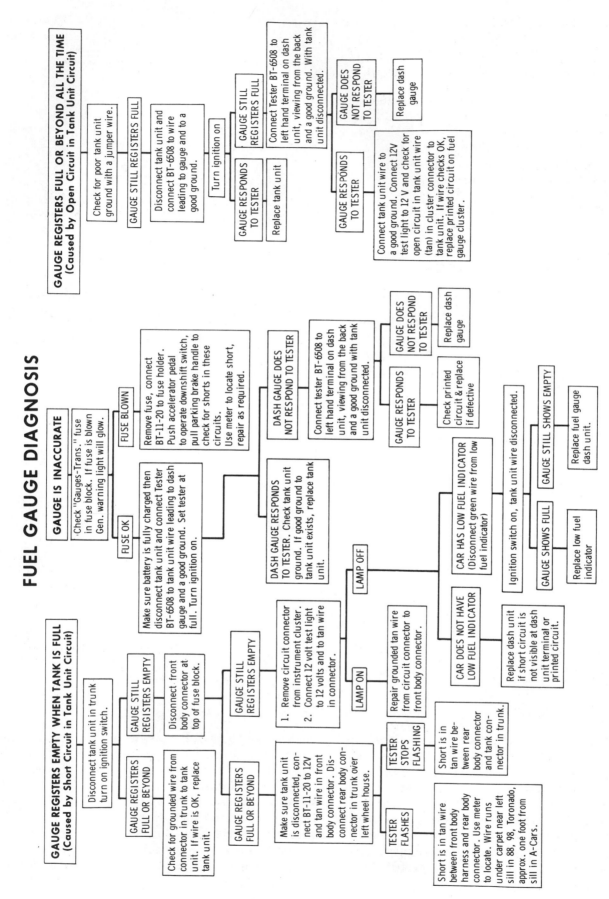

Fig. 12-33 Fuel gauge diagnosis flow chart (Oldsmobile Division, General Motors Corporation).

Electric oil-pressure and temperature gauges work in a similar manner. The design of the engine unit is their primary difference. Oil-pressure-gauge senders have a spring-loaded diaphragm. Diaphragm movement caused by oil pressure pushing the diaphragm toward the spring changes the instrument circuit resistance proportional to the diaphragm movement. Sender resistance is low when oil pressure is high, giving a high instrument reading. The temperature gauge sender has a bimetal spring that changes resistance proportional to engine heat. The free end of the bimetal spring in the sender is attached to a variable resistance so the instrument circuit resistance is changed proportional to the engine temperature. When the engine is hot, the circuit resistance is low, which will give a high instrument reading.

If the sending unit end of the wire is grounded, the normal reading will always be high. If no current flows, the reading will always be zero. Some service manuals give resistance values that can be temporarily inserted in the circuit in place of the sender to check gauge accuracy. These resistance values are also helpful in troubleshooting gauge problems.

The vehicle ammeter is connected in the part of the charging circuit that leads to the battery. Its purpose is to indicate the amount of current being put into or being taken from the battery. It does not indicate generator output. Ammeter wiring circuits are, therefore, made from large-size wires. The ammeter itself must also be of heavy construction to carry high current. Several ammeter movement types are used. All basically use the principle of induction. As current flows, it forms a magnetic field that is deflected by a permanent magnet in the instrument. High current flow causes high magnetic field deflection. The moving portion of the gauge is connected to an indicator needle and is held upright in its normal position. The needle moves to the right when the current is flowing to charge the battery and to the left when a discharging current flows from the battery.

Troubleshooting becomes routine when the technician understands the basic operating principles of these instruments and when the service manual instructions are followed. The biggest problem encountered in instrument troubleshooting in some vehicle models is to reach the instrument leads to check them, especially in a car equipped with air conditioning and a center console. In some later model vehicles, manufacturers have corrected this problem by designing the instrument panels so that they can be removed from the driver's side.

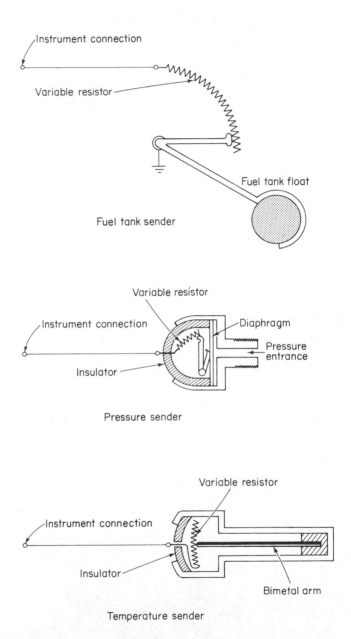

Fig. 12-34 Typical instrument tank and engine unit principles.

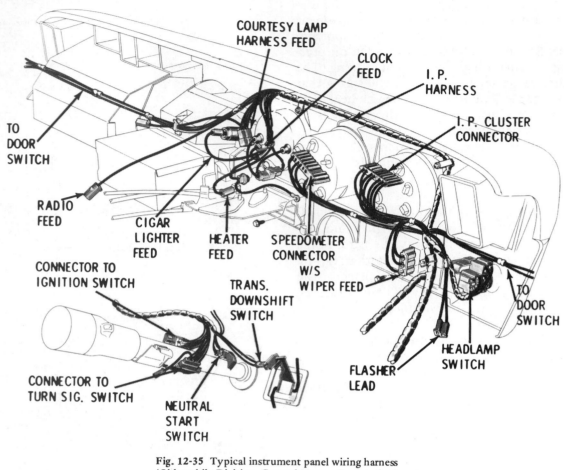

COURTESY LAMP
HARNESS FEED

CLOCK
FEED

I. P.
HARNESS

I. P. CLUSTER
CONNECTOR

TO
DOOR
SWITCH

RADIO
FEED

CIGAR
LIGHTER
FEED

HEATER
FEED

SPEEDOMETER
CONNECTOR
W/S
WIPER FEED

TO
DOOR
SWITCH

CONNECTOR TO
IGNITION SWITCH

TRANS.
DOWNSHIFT
SWITCH

HEADLAMP
SWITCH

CONNECTOR TO
TURN SIG. SWITCH

NEUTRAL
START
SWITCH

FLASHER
LEAD

Fig. 12-35 Typical instrument panel wiring harness
(Oldsmobile Division, General Motors Corporation).

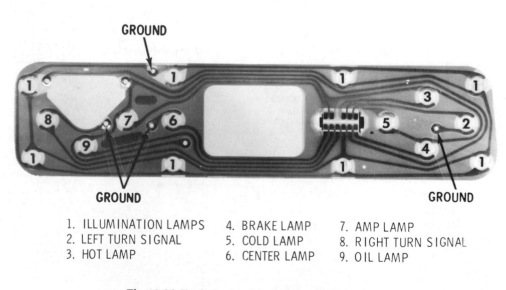

GROUND

GROUND

GROUND

1. ILLUMINATION LAMPS
2. LEFT TURN SIGNAL
3. HOT LAMP

4. BRAKE LAMP
5. COLD LAMP
6. CENTER LAMP

7. AMP LAMP
8. RIGHT TURN SIGNAL
9. OIL LAMP

Fig. 12-36 Typical printed instrument panel circuit
(Oldsmobile Division, General Motors Corporation).

ELECTRIC DOOR LOCK DIAGNOSIS
88-98 & TORONADO

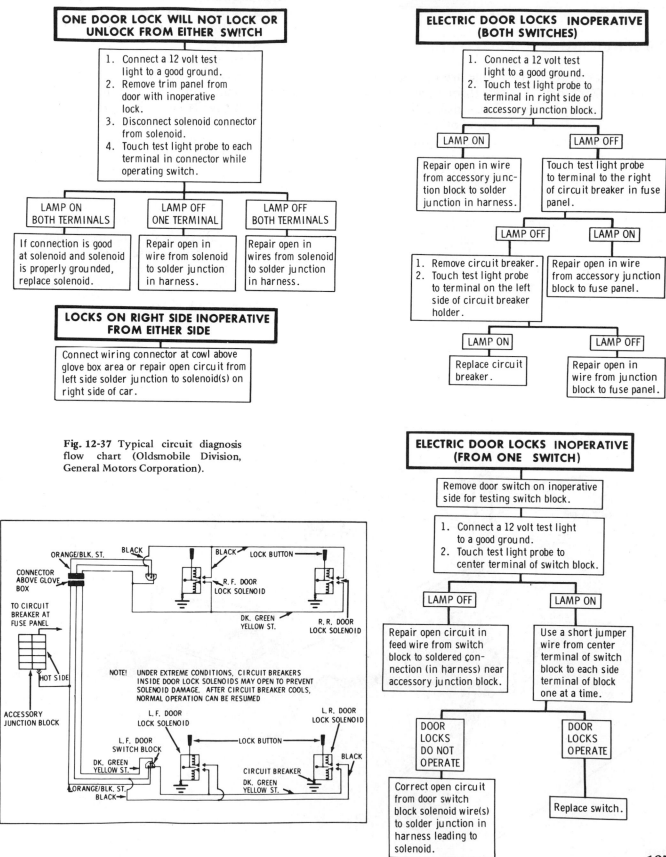

ONE DOOR LOCK WILL NOT LOCK OR UNLOCK FROM EITHER SWITCH

1. Connect a 12 volt test light to a good ground.
2. Remove trim panel from door with inoperative lock.
3. Disconnect solenoid connector from solenoid.
4. Touch test light probe to each terminal in connector while operating switch.

LAMP ON BOTH TERMINALS

If connection is good at solenoid and solenoid is properly grounded, replace solenoid.

LAMP OFF ONE TERMINAL

Repair open in wire from solenoid to solder junction in harness.

LAMP OFF BOTH TERMINALS

Repair open in wires from solenoid to solder junction in harness.

LOCKS ON RIGHT SIDE INOPERATIVE FROM EITHER SIDE

Connect wiring connector at cowl above glove box area or repair open circuit from left side solder junction to solenoid(s) on right side of car.

Fig. 12-37 Typical circuit diagnosis flow chart (Oldsmobile Division, General Motors Corporation).

ORANGE/BLK. ST.
BLACK
CONNECTOR ABOVE GLOVE BOX
BLACK
LOCK BUTTON
R. F. DOOR LOCK SOLENOID
DK. GREEN YELLOW ST.
R. R. DOOR LOCK SOLENOID
TO CIRCUIT BREAKER AT FUSE PANEL
HOT SIDE
ACCESSORY JUNCTION BLOCK
NOTE! UNDER EXTREME CONDITIONS, CIRCUIT BREAKERS INSIDE DOOR LOCK SOLENOIDS MAY OPEN TO PREVENT SOLENOID DAMAGE. AFTER CIRCUIT BREAKER COOLS, NORMAL OPERATION CAN BE RESUMED
L. F. DOOR LOCK SOLENOID
L. R. DOOR LOCK SOLENOID
L. F. DOOR SWITCH BLOCK
LOCK BUTTON
DK. GREEN YELLOW ST.
ORANGE/BLK. ST.
BLACK
CIRCUIT BREAKER
DK. GREEN YELLOW ST.
BLACK

ELECTRIC DOOR LOCKS INOPERATIVE (BOTH SWITCHES)

1. Connect a 12 volt test light to a good ground.
2. Touch test light probe to terminal in right side of accessory junction block.

LAMP ON

Repair open in wire from accessory junction block to solder junction in harness.

LAMP OFF

Touch test light probe to terminal to the right of circuit breaker in fuse panel.

LAMP OFF

1. Remove circuit breaker.
2. Touch test light probe to terminal on the left side of circuit breaker holder.

LAMP ON

Repair open in wire from accessory junction block to fuse panel.

LAMP ON

Replace circuit breaker.

LAMP OFF

Repair open in wire from junction block to fuse panel.

ELECTRIC DOOR LOCKS INOPERATIVE (FROM ONE SWITCH)

Remove door switch on inoperative side for testing switch block.

1. Connect a 12 volt test light to a good ground.
2. Touch test light probe to center terminal of switch block.

LAMP OFF

Repair open circuit in feed wire from switch block to soldered connection (in harness) near accessory junction block.

LAMP ON

Use a short jumper wire from center terminal of switch block to each side terminal of block one at a time.

DOOR LOCKS DO NOT OPERATE

Correct open circuit from door switch block solenoid wire(s) to solder junction in harness leading to solenoid.

DOOR LOCKS OPERATE

Replace switch.

197

12-6 SERVICING SPECIALIZED UNITS

Many devices in the automobile are operated with electricity. Each device is fed through an electrical circuit containing wires; a fuse, fusible link, or circuit breaker; and a switch. Some of the specialized electrical operating devices use motors, such as rear window defogger blower, power windows, power seats, concealed headlight doors, power radio antenna, and power-operated tops. Others make use of electronic control modules, such as automatic head lamp dimmers, anti-lock brakes and anti-wheel-spin controls. Specialized lighting devices include lamp monitors and lights that turn on at dusk. Trunk locks, electric door locks, electric seat-back release, and speed controls are specialized electrical units using remote-controlled solenoids.

Indicators are used to alert the driver to an abnormal condition; these indicators include a low-washer-fluid-level indicator, a seat belt warning system, a key-in-lock warning system, a parking brake set light, a head lamp warning system, and a starter–seat belt interlock.

Electrical circuits operating specialized units are tested in the same manner as are all other electrical circuits in the automobile. Electrical power must be available at the operating unit when the switch is on and the circuit must not have excessive voltage drop. The thing that usually confuses the technician while he is troubleshooting these items is his inability to follow the schematic wiring diagram to locate the correct circuit and correct junctions. Circuits can be identified from wiring diagrams by following procedures previously discussed. Specialized test equipment may be required to accurately diagnose problems in some of these circuits, but most electrical system problems can be accurately diagnosed using a test light, a voltmeter or an ohmmeter.

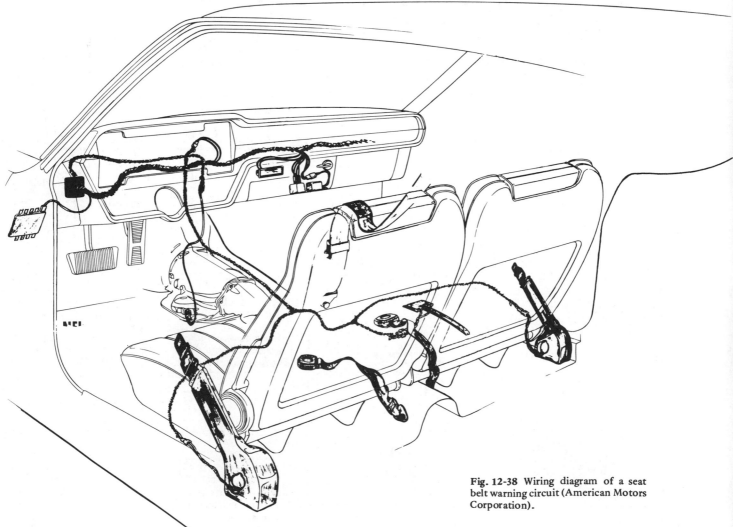

Fig. 12-38 Wiring diagram of a seat belt warning circuit (American Motors Corporation).

TAILGATE WINDOW DIAGNOSIS (CUSTOM CRUISER)

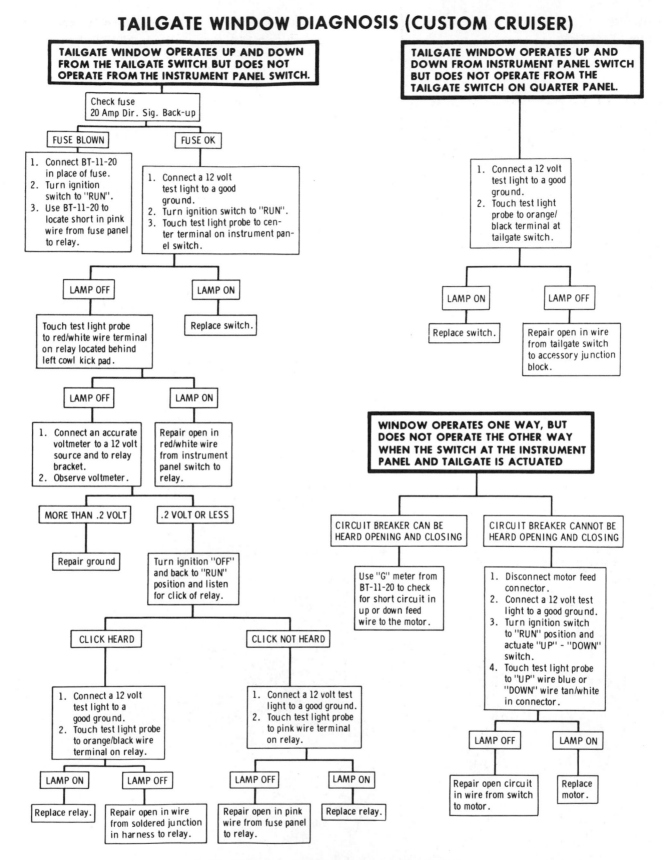

TAILGATE WINDOW OPERATES UP AND DOWN FROM THE TAILGATE SWITCH BUT DOES NOT OPERATE FROM THE INSTRUMENT PANEL SWITCH.

Check fuse
20 Amp Dir. Sig. Back-up

FUSE BLOWN

1. Connect BT-11-20 in place of fuse.
2. Turn ignition switch to "RUN".
3. Use BT-11-20 to locate short in pink wire from fuse panel to relay.

FUSE OK

1. Connect a 12 volt test light to a good ground.
2. Turn ignition switch to "RUN".
3. Touch test light probe to center terminal on instrument panel switch.

LAMP OFF

Touch test light probe to red/white wire terminal on relay located behind left cowl kick pad.

LAMP ON

Replace switch.

LAMP OFF

1. Connect an accurate voltmeter to a 12 volt source and to relay bracket.
2. Observe voltmeter.

LAMP ON

Repair open in red/white wire from instrument panel switch to relay.

MORE THAN .2 VOLT

Repair ground

.2 VOLT OR LESS

Turn ignition "OFF" and back to "RUN" position and listen for click of relay.

CLICK HEARD

1. Connect a 12 volt test light to a good ground.
2. Touch test light probe to orange/black wire terminal on relay.

LAMP ON

Replace relay.

LAMP OFF

Repair open in wire from soldered junction in harness to relay.

CLICK NOT HEARD

1. Connect a 12 volt test light to a good ground.
2. Touch test light probe to pink wire terminal on relay.

LAMP OFF

Repair open in pink wire from fuse panel to relay.

LAMP ON

Replace relay.

TAILGATE WINDOW OPERATES UP AND DOWN FROM INSTRUMENT PANEL SWITCH BUT DOES NOT OPERATE FROM THE TAILGATE SWITCH ON QUARTER PANEL.

1. Connect a 12 volt test light to a good ground.
2. Touch test light probe to orange/black terminal at tailgate switch.

LAMP ON

Replace switch.

LAMP OFF

Repair open in wire from tailgate switch to accessory junction block.

WINDOW OPERATES ONE WAY, BUT DOES NOT OPERATE THE OTHER WAY WHEN THE SWITCH AT THE INSTRUMENT PANEL AND TAILGATE IS ACTUATED

CIRCUIT BREAKER CAN BE HEARD OPENING AND CLOSING

Use "G" meter from BT-11-20 to check for short circuit in up or down feed wire to the motor.

CIRCUIT BREAKER CANNOT BE HEARD OPENING AND CLOSING

1. Disconnect motor feed connector.
2. Connect a 12 volt test light to a good ground.
3. Turn ignition switch to "RUN" position and actuate "UP" - "DOWN" switch.
4. Touch test light probe to "UP" wire blue or "DOWN" wire tan/white in connector.

LAMP OFF

Repair open circuit in wire from switch to motor.

LAMP ON

Replace motor.

Fig. 12-39 Flow diagram of a power window diagnosis (Oldsmobile Division, General Motors Corporation).

Basic electrical diagnosis procedures are used to correct electrical problems in the specialized electrical units. First the fuse is checked and replaced if necessary. If the fuse is good the lead wire is disconnected at the operating unit and the lead is checked with the test light or voltmeter to determine if electrical power is being conducted to the unit. If power is available at the unit the problem is in the unit or its mechanical linkage and so the unit must be removed for replacement or repair. If power does not arrive at the unit and the fuse is good the wiring circuit should be separated at one of the wiring harness junctions and the circuit operation checked at the junction. The technician can use this procedure to break the circuit into small segments to isolate the problem point. When the problem is found it can be repaired by soldering with rosin core solder or by insulating with electrical tape. Sometimes it is more practical to remove the wire from the junction at each end and install a new wire between the junctions.

Using the principles described in the chapters dealing with electrical components, the technician should be able to rapidly locate and repair electrical problems that cause complete electrical unit failure. A partial failure or intermittent failure is often very difficult to locate, especially when the unit is functioning normally at the time the customer brings the vehicle in for service. In this case the technician should attempt to produce the malfunction by moving the wires and switch so the fault can be identified exactly, he can then repair it and recheck his work to make sure the unit now functions correctly.

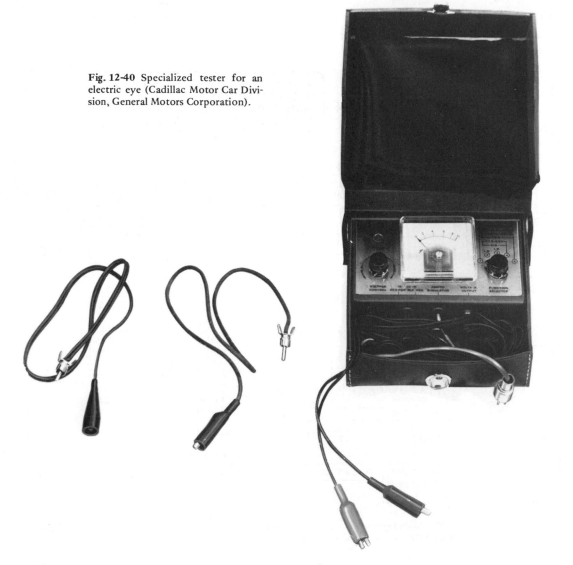

Fig. 12-40 Specialized tester for an electric eye (Cadillac Motor Car Division, General Motors Corporation).

REVIEW QUESTIONS

1. What is a device called that restricts the flow of electricity?

2. What is a device called that increases the flow of electricity?

3. How can a circuit be tested to locate a ground without blowing a second fuse?

4. A voltmeter is connected in place of a burned out fuse. With the switch off it shows battery voltage. What does this indicate?

5. What is the most common cause of one light malfunctioning?

6. What is the most common cause of a whole set of lights malfunctioning at once?

7. What is the name used for a remotely controlled switch?

8. What is the name used for an electrical device used to provide mechanical movement?

9. What is usually done to correct a system with a non-functioning electrical component?

10. The instrument lamps will light. After a few minutes the fuse burns out. What will cause this malfunction?

Glossary

Accessory. A device that performs a secondary function.

Actuate. To move or produce movement.

Aftermarket. The sales market designed for the consumer after he purchases a product from the dealer.

Air Gap. A small space between two parts.

Ambient Temperature. The temperature of the surrounding air.

Ammeter. An instrument connected in series in an electrical circuit to measure current flow.

Ampere. A measure of the rate of electrical current flow.

Ampere Turns. A measure of electromagnetic strength. The current flow times the number of winding turns in the coil.

Arc. A spark caused by an electrical current flow across an air gap.

Armature. A moving conductor within a magnetic field.

Atmospheric Pressure. The surrounding air pressure produced by the total weight of the atmosphere.

Atom. The smallest particle of an element. Made of protons, neutrons, and electrons.

Available Voltage. Maximum voltage an ignition system is capable of producing.

Balast. A resistor made of a material that maintains a constant resistance regardless of its temperature.

Barrel. The opening in a carburetor through which air/fuel mixture enters the intake manifold.

Battery Post. The terminal of the battery on which the electrical cables are attached.

Battery Post Adapter. A connector placed between one of the battery posts and the battery cable that is used with test equipment. It is sometimes called a battery post knife switch.

Beam. A stream of electrons within an electron tube that produces a pattern on the tube screen. Also the light produced by a lamp with the light focused in one direction.

Bearing. The surface that supports a load. In vehicles it supports a moving load with minimum drag.

Bendix. A starter drive type that uses inertia to engage the drive pinion.

Bimetallic Spring. A coil or leaf spring made of a double strip of two different metals. When it is heated or cooled it will bend.

Block. The large casting that forms the engine base.

Bond. An attracting force between atomic elements that allow them to combine to form different molecules.

Bore. The diameter of a hole. The carburetor opening often called a barrel.

Boss. A heavy cast section that is used for support, such as the heavy section around a bearing.

Bowl. A compartment in a carburetor containing a specified level of gasoline.

Breaker. A switch that is automatically opened by heat, high current, or mechanical action.

Bridge. A connection across a gap. A group of diodes that go between the stator and the electrical system.

Brush. A carbon compound connector that slides against a moving surface to form a good electrical connection.

Bumping. Very short snaps of the starter switch that will turn the engine slightly each time. It is used to position the crankshaft for ignition timing.

Bypass. To connect around some restriction such as a thermostat, valve, switch, circuit, etc.

C

Cable. Secondary ignition wires or large diameter wires connected to the battery.

Cam. A raised or flattened section on a rotating cylinder or disc that is used to provide a timed mechanical movement.

Camshaft. The engine shaft that controls the valve action in the cylinder.

Canister. An enclosed can containing activated charcoal or carbon used in the evaporative emission system to absorb hydrocarbon vapors when the engine is not running.

Cap. A cover. Holds secondary cables in a distributor assembly.

Capacitance. The ability to store electrical energy on conductors that are close together but insulated from each other.

Capacitive Discharge. A type of electronic ignition system that produces a secondary spark when a large condenser is triggered to release its stored energy through the coil primary.

Capacitor. A device consisting of two metal plates in close proximity to each other with an insulator between. Electrons readily collect at one plate and holes collect at the other.

Capacity. The amount of electrical energy a battery can deliver.

Carbon Pile. Carbon plates that can be pressed together to reduce the electrical resistance through them so they will carry a large electrical current.

Carbon Track. A mark across an insulator produced by an arc.

Case. An enclosure or box.

Cathode Ray. A beam of electrons emitted from a hot negatively charged metal part.

Chamber. An enclosed volume.

Charge. To force electricity through a battery to condition it so it will be able to produce electricity. Also the air/fuel mixture taken into the cylinder on the intake stroke.

Chassis. The supporting framework upon which active components are mounted.

Check Valve. A valve that will allow flow in one direction and will stop flow in the opposite direction.

Chip. A small solid state semiconductor device, usually an integrated circuit.

CID. Cubic inch displacement.

Commutator. A segmented ring of a starter to which the armature windings connect and upon which the brushes ride to transfer electrical current between the rotating armature and the stationary case.

Compression. The pressure that builds up in the combustion chamber as the piston moves toward top center when both valves are closed.

Condenser. An electrical component that can store a small electrical charge.

Conductor. A part that will carry electricity.

Console. An instrument display panel with operating controls.

Contacts. The parts of a switch that make and break the electrical circuit.

Contact Finger. A spring on the distributor rotor that touches the center button in the distributor cap.

Continuity. The result of a closed circuit through which an electrical current can flow.

Core. The metal center of a coil.

Corrosion. A combination of a metal and oxygen or water that causes the surface of the metal to disappear.

Crankshaft. The primary rotating member of an engine that is turned by the pistons and connecting rods.

Crimp. To bend over to make a tight junction.

Crossfire. Ignition secondary arcing across an insulation to fire the wrong spark plug.

Cubic Inch Displacement. The volume sweep by the pistons as the crankshaft rotates one revolution.

Current. Electrical flow in a conductor.

Cut-out. An automatic relay-type switch that opens to prevent an electrical drain when the engine is not operating on systems that use a commutator rectified generator.

Cycle. A complete circle back to the beginning. In engines, a series of events, intake, compression, power, and exhaust.

Cycled. Normalized regulator operation created by causing alternating charge and discharge.

D

Dash. A term used for the front part of the passenger compartment below the windshield.

Decay. To gradually lose its energy.

Delta. A triangular shape.

Diagnose. To determine the cause of a malfunction through analysis of data observed on test equipment, troubleshooting charts, and knowledge of the operating principles of the system.

Diaphragm. A flexible membrane on one side of an enclosed chamber.

Dieseling. A name used for firing after a hot engine is turned off. The ignition of the charge results from hot spots in the combustion chamber.

Diode. A semiconductor that allows current to flow in only one direction.

Discrete. An electrical device assembled from a number of electrical components.

Draw. The amount of current being used by an electrical device.

Drivability. Smoothness of engine operation at all vehicle speeds and loads.

Dwell. The number of degrees the distributor cam turns while the ignition contact breaker points are closed.

E

Electricity. The flow of electrons through a conductor.

Electrodes. The ends of charged conductors.

Electromagnet. A magnet made with a coil wound around a soft iron core. It becomes magnetized when electrical current flows in the coil.

Electromotive Force. A force produced by the interaction of current carrying conductors and magnetic fields.

Electron. The smallest known negatively charged particle.

Emission. Gaseous material expelled. Usually refers to harmful gases being expelled from an engine.

End Plate. The part of a starter that supports the armature bearings.

End Play. Free endwise movement without binding.

Energize. To fill with energy as a result of electrical current flow.

F

Fiber Optics. Plastic strands that carry light.

Filter. A device to remove particles from a fluid.

Flare. The brightening and dimming of lights as the engine speed changes. It is caused by changes in the electrical system voltage.

Flash Over. Arcing across insulation.

Flow Chart. A step-by-step procedure used in troubleshooting.

Flux. A substance applied during soldering or welding to free oxides.

Forward Bias. Voltage applied to a semiconductor in the direction allowing current to flow.

G

Galvanometer. A sensitive instrument that indicates differences in electromagnetic force.

Gap. A space between objects or parts.

Gasket. A sealing substance between stationary parts that prevents leakage.

Gassing. Formation of bubbles in the battery electrolyte during charging.

Ground. To connect an electric circuit to the vehicle frame or metal structure.

Growler. A coil wraped around the center of a U-shaped core that produces a continually changing magnetic field when the coil is connected to an AC voltage.

H

Hair Spring. A very fine spring coiled in a plane so the diameter of the coil keeps expanding as it is wound.

Hanger-Spring. Stationary connector at one end of a spring.

Heat Sink. A metal block that absorbs heat from an electrical device and radiates the heat to the surrounding air.

Helix. Spiral grooves along and around a shaft.

Hole. An electron missing from an atom.

Hybrid. An electric circuit combining discrete and monolithic components.

Hydrometer. A floating device that measures specific gravity of a fluid by the depth the float sinks into the fluid.

I

Idler. A free running pulley or gear that is used to transfer power or maintain tension.

Inductance. The process of an electromagnetic force being produced in a conductor located in a moving magnetic field.

Installation. The way a component is placed in an assembly.

Insulation. Nonconducting material surrounding a conductor to prevent short circuiting.

Insulator. A device that does not conduct electrical current.

Ion. A atom having excessive or missing electrons and therefore no longer has a neutral electrical charge.

Ionization. The process of forming ions.

J

Jumper. A wire with clips on each end that can be used to bypass electrical components for testing purposes.

Junction. An electrical connection between two conductors. Also the area between P and N semiconductor materials.

K

Keeper. A bar placed across a magnet that helps to retain the magnetism of the magnet.

Knife Switch. A test device placed between one battery post and the battery cable. It is used as an easy means of inserting and removing an ammeter from the circuit.

L

Laminated. Made of layers of thin material—soft steel in electromagnetic devices.

Lamp. A light bulb.

Lead. A connecting wire.

Lines-Of-Force. Lines produced when iron filings are sprinkled on a paper covering a magnetic field.

Load. A electrical device that uses current.

Lobe. The high portion of a cam.

M

Magnetic. Surrounded by a magnetic field.

Malfunction. A fault or improper operation.

Microfarad. A measure of the capacity of a condenser.

Misfire. Partial or intermittent nonfiring of one cylinder on a running engine.

Monolithic. Made from one piece.

N

Neutron. A small neutrally charged particle in the nucleus of an atom.

Nipple. A hollow metal connection point to which a hose is attached.

Normally Closed. A switch or valve that is closed in its static nonoperating position.

Normally Open. A switch or valve that is open in its nonoperating static position.

Nozzle. A hollow part through which fluid flows or is sprayed into a gas.

O

Ohm. A unit of electrical resistance.

Ohmmeter. A device used to measure the resistance of an electrical component.

Open. A separated connector. No current will flow.

Output. The amount of current being produced by the charging system. Usually the maximum possible current.

Out-Of-Round. Not a true circle when it should be.

Overrunning Clutch. A clutch that will run freely in one direction but lock when turned in the opposite direction.

Owner's Handbook. A book supplied with each new automobile that describes the features of the automobile and the recommended maintenance schedule.

Oxidation. The chemical combination of a material with oxygen.

P

Panel. A surface upon which instruments and other electrical devices are mounted.

Parallel. Circuits running adjacent to each other between electrical devices but not touching each other.

Part Throttle. Engine operating speed between idle and full throttle. Generally considered to be highway cruising speed.

Phase. Uniform oscillation of the voltage in one set of alternator windings.

Pick-Up. The end of an electrical instrument test lead used to attach the instrument to the circuit being tested.

Points. The contact breaker that interrupts the primary ignition circuit.

Polarize. To line up in a known way, such as magnetic fields or electrical charges.

Pole. The location in a magnet where all the magnetic lines of force come together.

Pole Shoe. A soft iron laminated part used to concentrate the lines of magnetic force.

Ports. Openings through which liquids or gases flow.

Power. The amount of work done in a specific period of time. One horsepower equals 33,000 ft lbs per min.

Printed Circuit. A thin coating of electrical conducting material on an insulating board. Used in place of wires to connect electrical units attached to the board.

Proton. A positively charged particle in the nucleus of an atom.

Pulse. A surge of voltage in a circuit.

R

Race. The inner and outer running surface of a ball, roller, or needle bearing.

Rate. A quantity of one thing measured in terms of a quantity of a different thing.

Read Out. An observed instrument reading.

Rectification. The act of changing an alternating current to a direct current.

Regulator. An electrical device used to control the charging system by controlling the field strength to limit maximum charging system voltage.

Relay. A remotely operated switch that carries a heavy current.

Reluctance. The resistance to becoming magnetized.

Remote. Operated from some distance.

Required Voltage. The ignition secondary voltage that is needed to produce an arc or spark across the spark plug electrodes.

Resistance. Something that limits the flow of electrical current.

Resistor. A conducting device that retards the flow of current.

Reverse Bias. Voltage applied to a semiconductor in a direction that prevents current flow.

Rheostat. A variable resistance. Sometimes called a pot.

Ring Gear. The gear around the flywheel or drive plate attached to the engine crankshaft. The starter pinion engages in this ring gear to crank the engine.

Rise Time. The time required to increase the voltage sufficiently to produce a spark between the spark plug electrodes.

Road Load. A load applied to an engine that simulates an engine load that would be required for highway cruising speeds.

Rotor. The part of a distributor that directs the secondary voltage to the proper spark plug. The part of an alternator that contains the field windings and rotates within the stator.

S

Secondary. The high voltage side of the ignition system.

Semiconductor. An electrical component that will conduct under some conditions and will insulate under other conditions.

Sender. The sensing unit of an electrical instrument circuit.

Series. A single path through a number of items, one after another.

Service Manual. A paper-backed book produced by the automobile manufacturer each year that shows the correct servicing procedures.

Set Screw. A screw in the side of a member on a shaft. The screw is tightened against the shaft to prevent movement between the member and the shaft.

Short. An electrical path that breaks out of the circuit, bypassing back to the electrical source.

Shunt. A device that produces a bypass function.

Sine. A trigonometric function.

Slip Rings. Metal conducting bands around the alternator rotor shaft through which field current can be received from stationary brushes.

Snap Action. A movement which, once started, moves immediately through its full travel.

Solenoid. An electrical device used to produce endwise movement.

Spike. The high point on an ignition scope secondary pattern at the point opening signal preceding the spark across the spark plug gap.

Splice. To make an electrical connection between two wires.

Splines. Sized grooves on a shaft and in a hole that match to prevent torque slippage.

State-Of-Charge. The percentage of full battery charge.

Stroke. Piston movement from one extreme limit to the other.

Suppress. To reduce or dampen.

Surge. A transient high voltage in an electrical circuit.

Switch. An electrical device used to close or open an electrical circuit.

T

Tab. A short projection on a part.

Tang. A lip or projection from an object surface.

Technician. A specialist in the technical details of automotive service.

Temperature Compensation. Controlled by a device that changes operating conditions as the temperature changes.

Terminal. The end of a circuit wire that is attached to a junction.

Test Light. A light used to check electrical continuity or the presence of voltage.

Thermister. An electrical device that changes its resistance as its temperature changes.

Thermostat. A device used to maintain constant temperature.

Thermostatic Arm. An arm that changes its angle as the temperature changes.

Through Bolts. A long bolt connecting between the outer parts of a device.

Timing. The number of crankshaft degrees from the piston top center when the spark plug ignites the combustion charge.

Torque. The twisting force on a shaft measured in pound feet.

Transient. An unusual momentary random high voltage in an electrical circuit produced by the interaction and location of electrical components.

Transistor. A semiconductor solid state electrical switch.

V

Vacuum. A pressure less than atmospheric pressure.

Volt. A unit used to measure electromotive force.

Voltmeter. An instrument used to measure voltage.

W

Winding. A long single strand of insulated wire turned evenly around a core.

Z

Zener Diode. A diode that will allow reverse current to flow at a designed voltage.

Electrical Symbols

Alternator	
Ammeter – test	A
Ammeter – vehicle	
Battery	
Carbon pile	
Coil	
Coil – electromagnet	
Coil – ignition	
Condenser	

Conductor – current out	⊙
Conductor – current in	⊕
Connector – junction	
Contact points	
Diode	
Fuse	
Ground	
Junction – fixed	
Lamp bulb	

Ohmmeter	
Resistor – fixed	
Resistor – variable	
Starter	
Switch	
Terminal – test lead	
Transistor NPN	
PNP	
Voltmeter	V
Zener diode	

Index